Theatre and its Audiences

Methuen Drama Agitations: Text, Politics and Performances

Theatre has always offered immediate responses to political, social, economic, and cultural crisis events that are local, national, and global in dimension, establishing itself as a prime medium of engagement. Methuen Drama Agitations interrogates these manifold intersections between theatre and the contemporary: What is the relationship between theatre and reality? Which functions does the theatre perform in public life? Where does the radical potential of the theatre reside and how is it untapped?

Methuen Drama Agitations addresses issues from across a number of spectrums, including contemporary politics, environmental concerns, issues of gender and race, and the challenges of globalization. The series focuses on text as much as performance, on theory as much as practice. It investigates the lively dialogues between theatre and contemporary lived experience.

Series Editors

William C. Boles (Rollins College, USA)
Anja Hartl (University of Innsbruck, Austria)

Advisory Board

Lynnette Goddard (Royal Holloway, University of London, UK)
Anton Krueger (Rhodes University, South Africa)
Marcus Tan (Nanyang Technological University, Singapore)
Sarah J. Townsend (Penn State University, USA)
Denise Varney (University of Melbourne, Australia)

Theater of Lockdown: Digital and Distanced Performance in a Time of Pandemic
Barbara Fuchs

Theater in a Post-Truth World: Texts, Politics, and Performance
Edited by William C. Boles

Performing Statecraft: The Postdiplomatic Theatre of Sovereigns, Citizens, and States
Edited by James R. Ball III

Contemporary Black Theatre and Performance: Acts of Rebellion, Activism, and Solidarity
Edited by DeRon S. Williams, Khalid Y. Long and Martine Kei Green-Rogers

Performing Left Populism: Performance, Politics and the People
Edited by Goran Petrović Lotina and Théo Aiolfi

Performing the Queer Past: Public Possessions
Fintan Walsh

Forthcoming Titles

Performance and Activism in 21st-Century Workers' Movements: Organizing Resistance
Rebecca Hillman

Theatres of Disruption in 21st-Century Britain: Plays and Performances in Turbulent Times
Ellen Redling

Theatre and its Audiences

Reimagining the Relationship in Times of Crisis

Kate Craddock and
Helen Freshwater

methuen | drama
LONDON • NEW YORK • OXFORD • NEW DELHI • SYDNEY

METHUEN DRAMA
Bloomsbury Publishing Plc
50 Bedford Square, London, WC1B 3DP, UK
1385 Broadway, New York, NY 10018, USA
29 Earlsfort Terrace, Dublin 2, Ireland

BLOOMSBURY, METHUEN DRAMA and the Methuen Drama logo are trademarks of Bloomsbury Publishing Plc

First published in Great Britain 2024

Copyright © Kate Craddock and Helen Freshwater, 2024

Kate Craddock and Helen Freshwater have asserted their right under the Copyright, Designs and Patents Act, 1988, to be identified as authors of this work.

For legal purposes the Acknowledgements on p. viii constitute an extension of this copyright page.

Series design by Ben Anslow
Cover image: Audience members at GIFT 2013. Photo by Richard Kenworthy
(© Kate Craddock, 2013)

All rights reserved. No part of this publication may be reproduced or transmitted in any form or by any means, electronic or mechanical, including photocopying, recording, or any information storage or retrieval system, without prior permission in writing from the publishers.

Bloomsbury Publishing Plc does not have any control over, or responsibility for, any third-party websites referred to or in this book. All internet addresses given in this book were correct at the time of going to press. The author and publisher regret any inconvenience caused if addresses have changed or sites have ceased to exist, but can accept no responsibility for any such changes.

A catalogue record for this book is available from the British Library.

Library of Congress Cataloging-in-Publication Data.
Names: Craddock, Kate, author. | Freshwater, Helen, author.
Title: Theatre and its audiences : reimagining the relationship in times of crisis / Kate Craddock and Helen Freshwater.
Description: London; New York: Methuen Drama, 2024. | Series: Methuen drama agitations : text, politics and performances | Includes bibliographical references and index.
Identifiers: LCCN 2023022767 (print) | LCCN 2023022768 (ebook) | ISBN 9781350339163 (hardback) | ISBN 9781350339170 (paperback) | ISBN 9781350339187 (ebook) | ISBN 9781350339194 (pdf)
Subjects: LCSH: Theater audiences–Great Britain. | Theater–Public relations–Great Britain. | Theater–Great Britain–History–21st century.
Classification: LCC PN1995.9.W6 .C73 2024 (print) | LCC PN1995.9.W6 (ebook) | DDC 792.0941–dc23/eng/20230821
LC record available at https://lccn.loc.gov/2023022767
LC ebook record available at https://lccn.loc.gov/2023022768

ISBN: HB: 978-1-3503-3916-3
PB: 978-1-3503-3917-0
ePDF: 978-1-3503-3919-4
eBook: 978-1-3503-3918-7

Series: Methuen Drama Agitations: Text, Politics and Performances

Typeset by Deanta Global Publishing Services, Chennai, India

To find out more about our authors and books visit www.bloomsbury.com and sign up for our newsletters.

Contents

Acknowledgements viii

Introduction: conventions, interruptions and change 1

1 Performance's place in time: on duration, speed and intervals 25
2 Spatial relationships: exclusivity and inclusivity 57
3 Technologies, connection and copresence 87
4 Honesty, secrets and lies: how theatre communicates with audiences 119
5 On the present and future needs of audiences: care, access and sustainability 147

References 175
Index 205

Acknowledgements

Helen would like to thank Stephanie Pitts and Sarah Price, wonderful colleagues on the Understanding Audiences for the Contemporary Arts project; Matthew Reason and Lynne Conner for their patience and thoughtful questions on earlier work which led directly to this book; Mark Dudgeon at Bloomsbury for helping Kate and I clarify our early ideas and the book's parameters; my colleagues at Newcastle whose work in and on theatre and performance keeps surprising and inspiring me: Zoe Cooper, Kate Chedgzoy, James Cummings, Kate De Rycker, James Harriman-Smith, Ros Haslett, Jennifer Richards, Jo Robinson, Emma Whipday and Margaret Wilkinson. Particular thanks are due to the people who were sat in the management boat alongside me when the Covid storm hit, especially Sherelle Coulson, Lesley Lant, Geoff Poole, Heike Pichler and Jennifer Orr. Thanks also to Lu Kemp, who has always walked the walk, and to Jo Underwood for the most helpful listening; to my Dad, who has always shown me that actions speak louder than words; Mum, who taught me that change is always possible; and my family bubble who lived through lockdown with me – Ian, Leo, Bea and Mark.

Kate would like to thank the consortium partners on *Horizon – Performance Created in England* for their invaluable insight, conversation and friendship over the last three years: Aaron, Amy, Hannah, Kate, Matthew, Paul, Pelin, Pippa and Tarek. A huge thank-you to the GIFT team for all the discoveries we made when we moved the festival online – Hannah, Jason, Kate, Melanie, Rachel and Simon – and a very special thanks to all the artists and audiences who took the leap with us. Thanks to the many artists and cultural sector colleagues for the endless hours of online conversations across multiple networks that have inspired so much of my contribution to this book: the participants from FIELD, The Festival Academy community, GENERATE peers, Imagining Futures network, UK Festival Directors network and my Wear and Tyne Festivals friends. Finally, thank you to Kit for being my constant in a changing world.

Introduction

Conventions, interruptions and change

It's 22 March 2020. I go to Sainsbury's after dropping my daughter at school – the last day she'll go to school for five months, but I don't know that then. The shop is very busy but there's almost nothing on the shelves. Entire aisles have been cleared of stock, as if a swarm of locusts have been through the store and consumed everything edible, as well as every last bar of soap. Bewildered shoppers rush up and down. No one is talking to each other. I walk home empty-handed, dazed. Is this it, I think – is this the beginning of the end?

This book is a product of our shared preoccupation with the relationship between performance and its audiences. It has developed out of our own long-term relationships with performance: our fascination with its past, frustrations with its present and hopes for its future. It is a product of our belief that change is possible, as well as an increasing sense of urgency. It is also a product of our experience of the impact of the Covid pandemic. The spread of the Covid virus across the world generated loss, fear, stress and hardship on a global scale, touching every aspect of our lives. Theatre and performance was especially hard hit by governmental 'stay at home' orders and the decisions to close all but essential public spaces and services, resulting in the permanent closure of some theatre companies, widespread redundancies and sudden loss of income for the enormous number of freelance artists usually employed across the sector.

Given the human cost of Covid, it is hard (and no doubt impossible for some) to see these events as having any kind of productive or positive outcome. Yet the disruption did provide an opportunity to take stock of what is core to the experience of watching or witnessing performance, and enabled a re-evaluation of performance's place in our lives. It allowed us to identify what we most missed about theatre-going, and what seemed to us most valuable about the experience. In this moment of extremity, the content of performance was reframed, its meaning remade in a world marked by newly shared awareness of our universal precarity and fragility. The early months of the pandemic were also marked by a sense that we were glimpsing the way in which apocalyptic societal breakdown could play out in our cities and communities. The panic buying which marked the first weeks of the crisis generated sudden awareness of the fragility of the supply systems and services which sustain modern urban life. Everything which we had taken for granted – food in the shops, water, electricity, gas, emergency and medical support systems, waste collection services – all seemed under threat. In abandoned theatres, crew left 'ghost lights' burning on empty stages. Images of these lights – a standard safety feature designed to prevent accidents in dark auditoria – offered powerful reassurance: that this moment was just a pause, that the traditions of the stage would continue, that these spaces would be occupied again. As lockdown lifted, the impulse to fulfil the promise of these lights, and to return to 'business as usual', has clearly been powerfully felt.

We argue, however, that the pandemic was not a pause, but a teachable moment. In this, we follow activist and author Arundhati Roy's argument, articulated in 'The Pandemic is a Portal', published in early April 2020. Roy's powerful article captures the extremity of the impact of the virus in India. It registers and reflects upon the desire to find meaning in the meaningless, the scramble to adjust to a new reality and to connect the past with a future which has suddenly become unrecognizable and unknowable. Roy acknowledges the difficulty of processing the reality of sudden and irrevocable loss, and the desire to get back to normality. But she asserts that we need to resist this urge. Instead, she argues, we need to take up the opportunity the pandemic offers. We need to accept its invitation to imagine an alternative future, and step through the portal of the pandemic into a future in which we leave prejudice, greed and disregard for the natural world behind. As Roy's article indicates, Covid can and has been interpreted as a symptom of broader systemic stress at environmental as well as human levels. It also made inequalities starkly apparent. As the crisis lengthened, the gulf widened between those who were relatively well insulated from the disruption and those who were most vulnerable to the threat it posed to health, well-being and livelihoods. For those invested in the future of theatrical performance, Covid has provided discomforting revelations about access, inequalities and assumptions built into our spaces, conventions and traditions, as well as salutary lessons about what performance offers its audiences. It taught us, above all, that it is possible to do things differently.

Taking the long view: on convention

As we move on from the Covid crisis, we argue that it is essential to learn these lessons. Part of this process necessarily involves a thoughtful, critical reckoning with the cultures of performance practice and audiencing that we have inherited. As Helen has observed elsewhere, histories of theatre audiences sometimes have a tendency to mythologize past practices, drawing unfavourable comparisons between audiences past – unified, active, powerful – and the passivity of present-day audiences (Freshwater 2022). This book attempts to resist the lure of nostalgia in its account of past practices but recommends revisiting the past in order to encourage careful consideration of where we want to go from here.

This book focuses on the institutionalized conventions of theatre-going, which frame and often determine the nature of the relationship between performance and its audiences. We believe that this kind of critical consideration is urgently needed in the aftermath of the Covid pandemic, when we witnessed a significant shift in understanding of this relationship. The book aims to provide this by positioning the disruption, insights and opportunities provided by the pandemic in the long durée of theatrical audiencing. It places discussion of the changes forced by the Covid crisis alongside accounts of historical conventions: both those subject to immediate change and those which preceded and produced the pre-Covid status quo. It identifies the shifts in norms that are increasingly visible across contemporary practice, and how these point to a more equitable future for the relationship between theatre and its audiences. We hope that this book will provide readers with an opportunity to contemplate – and potentially alter – their own cultural practices as practitioners and/or future audience members. We are interested in change that has occurred in the past, but also in changes to come: changes which we (and you) can bring about.

Viewing the impact of Covid historically does, of course, provide opportunities to compare and contrast theatre's response to comparable periods of crisis and disruption. Though critics and theatre makers have declared that British theatre is in crisis at conferences and in print at regular intervals since the end of the 1980s (Lavender 1989; Delgado and Svich 2002; Turnbull 2008), the scale of the Covid crisis was clearly something new. Critics found themselves reaching into the more distant past for historical antecedents in an attempt to communicate and quantify the extent of Covid's impact. Articles compared the extent and duration of disruption with that of previous crises, such as the closure of public theatres during outbreaks of the plague in the sixteenth and early seventeenth centuries; the closure of London theatres between 1642 and 1660 following an order from the Puritan-led parliament; and the government's decision to order all theatres to close at the start of the Second World War in 1939 – a decision which was quickly reversed (Clarke and Smurthwaite 2020). For readers in early 2020, it was comforting, perhaps, to know that the theatre survived these historical ruptures. The articles invite us to conclude that if the theatre survived the Black Death, the Puritans and the Second World War, then surely we can get through this, as the theatre becomes a proxy for individual survival and the re-establishment of the recognizable rhythms of everyday life, the luxuries of gathering and entertainment.

Here, however, we have chosen to focus upon the historical establishment and emergence of long-standing conventions, rather than comparing the experience of Covid with the impact of earlier crises upon the theatre. There are several reasons for this. The way in which

Covid shuttered theatre venues across the world within days of each other makes its impact unique – unprecedented, even. Previous periods of war and plague had a local rather than global impact on the theatre. While venues in one city might be closed, theatres were open elsewhere; private gatherings for performance continued where large public venues had to close; performers could tour to find audiences (Carlson 2022). In contrast, the speed and frequency of twenty-first-century international travel allowed Covid to spread across the globe within weeks. The constraints on movement outside the home and gathering in private precluded the kinds of activity which had sustained performance when large venues were closed in the past. Comparing Covid to past crises only gets you so far. We also believe that while recalling the ways in which theatres endured past adversity may be comforting, it does not help us face the need for change in the present. So, here we focus upon historical norms, traditions and conventions rather than exceptional periods of historical disruption. This allows us to reflect upon what Covid can tell us about how these inherited attitudes and practices have determined the relationship between audience and performance, and how this relationship can be reimagined for the future.

The following chapters include examples of different types of audience–performance relationship from the fourteenth century to the twenty-first. This does, of course, mean that we cannot engage in detail with each example – and that we will inevitably omit much more than we can include. Nevertheless, we believe that there is value in focusing upon the cultural history of theatrical spectatorship over the long term. Here, the insights provided by the editors of Bloomsbury's recent *A Cultural History of Theatre* series prove instructive. In their 2015 'Prospectus' for the series, Christopher Balme and Tracy C. Davis explain their decision not to give audiences their own chapter in each volume. They propose that theatre history has tended to focus disproportionately on moments of 'epistemic breach' in relation to traditions of audiencing and spectatorship, arguing that patterns of audience behaviour and conventions may persist over centuries or more, with deeply embedded traditions militating against sudden change (417). We concur, but would add that the long endurance of institutionalized approaches, cultural assumptions and learned behaviours does not mean that change does not occur. The scale and range of cultural adaptation brought about by the Covid crisis – and the uncomfortable awareness that we have been living through a cultural moment which is undoubtedly 'historical' – also provides a new appreciation that shifts in behaviour are possible, and that they can happen overnight. Taking the long view, and engaging with key innovations from the medieval period to the present day – as this book does – brings the significance, scale and speed of cultural changes in conventions governing audience behaviour into focus.

The view from the north: on material, location and form

The book's purview is broad but is determined by significant parameters. It focuses upon the material conditions which determine the nature of the relationship between performance and its audiences. This is not to dismiss the formative power of the discourse that surrounds and comments upon encounters with performance. Anti-theatrical prejudices about the pliability and volatility of audiences are as old and long-lived as theatre and performance, but they also live on in contemporary debates about twenty-first-century theatre etiquette (Heim 2016; Sedgman 2018). This focus does not signal lack of belief in the importance of asking audiences for their thoughts on their experiences in the theatre, either. Since the publication of Helen's *Theatre & Audience* in 2009 (which detailed the surprising paucity of explicit scholarly engagement with the responses of theatre audiences), there has been an explosion of scholarly publication in this area. There is now no need to complain about this gap in scholarship, or the methodological naiveté of making strong assertions about audience response with no reference to actual audiences. In the last ten years numerous publications have demonstrated that empirical studies which engage directly with audience members can yield rich insights

(Sedgman 2016; Pitts and Price 2020; Snyder-Young and Omasta 2022; Reason et al. 2022). This field of study is also marked by an extraordinary flourishing of methodological inventiveness and self-reflexivity in recent years (McDowell 2022). But the historical scope of this book militates against asking the audience directly: they are too distant, too numerous, too dead. Instead, in what follows, we attend to the tangible material conditions and conventions which determine and delineate the audience experience. We focus our attention upon the ways in which approaches to the use of space, time and technologies, and the provision of opportunities to interact and contribute, shape the form of the relationship between performance and its audiences. The assertion that 'a man walks across this empty space whilst someone else is watching him, and this is all that is needed for an act of theatre to be engaged' is clearly helpful when setting out an artistic approach which does away with one or more of the above (or, some readers might note, when beginning a book on theatre and audiences). But this encounter never takes place in an empty space, no matter what Peter Brook or other directors might say (1968: 11). Theatre and performance are necessarily dependent upon location in a designated building, space or institution. The details of scenography have a huge impact upon reception, as do plot, character, sound and script. They are defined by the time of day, time of year and the season they take place in, by how long they last and how this duration meets or frustrates audience expectations.

This book focuses upon theatre and performance made in Britain. We recognize that this means that we cannot address the ways in which British theatrical conventions have been shaped by intercultural exchange, transnational entanglements, networks and forms of cultural appropriation – interactions that have been highlighted by new approaches to historiography in theatre and performance studies, and a wave of valuable, much-needed scholarship (Bullock 2017; Katritzky and Drábek 2019; Balme 2020; Fischer-Lichte et al. 2022). We also acknowledge that this focus upon the performance practice of a single nation does not reflect either the way that digital innovation made geography seem irrelevant (Fuchs 2022: 27), or one of the most important lessons of the Covid crisis, our global interconnection. We gained access to this interconnection through new levels of access to performance works taking place across the world, but also through the opportunity to experience the thrill of being part of an international audience. The experience of suddenly and unexpectedly finding ourselves in a temporary, global community of spectators will stay with us. But the broad range of historical examples we examine here, and our interest in provoking new approaches to theatre and performance in the UK, necessitates a tight geographical focus.

The focus upon work made in Britain is also indicative of our lived experiences of theatre-going and immersion in the British performance scene. We have first-hand experience of observing the way in which contemporary practitioners making work in the UK observe and utilize long-standing theatrical conventions, and how they seek to challenge and change them, too. We have been to many of the spaces and recent events that we write about, while Kate's experience of working with international artists as director of GIFT (Gateshead International Festival of Theatre) provides her with particular insights into the specificities of the British way of working. What may seem self-evident or unremarkable to performance practitioners who are based in the UK long-term can seem peculiar, frustrating or even alarming to someone who has not worked in the country before, or has been based elsewhere for a long period. This knowledge feeds into our analysis here.

It is also important to acknowledge our location in more specific terms, too. We both live and work in Newcastle upon Tyne, in North East England: Kate grew up in the city, while Helen moved here in 2011. The city's theatre and performance scene has a particularity of perspective which is important to acknowledge as it informs our perspectives and the analysis we offer. Situated on the periphery of England, at a considerable distance from London and other major cities, it has a complex, sometimes contradictory, cultural relationship to its industrial past, to the broader North East region and, at times, to its status as English (Niven 2019). The city's theatre scene is diverse but tight-knit, while attitudes towards the history of the region and its performance traditions are representative of a conflicted mixture of pride and shame that can be detected more broadly in the region (Latimer 2022). This positioning inflects the book in a number of ways. We are alert to the tendency to refer to 'British theatre' when it would be more appropriate to use the label 'English' (Harvie 2018: 587), and to the range of distinct 'Englishes' that can be elided and subsumed by that singular category. We are also aware of the long-established dominance of London in British theatre culture. Work made by and for people based in the capital has long received disproportionate amounts of funding, newspaper-column inches and scholarly attention, underpinned by the enduring belief that work made elsewhere is not worthy of the same time and investment (Latimer 2022: 43; Cochrane 2011: 2). There are, of course, important studies to be found that engage with performance made in Wales, Northern Ireland, Scotland, towns and regions in England and rural areas – and late 2022 saw a major shift in the English funding landscape, with Arts Council England (ACE) announcing a rebalancing of their support for arts organizations away from the capital, and support for the relocation of major organizations to bases in the regions (Robinson 2016; Lewis 2018; Brown 2019; Maguire 2020; Jowett 2022b; Nicholson 2023). Although this is a very recent development, it has the potential to be a significant change in policy, particularly if it represents the first move in a more sustained commitment. When we turn to consider the past, however, it is clear that the dominance of the British capital in theatre historiography will determine the information available to us for many years to come, despite recent efforts at rebalancing the emphasis upon the UK capital. We attempt to counter this imbalance in our accounts of work that we have experienced elsewhere in what follows, but we recognize how our own positioning in the North East of England defines and delimits the analysis we offer: an awareness of our 'locatedness' that was enhanced by the restrictions on movement and travel introduced during the Covid crisis.

Awareness of the way in which our location informs our understanding of the past, present and future of British theatre and performance goes hand in hand with a consideration of the boundaries and borders of the forms we are focusing upon in this book. Theatre's use of digital platforms to share and create work during periods of lockdown has resulted in a renewed focus upon what does and does not count as theatre. Critical responses to theatre's use of technology during the pandemic have returned to questions of categorization as the pandemic has moved from an acute to a chronic phase. These circle around the nature of online or virtual theatre's relationship to forms of performance which are perhaps more clearly recognizable as theatre. They ask: if we understand theatre as performance which brings together groups of performers and spectators in spaces specifically designed to frame and accommodate the work, is theatre online really theatre? Engagement with this question has an undeniable appeal – particularly for people who have a long-standing attachment to theatre and care deeply about its development and future. For academics, it is the equivalent of scholarly catnip: an opportunity for display of our knowledge of theatres past and present, as we consider what is central, and most valued, about the form. Yet this question, toothsomely complex as it is, can quickly morph into broader boundary-policing. Is theatre really theatre if it is only watched by a single spectator? Is it theatre if there's only one performer? Is it really theatre if it doesn't happen in a theatre? Is it theatre if we are viewing it through a screen? (Worthen 2021; Carlson 2022). These questions also preoccupy many people working in the live arts, alongside profound concerns about the impact of the crisis upon the livelihoods of artists and the survival of live performance as an art form (Crouch 2023). This book is also informed by deep concern about these issues, but neither of its authors has any interest in policing the boundaries of what does and does not count as performance or theatre. We prefer to take our cue from practitioners: if artwork is presented as theatre or performance by the organization or individual who made it, then it is surely not our role, as curators or as critics, to say that it does not belong.

Still, we need to acknowledge that our personal preferences for particular types of experience in the theatre will inevitably shape our hopes for the future of performance, and that these hopes will frame our understanding of the histories and narratives we are writing in turn. Most – if not all – of the books published in the last ten years in theatre and performance studies that engage explicitly with questions of spectatorship and audiencing follow Susan Bennett in her investment in the idea of the 'productive and emancipated spectator' (1997: 1). We are no different in this respect. But these preferences do not, we hope, override a broader appreciation and fascination with theatre and performance in all its forms. We consider ourselves to be theatre omnivores: we enjoy sitting in the dark as well as being invited to contribute, and we like intimate as well as large-scale work. We can be charmed by performances that are made by people who don't know much about theatre traditions, as well as impressed and energized by those that depend upon high levels of audience and performer expertise. We get a thrill from shows which are intended to disturb as well as those that are designed to divert and entertain. From *Tanz* at Battersea Arts Centre to *The Lion King* at the Sunderland Empire; Ben Lewis' *Don Quixote: Man of Clackmannanshire* at Perth Theatre to *I am from Reykjavik* by Sonia Hughes in Edinburgh's Holyrood Park; *39 Horses* by Izaak Gledhill, experienced in a taxi parked outside Newcastle's fringe venue Alphabetti Theatre to *Arcadia* by Deborah Warner at the partially constructed The Factory in Manchester; primary school Christmas plays to *The Dante Project* at The Royal Opera House (examples of performances we've attended in the process of putting this book together) – we appreciate them all.

Our approach is also informed by our professional backgrounds. Helen has been interested in audience response to theatre and performance, and how we think about and study it, since the late 1990s when she first began to research forms of theatre censorship; Kate has long experience of getting performance made and shared with audiences. As a maker, Kate's work often disrupts audience conventions, and between 2005 and 2011 she used Skype as a tool to bring globally dispersed performers together for performance events as co-director of mouth to mouth international performance collective. As a curator, Kate regularly sites performances in locations where audiences might least expect to encounter them. Kate drew on these experiences when deciding to put GIFT online when Covid hit in 2020. Here we offer insights that combine the lived experience of a performance practitioner, director and curator with the perspective provided by scholarship and research. Our authorial partnership weaves together two distinct voices and sets of expertise across the book. Kate's experience and insight have informed the whole of this book, and she leads on the final chapter. Helen wrote Chapters 1 to 4 with contributions from Kate.

On structure

The first four chapters of this book are arranged into discussions of the questions of where, when and how audiences have experienced live theatrical performance in the past. They address the impact of the pandemic on space, time, technology and communication in our daily lives as well as on our understanding of what it means to be a member of an audience. Chapter 1 focuses upon time. The early days of the Covid crisis generated a powerful sense that time had been disrupted by the measures taken to limit the spread of the virus. Everyday routines and activities were paused and then rescheduled and relocated to new times and frequencies. The proliferation of online performance (available, it seemed, for consumption at all times of the day and night in the early weeks of lockdown) challenged previously shared understandings of where performance belongs in time as well as space. This chapter examines how we conceive of this place in terms of duration, frequency and placement in our days, weeks and years, and asks whether the temporal norms that have governed performance over centuries have changed as much as we might imagine. It discusses performances fast and slow, long and short, analysing productions of unusual brevity as well as those that stretch or challenge expectations regarding the length of time that an audience can reasonably be expected to concentrate upon a single performance. Engaging with the question of how timing and duration impact the relationship between performance and its audiences, it highlights areas of innovation and practice which have not received as much attention as they deserve, arguing that time is an important factor when thinking about access and inclusivity.

Chapter 2 concentrates on space. When the British government issued the order to stay at home in March 2020, auditoria closed overnight. In the months of lockdown that followed, boundaries between life and work, school and home, the public and the private, were radically redrawn. Covid cast us out of buildings which have long been associated with audiencing and forced a radical reassessment of the kinds of spaces in which a performance can take place. Audiences and performers sought out new spaces to gather in the middle of this broader spatial reordering. This chapter reflects on how traditions of design, architecture and conventions regarding the proper location of theatrical display have created and conditioned audience expectation. It offers critical perspectives on some of the most commonly held ideas about the configuration of space in historic theatres and explores earlier attempts to change spatial relationships with audiences for theatre and performance, examining what the issues have been with these efforts. It maintains that we should reconsider how we think about the relationship between space and audience experiences of privacy and publicness, transparency and exposure, and distance and proximity.

Chapter 3 focuses upon technological innovation. It argues that British performers and theatres have been quick to exploit new technology in the past, yet ambivalence about the impact of new technologies on audience experience also persists. The tension between these two positions became apparent as the pandemic forced speedy adoption of new technologies, pushing many to get to grips with the potentials – and limitations – of unfamiliar digital platforms and tools. This chapter looks at how histories of lighting express this tension, exploring how concerns about exposure, anonymity and voyeurism play out when theatre takes place in the digital realm or uses approaches to participation which are deemed to be modelled upon digital culture. It proposes that a negative and dismissive position towards the use of digital platforms fails to appreciate their potential to provide experiences of copresence, to develop and sustain relationships between practitioners and spectators and to provide greater accessibility.

Chapter 4 focuses on the forms of communication that performers and organizations have used to create, develop and maintain relationships with audiences in the past. It assesses the strategies used to attract audiences and considers how theatres approach the establishment of contracts, conventions and boundaries with audiences, considering how explicit statements about audience behaviour may facilitate communication and better relationships, as well as creating barriers. It provides critical discussion of the use of relationship marketing, exploring how theatres and performance practitioners have sought to develop relationships which move beyond superficial engagement with this model. It touches upon moments when theatres have been less than honest and direct with audiences, as well as models of clarity and transparency. It closes by contemplating the parallels between the relationships that can develop between an organization and its audience, and those we foster and value elsewhere in our lives.

The suggestion that the Covid crisis can be interpreted as a period of 'dark festival' runs across these four chapters. Chapter 1 proposes that the crisis transformed our experience and understanding of time – and theatre's place in time – in ways that mirror the productive disruption common to festival time. Chapter 2 focuses upon the spatial disruption wrought by the pandemic, and how it demonstrated – as festivals often do – that it is possible to approach the question of where we meet to view performance afresh: an issue which is then explored in further depth in Chapter 3, as we contemplate how technology changes our understanding of copresence. Chapter 4 touches upon lessons to be learned about communication, inequality and power from the licensed disruption inherent in festival. In our use of the concept of festival, we follow Marjana Johansson's understanding of the form as inherently political, productive as well as reflective of social and material reality. As she observes:

> Festivals tend to be thought of as being organized at a given time in a given place, but we should also consider festivals as *organizing*

[. . .] bodies, feelings, social hierarchies, and cultural and social value.
[. . .] festivals also shape patterns of exclusion and inclusion and can
be mobilized to protect established boundaries as well as to transgress
them. (2020: 68)

Still, before we go further, we should acknowledge that Covid is, of course, not like a festival – dark or otherwise – in ways that should not be ignored. The crisis cannot be thought of as celebratory or convivial. Instead of encouraging public gatherings, its presence made even the smallest of group meetings unthinkable – even illegal – for months at a time. The crisis shares little with other events that have occasionally been labelled 'dark festival', such as the increasingly popular annual festival of Halloween, or annual Goth gatherings (Clark 2005: 187; Spracklen and Spracklen 2018: 24). With Covid, death arrived without any of the props, costumes or make-up associated with modern Gothic's theatrical culture and sensibility, or the safety of the licensed and boundaried rituals of trick or treat (Jones, Poore and Dean 2018). Rather, in labelling the crisis a 'dark festival', we recall Richard Schechner's definition of 'dark play', in which play becomes heightened through risk of injury and death; the lines between the real and the imaginary are blurred or indistinguishable; and deception and deceit are integral to the experience (2002: 106–9). As we discuss in the chapters to follow, the Covid crisis was characterized by intense awareness of mortality and vulnerability, as well as difficulty in perceiving what did and did not constitute risk, or reliable information. And, as we discuss in Chapter 4, the crisis called the honesty and integrity of the authorities into question. Still, there are limits, too, to the parallels with this model. Though Schechner's exemplars dice with death and injury, as they break rules, transgress social mores and test out the boundaries of their endurance, relationships and identities, the dark games they play are short-lived: lasting seconds, minutes, hours. Moreover, though dark play sometimes produces results which may be unwanted or overwhelming, it is clear that those who instigated it have actively chosen to do so. In contrast, the darkness of Covid offered neither the comfort of temporal boundaries nor the certainty that it had been started deliberately, or for a definite purpose, despite ongoing speculation as to the source of the virus. Covid was terrifying because it was immediately apparent that no one was in control. The crisis had no clear end and no obvious meaning to offer. The darkness it called up was that of an abyss, into which the world had unwittingly plunged. In what follows we use the concept of 'dark festival' to explore the ways in which Covid enabled the exploration of alternative ways of being; to challenge the norms which govern our experience of time, space, technology and communication; and the implications of these challenges for our understanding of the relationship between audiences and performance.

The final chapter focuses on the future. Drawing on key learnings that are emerging from the late-Covid moment in 2022, and on those expectations and experiences that are more established from the pre-Covid past, it offers a vision for how the relationship between theatre and its audiences could be redefined. The chapter points to 'care', 'access' and 'sustainability' as being the key guiding principles that came to the fore throughout the pandemic and are currently reshaping accepted norms. Weaving together observations from recent contemporary performance works – where a more equitable relationship is apparent – with critical conversations and efforts that emerged during the pandemic, it suggests how the choices being made by current practitioners are changing how theatre will be experienced in the future.

On interruption

This book is as much a product of our lived experience of the pandemic as our professional lives. It is important to acknowledge that it was written in less than ideal conditions. We both suffered personal and professional losses during the first months of the Covid crisis, and both of us had to attempt to educate and entertain our primary-school-age children during school closures, which lasted from March 2020 through to March 2021 – while also attempting to manage the impact of the crisis upon our working lives. We have both had Covid more than once and the creative and critical projects we were pursuing prior to the pandemic were derailed and reconceived on numerous occasions: an experience shared by many others working in research and the cultural sector during the pandemic. The short memories which interrupt each chapter serve, we hope, to highlight the way in which our analyses are framed by our personal and professional experiences from the first year of the pandemic on. This approach is also inspired by the form and content of playwright Sarah Ruhl's *100 Essays I Don't Have Time to Write: On Umbrellas and Sword Fights, Parades and Dogs, Fire Alarms, Children, and Theater* (2015), and by Erin Sullivan's discussion of how the experience of viewing performance online, at home, enables a form of reception in which the act of audiencing is mixed up with rhythms of our everyday lives (2020: 114).

The memories we present capture moments from 2020, 2021 and 2022 that we recall strongly but are, in many ways, mundane. They reflect Lauren Berlant's insights into the way in which the 'ordinariness' of crisis – its situation in the banal and everyday – can lead to a state of helpless acceptance in the face of challenges at a scale that cannot be addressed on an individual level (2011: 10). Yet, we also wanted to place these memories amongst the text because we recognize that it is extremely tempting to forget about the experiences we lived through during the pandemic – and that earlier pandemics have also been subject to collective cultural amnesia (Honigsbaum 2016). The desire to return to 'normal' and to put the loss and fear experienced in the past few years behind us is, of course, very powerful. Acknowledging and retaining our memories, the mental pictures which flash up from a time of crisis, feels more important than ever.

These memories also function to highlight the significance of interruption. We are accustomed to thinking of interruptions as an unwelcome nuisance, a threat to productivity or focus or as a pause to be patiently endured before activity can continue. But we want to suggest that we should attend to their content and value, as well as registering their impact. For example, interruptions can serve to remind us of what our minds and bodies require. In the theatre, intervals provide time to check in with those we are sharing the experience with, as well as allowing us to attend to the needs of our bodies: to stretch, to find a toilet or to have a drink. They are an acknowledgement that we can maintain focus and remain immersed in the work of spectatorship only for a limited period of time. Beyond the theatre, interruptions that delay journeys and the smooth functioning of communication technologies remind us that large-scale systems are vulnerable, too. When interruptions come directly from others, they often are an expression of need: requests for help, for information or simply for attention. Covid can be interpreted as a planetary-level interruption: an intervention from a distressed and imbalanced system which desperately needs our attention and care. Interruptions may frequently be unwelcome, but they may also be telling us something we urgently need to know.

Consideration of the significance of interruption can also help us contemplate the variety of ways that historical and cultural change is conceptualized. We can think in terms of evolution, progress and paradigm shifts, or revolution, stages of crisis, disjunctions and ruptures (Postlewait 2009: 259). Here, however, we want to acknowledge and highlight the fact that we are writing about *times* of crisis: plural rather than singular. In this respect, the book takes a different approach to some other recent publications which address this issue. Perhaps the best example is another book in this series – Barbara Fuchs' *Theater of Lockdown: Digital and Distanced Performance in a Time of Pandemic* (2022). Fuchs' subtitle, with its emphasis upon the singular 'Time of Pandemic', is indicative of the tight focus of her work. Still, as we pieced together this book across 2021 and 2022, it became clear that it is more appropriate to think of *times*, rather than time. Crisis can no longer be considered a distinct period of fear, insecurity and instability which we will pass through. Instead, we seem to be caught in 'Permacrisis': the Collins Dictionary's word of the year for 2022 (Sherwood 2022). In 2022, the reality of the climate crisis made itself felt more strongly than before, provoking a new level of disruption and protest; the Russian invasion of Ukraine in February 2022 brought war to Europe and created sudden rises in global energy prices; inflation aggravated the cost-of-living crisis; pay's failure to keep pace with the cost of living provoked strikes in essential services; the Conservative Party churned through leadership battles, creating political instability and preoccupying the government; financial crisis resulted from market responses to the government approach to borrowing; the National Health Service (NHS) seemed to be grinding to a halt. Crisis seems to follow crisis, each feeding into the others. This awareness of interlinked, enmeshed and cascading crises – plural rather than singular – is shared by other critics who have published on the relationship between British theatre and crisis in recent years (Angelaki 2017; Wallace and Escoda 2022). We also share an understanding of crisis as a turning point which carries within it the potential for change with these critics.

We realize that having the space and time to write a book during 2022, in the midst of these interlinked and apparently interminable crises, is a measure of relative privilege. Yet, this period made us more aware than ever before of the precarity of our positioning as academics and practitioners. Colleagues in University departments dedicated to theatre and performance across the UK were made redundant; the British Council suffered extreme cuts; audience appetite for attending live events was impacted by the increased cost of fuel and food (Jowett 2022a; Hemley 2022; Mantell 2022). Moreover, we have often been made anxiously aware that the Covid crisis itself is not yet over. In Britain it has just moved from an acute to a chronic phase: the notion that its impact has been contained within one discrete and completed historical moment is clearly untenable. So, although this book is primarily concerned with the new perspectives that Covid has provided, its title acknowledges that the virus is one of many global challenges and that we are still living in 'Covid time'.

19 July 2022. I've been inside all day, mostly lying on the sofa. I've closed all the curtains and the windows but it's still too hot to work, to move, to think. Now I need to go and get my daughter from school. I cover up:

a long skirt, long sleeved shirt, a floppy hat. When I step outside it's like entering a furnace. The heat seems to be rising from the tarmac and beating off the walls. I've never felt anything like it before.

On change

We must, of course, acknowledge the challenges inherent in any attempt to write analytically about, and to, the present moment and the very recent past. New information and experiences unsettle the development of smooth narration; the present arrives in a jumble of action and inaction; no one has sorted the significant and insignificant, the meaningful from the meaningless; and there is as yet no settled version of events to correct or update. The sudden burst of media attention given to examples of audiences behaving badly in April 2023, as we finalized these pages for publication, is indicative of this issue (Healy 2023). This effect is amplified, of course, by the volume and churn of social media, which generates a cacophony of voices and perspectives. Indeed, some critics have argued that the lack of temporal distance makes it impossible to examine the contemporary moment historiographically, and that the networked simultaneity of the contemporary moment does not map on to the chronological logic of conventional historiography, which presupposes a linear movement that necessarily invokes a 'before', and an 'after' (Warstat 2020: 385–6). Writing this book – which covers past, present and hopes for the future – has involved reflection on how we understand their relationship. It was inspired, in part, by recent experience of examining some of the most dominant and influential histories of audiencing, and interrogating some of the most well-worn stories about the past experience of watching or witnessing the performing arts. This analysis highlighted the role that nostalgia, myth-making and hope for the future play in evocations of theatres past, as well as detecting disciplinary blind spots, distortions in the record created by the desire to defend and promote performance, and complexities elided by the construction of a good story. It has also involved facing discomforting questions. In a historical moment which is characterized by fears for the future of democracy, the possibility of nuclear annihilation and climate breakdown, what is the point of concerning ourselves with theatre's future – or its past? Who – or what – is this work for? We are not alone in feeling that there is an urgent need to address these questions (Wiles 2021). The editors of recent collections which address the direction and purpose of theatre historiography also engage directly with them. Jo Robinson and Claire Cochrane (2019) declare that the discipline needs to become more diverse, collaborative and inclusive, becoming broader in its international reach, more expansive in the practices it focuses upon, and more open to collaboration and input from outside the academy. Tracy C. Davis and Peter W. Marx (2020) push for the discipline to set aside its long preoccupation with the distinctions between theatre and performance, arguing that not only are the two interdependent but that this debate can also be seen as irrelevant when viewed from a global perspective. Both assert that we need to move beyond a historiographical approach which is governed by linear or grand narratives and dominated by publications which focus upon singular individuals – whether actors, directors or playwrights. Clearly, it is long past the time when we should be dedicating our energies to storying the achievements of dead white men. Instead, these collections propose that the discipline needs to accommodate a broader range of methodologies and conceptualize theatre history itself in different ways. Davis and Marx state that we should approach theatre history as a collage, a product of a range of different perspectives (2020: 1), while Robinson and Cochrane use the rhizome as metaphor and model for an invisible but interlinked network, which operates both as a storage bank of shared cultural knowledge and the basis for new growths in study and understanding (2019: 9–10).

Answering the question of who this work is for, however, involves acknowledging that this book is addressed to the future, rather than the past. A reckoning with profound cultural change can animate and energize. Covid can be interpreted as a portal – a gateway from one world to another – and, as noted earlier, we consider Roy's insights to be inspiring and prescient. In the context of discussion of concerns that might be raised by a move to deliver performance solely via pre-recorded video, Esther Neff argues that we should view the pandemic situation as a 'one-time-only' experiment (2022: 43) – an experiment which would suggest that it is possible to brush aside concerns about form in favour of focus upon aesthetics and the values that the work expresses. We propose that rather than viewing the pandemic experience as a singular event, it would be more appropriate to think of it as a rehearsal: an opportunity to assess our readiness and prepare for the future. Changes to come in the way of life that has supported traditions of performance practice to date may be incremental or sudden – and take forms as yet unclear to us – but they are certain to arrive. The stark revelations afforded by this supremely teachable moment present us with compelling evidence of the need to take stock of our past practices and to move with purpose towards a new kind of relationship between audience and performance. But in the time since the publication of Roy's article in April 2020, we have had time to reflect upon how cultural change comes about, and the speed at which these changes take place. We can, of course, identify 'the Before Times', a term from science fiction that now has currency as shorthand for our pre-Covid lives (Gillespie 2021; Merriam-Webster 2022). Still, it is important to remember that the temporal cut off between 'before' and 'after' is not perhaps quite as distinct as the melancholy grandeur the phrase seems to suggest. What's more, innovation in the theatre does not occur in the same way as biological processes, despite the enduring and problematic tendency in theatre and performance studies to conceptualize the theatre as a living body: as being 'alive' or 'dead'. Instead, it is a network, as Sarah Bay-Cheng and Amy Holzapfel point out in their article 'The Living Theatre: A Brief History of a Bodily Metaphor' (2010: 27). Traditions and conventions in theatre and performance practice do not 'die' – they transition between being emergent, dominant and residual cultural forms, as described by Raymond Williams (1977: 121–6). Some are clearly old-fashioned, even passé; while dominant forms are the status quo, the unremarkable mainstream. Experimental innovations are often the focus of censorious anxiety, struggling for recognition and acceptance. Though our cultural lives were profoundly altered when we entered lockdown in March 2020, what we experienced in the immediate aftermath of this upheaval was a pause in dominant and residual types of theatre-making, which made emergent forms more noticeable. Digital performance and livestreaming had substantial histories of their own before the lockdown conditions made them more visible and accelerated their development (Dixon 1999a; Aebischer, Greenhalgh and Osborne 2018; Masura 2020). Covid did not bring them into being. It just made more people aware of their existence, potentials and limitations. The crisis has expanded our understanding of what theatre and performance can be; what audiences can be; and what their relationship to performance might be. Covid also demonstrated that disruption does not only give emergent forms a boost. The solutions which some companies came up with in the summer of 2020 when distanced gathering was possible again were reminiscent of residual forms of theatrical experience: taking place outdoors and making use of the street rather than the stage.

We hope this book demonstrates the value of bringing scholarly and current cultural sector perspectives together. It is a product of fascination with the variety of historical conventions, the way that they have come to develop and shift, and how they inform current practice. But it is also driven by our need to engage with how things can be different in the future, and the urge to inspire future change. This focus on material conditions and tangible opportunities – rather than cultural discourse – is compelled in part by the realization that our particular cultural and historical moment demands decisive action from those in positions of power. We have written this book in the hope that it will provide readers with space to contemplate the future forms of theatrical performance and audience engagement – and reinvigorate desire to bring about change.

1

Performance's place in time
On duration, speed and intervals

This chapter proposes that the Covid crisis can be interpreted as a period of 'dark festival', in which the norms of spectatorship were overturned, transforming our understanding of theatre's place in time. Fresh from this experience of temporal disorientation, it considers how we conceive of performance's place in time in terms of duration, frequency and its place in our days, weeks and years, and asks whether the temporal norms that have governed performance over centuries have changed as much as we might imagine. Reflecting on how timing and duration impact the relationship between performance and its audiences, it highlights areas of innovation and practice which have not received as much attention as they deserve to date, arguing that time is an important factor when thinking about access and inclusivity. It touches upon performances fast and slow, long and short, analysing productions of unusual brevity as well as those that stretch or challenge expectations regarding the length of time that an audience can reasonably be expected to actively engage with performance.

During the pandemic, the experience of unnerving changes in the perception of time was broadly shared. The curious, distorted perception of time during lockdown periods of the crisis was one of the most remarked upon aspects of the experience. For those of us obliged to stay at home, many of the usual divisions in our days were removed. Without the temporal anchors provided by the daily routine of journeys to and from work, regular shopping trips, weekly gatherings for worship or for leisure activities, many felt unmoored and adrift on a vast sea of undifferentiated time. The distinctions between days and weeks, weekdays and weekends, morning and night, began to blur. In these conditions, people reported temporal disorientation, becoming unclear about which day of the week it was and feeling as if time was passing either too quickly or too slowly. The passing of time seemed paradoxical and contradictory: extremely slow on an hour-by-hour basis but then also vanishingly fast – as though a year had been swallowed all at once.

Time, however, was also one of the areas which highlighted profound inequalities. It seemed that one had either too much of it or too little. Some professions were pushed into frantic activity. People working in the NHS and in the care system found themselves overwhelmed by the expanding volume of extreme and challenging activity (Clarke 2021); working parents attempting to entertain, educate and care for bored and anxious children suddenly found themselves without a moment to pause. Others, child-free in secure employment and able to work from home, were also struggling with the sudden lack of routine and structure. Events which we use to mark major life stages – weddings, funerals, parties – were either postponed or held online in unrecognizable forms. Many teenagers, passing through the UK's rites of educational passage, felt as though Covid had effectively stolen time, denying them the experiences and events which usually mark this period out: examinations; final days in school with their year group; proms and end-of-year parties. The sudden lack of novel, significant or memorable occasions, and the removal of methods of marking time through transitions between different spaces, was experienced by many as a deep boredom, and a sense that days were passing by monotonously without meaningful activity or distinctiveness. Alister Wedderburn surely speaks for many in his musings on 'Pandemic Time', in which he recalls that he found that the scale and scope of his life had shrunk dramatically during the weeks of lockdown at the start of the pandemic. His days began to revolve around meals and his daily walk: temporal markers which are usually for dogs rather than people (2020: 31). Writing in May 2020, Arielle Pardes captures this quality in her article 'There Are No Hours or Days in Coronatime'. Yet, Pardes argues that the distortions and pressures of 'Coronatime' were not simply a product of the monotony, anxiety and frustration associated with being cooped up at home. They were generated by lack of control and uncertainty about what would happen next. Writing from the middle of the first months of the crisis, she observes that the waiting enforced by Coronatime feels particularly crushing because we do not know how long it will last; whether a viable vaccine will be created; how the virus will develop; or when and whether the crisis will come to an end. Pardes notes that we are scared that there is no end in sight, but also that it might all come to an end too soon. Her article illustrates the way that tedium sat alongside a heightened awareness of human vulnerability and mortality, as well as a sharpened appreciation of the fragility of our systems of social and economic organization, in this early phase of the pandemic. The sudden arrival of the crisis wiped away the illusion that things will always go on as they have before. Change, in this case, did not arrive slowly or incrementally, giving us all a chance to adjust.

The challenge to mental health posed by this temporal disruption quickly became apparent. Both the World Health Organization and the NHS issued guidance which advised people to try either to keep to their existing routines or to generate new rhythms of behaviour (2020). The difficulty of doing so is recorded by numerous studies that surveyed the temporal impact of lockdown, both in terms of changes to the ways that time was being used, and in relation to perceptions of time. These studies note changes in the quality and quantity of sleep; decreases in quantity of physical activity; increases in screen time (particularly for children aged six to ten) as well as the perceived distortion of time – indicating the extraordinary levels of confusion and disruption caused by the crisis (Ogden 2020; Blume, Schmidt, and Cajochen 2020; Trott et al. 2022).

Our subjective experience of time is, of course, distinct from objective measures of its duration. Age, parenthood, physical exertion, emotional state, exposure to stimulants or depressants, immersion within activities – or interruptions – can all impact upon our perception of time (Draaisma 2004; Rutrecht et al. 2021; Wittman and Mella 2021; Fayolle, Gil, and Droit-Volet 2015). We know that individual people experience time differently from one another, and that time has been conceived of differently in different periods and cultures (Whitrow 1988). Studies demonstrate that our experience of time is also inflected by gender, class, race, sexuality and even our politics (Moskowitz, Olcaysoy Okten, and Gooch 2015; Edelman 2004; Ouellet, 2023). We are aware that other animals experience time differently from humans, and that human civilization has really, when it comes to planetary time, only just arrived (Healy et al. 2013; Chakrabarty 2021). We recognize that technology carries within it a distinct understanding of time – and that this has implications for our own experience of time (Landes 1983). We sense that machine time is different from human time, worrying about the disjunction between the two, and the possibility that our ability to maintain our grip on time – to sustain attention and focus – is being undermined by our encounters with devices and algorithms, which appear to be designed to steal time from us (Pettman 2016).

> *19 April 2020. We visit Druridge Bay, a ten-mile stretch of sandy beach on the North Sea coast. It's never busy but on this occasion it's completely deserted. We probably shouldn't be here. It's stretching the definition of local. We are the only people on the beach. Searching the tide line for shells, I find a large piece of dark green sea-glass, not long in the water. The edges are softened but you can still see the branding clearly – it's a green bottle of Newcastle IPA. I wonder what will be left of us when we're gone. How long will it take nature to break down the mess we've made?*

Time is at once the most metaphysical and the most mundane of matters, where awareness of our mortality and fear of ageing rub up against task list reminders and bullet journals. Discussion about time is often voiced in the language of concern. We worry that we do not have enough of it; that we are wasting it; that it is running out. To be professional involves awareness that time needs to be carefully measured and parcelled out. The metaphor 'time is money' has come to define and determine our understanding and everyday behaviours (Lakoff and Johnson 1980: 7–9), while time management has become big business in and of itself, with its own traditions, gurus, apps and classes (Claessens et al. 2007). Even the most thoughtful books on the subject remind us that, on average, each of us has only *Four Thousand Weeks* in which to pursue the activities that matter to us (Burkeman 2021). The knowledge that it is impossible to do everything that we want or need to do in the time we have is heightened by an ever-expanding volume of popular publications on 'the great acceleration': publications that continue to accumulate despite time use surveys which demonstrate that 'time poverty' is not a universal phenomenon, or getting significantly worse (Gleick 1999; Wajcman 2015; Colvile 2017; Sullivan and Gershuny 2018). This sense of time pressure is accompanied by a growing awareness that the continuing speed of change during the Anthropocene represents an existential threat to humanity as well as other life forms (McNeill and Engelke 2016). In response, calls to prioritize slowness across all aspects of culture have issued from the late 1980s on. From food to fashion, parenting to photography, science to scholarship, writers and practitioners have been promoting the benefits of resisting the 'cult of speed' (Honoré 2004; Stengers 2018; Chambers and Gearhart 2018). Recent years have seen a greater appreciation of the interconnection of time and politics. We know that power is usually won by those that have speed on their side (Virilio 1986 [1977]); that the denial of coevalness – the assertion that other civilizations are fundamentally behind the times – has enabled colonial violence and exploitation (Fabian 1983); and that being able to make others wait is a privilege enjoyed only by those with authority, influence and the law on their side (Tawil-Souri 2017; Stronks 2022).

Joanna died in late February 2020. Her funeral happened on the cusp of Covid. We sat at a distance from other families in the church at the end of our road. No one hugged. During lockdown we begin to include a circuit of the churchyard in our daily walks. As the weeks go on, a path has begun to be worn around the perimeter. The space gives me a chance to think about her, and about the presence of the dead. As I walk past the graves I look at the names and dates, the terse details which position the deceased in relation to their age, and other family members.

Occasionally we get given details of their profession, or how or where they died. So little remains here but the division between us and them feels thinner than ever: I've never been so aware of how easily the living can become the dead.

Time out of time: temporal disruption and the dark festival

Performance has a paradoxical relationship with time. On the one hand, it is commonly understood as a time-bound, ephemeral and transient art form. Each event possesses a unique, unrepeatable quality. It can feel alive with spontaneity and the electrifying sense of risk that only art made in the present moment can command. On the other, theatre can seem preoccupied – fixated even – with mortality, death and dying (Robson 2019). It allows us to confront collectively the worst things that might befall us, to face the brevity and fragility of existence, and to contemplate the inevitability of change and loss.

Repetition is central to performance's systems of production: from the memorization of lines and movement, run after run in rehearsal, and then repeated acts of presentation, as a single production is delivered many times over. Even after the end of a run or tour, successful productions are often revived, and the whole process starts again. Performance and theatre are also deeply preoccupied with the reliving of the past. Performance draws upon and re-enacts a broad repertoire of movement and gesture, while theatre often works with scripts written many years before, drawing upon long-established approaches to acting and systems of production. The UK is especially blessed – or cursed, perhaps – with a well-documented and much-exported historical theatre culture. Shakespeare looms over all areas of our theatre industry as companies return to his works time and time again. British theatre often takes place in buildings, which, as we note in Chapter 2, are redolent of performance past and have a long association with ghosts and haunting. Contemporary critics and directors can seem, however, to invest in the idea that successful performance offers audiences experiences which provide an alternative to the relentless forward press of linear time. For Steve Dixon, one of the benefits of the juxtaposition of live performance and digital imagery is its potential to generate an 'extratemporal' experience, allowing audiences to feel as though they are 'stepping to one side or outside of time' (2007: 537). Ann Bogart's brief foreword to the edited collection *Time and Performer Training* invokes a similar ideal as she urges theatre makers to cultivate awareness of the distinctions between 'horizontal' and 'vertical' time. She proposes that horizontal time is defined by clear distinctions between past, present and future, experienced by performance practitioners daily as they negotiate the press of time-limited projects, alongside the speed and demands of everyday life. Vertical time is experienced when we are fully present. Bogart argues that performance has the capacity to produce 'the experience of vertical time for the perceiver by [. . .] dropping an anchor into the endless flow of time, thereby creating a sense of eternity' (2019: 4).

Theatre festivals have long been seen as spaces in which these kinds of atypical temporal experiences are fostered. They appear to provide access to 'time out of time' (Falassi 1987: 7), a form of carnival time, set apart from the everyday, in which the usual rules and regulations do not apply. Festivals also test our understanding of how long our engagement with performance can – or should – last, and when it should occur during the day. As we have observed elsewhere, they produce curious and sometimes contradictory perceptions of the passing of time, appearing to stretch and compress experience simultaneously (Craddock 2019: 196). As discussed in the Introduction, the pandemic can be interpreted as a period of 'dark festival', in which the norms of behaviour and spectatorship were overturned, impacting our understanding of theatre's place in time in profound ways.

In the first phase of the pandemic, it seemed as though theatre's very existence was under threat: that it might not survive this time of crisis (Kirwan 2020). In March 2020, as productions were pulled and buildings and companies closed for business, it was easy to feel as if theatre was dying. But the death of theatre has long been hailed by scholars, critics, playwrights and directors many times before. As Rebecca Schneider remarks, announcements of the death of theatre, much like those of the death of the author, might be seen to function to bolster the health and longevity of the subject of concern (2001: 105). Indeed, for theatre enthusiasts lucky enough to have access to stable broadband in their homes, as well as good health, time and job security, the first few months of the Covid crisis were a theatrical bonanza. Theatre and performance companies and venues worldwide began to make their back catalogues of recorded productions available to watch online. Performances which few had had the opportunity to view in person suddenly became available to watch from home. Many were available 24/7: a boon for those suffering from the effects of insomnia and looking for distraction in the early hours. For an audience with nowhere to go, performance could be accessed at all times of the day and night. Pascale Aebischer's account of binge-watching past productions online during the early weeks of the pandemic draws out the curious impact that this had upon her perception of the artistic connections between the shows. She notes, 'precursors turn into successors, what follows after can change the meaning of what comes before, and dialogues between productions defy the laws of chronology' (2022: 25). For others, the deluge of archived performance in the first moments of the pandemic had the curious effect of making theatre seem as though it belonged in the past. As Gemma Allred and Benjamin Broadribb observe, the kind of distancing being experienced by audiences who were watching these productions was temporal and cultural, rather than social, as images of audiences and actors in close proximity to each other offered a nostalgic, backward-looking view of the theatre (2022: 3). The work that followed this initial archival outpouring represented a more significant challenge to the temporal norms which have determined the nature of the relationship between audiences and performers for most of theatre history. As we state in Chapter 3, digital and online forms of performance could hardly be considered new in 2020. They did, however, become newly visible in the absence of in-person offerings, energizing debate over the status of live performance: debate which usually included the assertion that theatre's meaning is bound up with its status as a live event, and the bringing together of the bodies of performers and spectators in shared time and space.

Performance's place in time

The conventions which determine the temporal aspects of the relationship between performance and audience can appear to be so ingrained – so unremarkable – that they are impossible to challenge, as Lyn Gardner acknowledges when questioning the standard 7.30 pm start time which almost all contemporary theatres in the UK now observe (2013). It is easy to imagine that temporal aspects of the relationship between theatre and its audiences are informed by the physical needs of the human body: the circadian rhythms that govern our activity and rest, and the limits of our ability to sustain speech, movement and attention. Yet, returning to the historical record indicates that expectations of when performance should occur, in terms of duration, sequencing, frequency and its proper place in our days, weeks, and years have been subject to significant variation across time, as traditions and norms shift and change. As Eviatar Zerubavel has demonstrated, the methods that we use to organize and manage the collective experience of time – minutes, hours, days, weeks, months and years – are arbitrary and artificial, and the distinctions between the working week and the weekend, and between sacred and secular time, are cultural constructs, subject to historical and geographical variation (2021). And, as historians have indicated, how the day is divided up, and understandings of which activities are appropriate during daylight and which after sundown, have changed from historical period to historical period (Ekirch 2006). The time that we spend with performance and its positioning in our days is delimited by these broader temporal norms and is also shaped by the perceived purpose of performance, and its social, political, spiritual or economic function.

It has been argued that the early modern period marks a significant shift in our understanding of time. Steven Connor asserts that 'modern temporality [. . .] begins with the replacement, during the late medieval period in Europe, of the cyclical, recurrent, or sacred time of religion, with a form of linear, progressive, and secular time centred not on God but on the State' (1999: 16). David Wiles' discussion of the impact of the transition from medieval to modern temporal eras in *Theatre & Time* draws upon a similar understanding. The pre-industrial year in Catholic Britain, Wiles observes, was punctuated by numerous religious holy days, including Palm Sunday, Whitsuntide, Pentecost, All Hallows Eve and Advent, and scripted theatre in this period was attached to these annual cycles as 'an extension of the richly textured drama of the year' (20). He proposes that modernity breaks this connection. Theatre is no longer 'part of the texture of sacred time', but instead becomes 'a transferable product which could take place at any moment in time when leisure became available' (2014: 21).

Changes in traditions of religious observance have certainly had a very significant part to play in performance's place in time. As we have noted elsewhere, scholars are particularly fond of citing the week-long duration of the ancient Greek City Dionysia festival as an example of civic and spectatorial investment in the theatre, linked to its status as a celebration of Dionysus, god of theatre, wine and transformation (Freshwater 2022). The religious pageants presented at the Corpus Christi festivals on the streets of English cities during the medieval period are also known for their length. Records indicate that the Chester cycle was presented over three days, with nine plays on the first day (including the fall of Lucifer and the Nativity), eight on the second (including the Passion and Crucifixion) and six on the final day (including the Resurrection and the Last Judgment). York's cycle took place on a very long single day, beginning at dawn and lasting around fifteen hours (Davis 1993, Fitzgerald and Sebastian 2018). The religious commitment that fuelled these events was also to result in their eventual silencing, however. The Corpus Christi cycles were subject to gradual but complete suppression during the second half of the sixteenth century, as part of the shift to Protestantism during the Reformation. The new Christian orthodoxy viewed theatrical performance as the work of the devil: a dangerous and potentially corrupting waste of time, rather than a tool which could be used to cement the status of the Church. And, as the commercial theatre became established in the late sixteenth century, tension grew between the obligation to congregate for worship and growing interest in gathering at the theatre, with the authorities only permitting performance on Sundays after the end of obligatory church attendance at 3.30 pm in the 1580s (Wiles 2014: 26). The linear, secular, State-centred time regime identified by Connor did not win out at this point, however.

The Puritan anti-theatrical prejudice which fuelled these debates ultimately resulted in the closure of the theatres in 1642. Debate over whether theatre should be permitted on Sundays reignited on their reopening in 1660. The year 1677 saw the introduction of a Sunday Observance Act, which curtailed commercial operations on the Sabbath. Commercial performance on Sundays in England and Wales was banned outright by the 1780 Sunday Observance Act and was only legalized again in the 1972 Sunday Theatre Act. Performers and audiences established systems for working around these constraints in the interim, including private theatre clubs (Brown 1929). Yet the extraordinarily lengthy debates held in Parliament in 1931 and 1953, as some MPs attempted to overturn the 1780 Act, provide a remarkable record of the extraordinary national attachment to Sunday's sacred status (Harline 2011). Presenting his case against legalizing theatre on Sundays in the House of Commons in 1931, the MP for Ashford, Roderick Kedward, asserted:

> I want to put this to the House, that there is something big and distinctive in Sunday and in the observance of Sunday, in this country. If you allow this Measure to pass and allow Sunday to be exploited, Prussianised, by all kinds of people for their own gain, you are going to undermine some of the very finest elements in this country. You are going to play fast and loose with the foundations upon which the greatness of this nation has been developed. [. . .] We should not turn

our backs because of any specious pleas about the liberty of the subject. It is not liberty that is being asked for to-night, but licence. I hope the House will reject the Bill.

Clearly, not everyone got the memo about the replacement of religious temporality with secular time.

Seasonality has also proved to be an enduring element in the annual cycle of engagement between performance and its audiences. In London, during the early seventeenth century, the seasons of the commercial theatres were referred to as 'terms' and 'vacations', labels borrowed from the scholarly and legal institutions from which many of the audience came. Theatre companies dependent upon the court toured the country during the summer as the aristocracy left London to avoid the plagues associated with the season (Stern 2007: 48). As Wiles notes, the migratory rhythms of audiences and performers changed as the eighteenth century brought better sanitation, reducing the scale of the summer exodus of the capital. Yet the rhythms of tourism and travel continue to influence the structure of the theatrical year. Many theatres still programme their work around distinct seasons, which are usually announced in the New Year and in early summer with some fanfare. Pantomimes continue to dominate the winter festive season, providing theatres with an annual financial boost, just as they did in the Victorian period (Davis 2007: 13).

Performance's position in the daily temporal pattern has also seen surprisingly little change. During the early modern period, performances at the open-air public venues mainly took place during the afternoon, starting at 2.00 or 3.00 pm and continuing for three to four hours. Visits to court and the homes of the aristocracy to deliver performance happened in the evening. The economics of theatre production drove this arrangement. The cost of lighting events in the evening meant that they were only for the privileged few. Achieving an adequate amount of light at night was a major and costly undertaking, as Martin White's study of negotiations over the cost of candlelight for seventeenth-century indoor playhouses indicates (2014). By the eighteenth century, start times had moved back to 6.00 pm (Van Lennep,

Avery, and Scouten 1965: lxix-lxx). Still, audiences did not have to turn up at a strictly prescribed time to enjoy the performance, and flexibility around entry times was still the norm for the best part of the nineteenth century, as theatres retained their status as relaxed, social spaces. Victor Emeljanow notes that the programming of most theatres in the period stretched from 6.30 pm until midnight, and it was not unusual for audience members to arrive later in the evening, making use of half-price tickets (2014: 55–6). This practice was phased out in many venues by the end of the century, however, as fixed start times of 7.30 and 8.00 pm were introduced, distinguishing mainstream theatres from Variety or Music Hall where spectators and performers were expected to come and go throughout the evening.

Performance has also found its way into the early morning and late into the night. Major theatre festivals now programme work around the clock. The pressure on space and time at the Edinburgh Festival Fringe free-for-all even results in work being offered in the early morning, from annual provisions of *Shakespeare for Breakfast* (available every year since 1991, with the exception of 2020 and 2021) to more short-lived offerings such as the 9.00 am *Breakfast Plays* at the Traverse Theatre (2016) and the *Continental Brechtfest* at the Royal Scots Club (1990), which advertised free coffee and croissants (rather surprisingly perhaps, given Brecht's thoughts on culinary theatre). At the other end of the day, 'Midnight matinees' made occasional appearances as fundraisers or special celebrations across the twentieth century and were a regular feature at seaside resorts such as Margate, Blackpool and Stonehaven during the 1950s (Vickers 1993; Marshalsay 1993; Clark 1998). Shakespeare's Globe has included two or three late-night midnight matinees in their summertime offer since 2006 (with start times of 11.59 pm for the avoidance of confusion). But these are the exceptions to the rule. The surprising level of uniformity in approaches to scheduling performance – outside of 'festival time' – suggests that we accept these norms without much thought. And, where divergence from these temporal conventions does exist, it does not usually receive much attention.

The re-establishment of afternoon performance as a regular part of theatre programming during the nineteenth century has certainly not attracted a great deal of scholarly notice. Susan Torrey Barstow, one of the very few theatre scholars to show an interest in the matinee, notes that its date and place of origin are attributed to a range of venues and individuals (2001). Writing in his memoirs, Squire Bancroft, manager of the Prince of Wales Theatre, asserted that his company 'really established' the form in 1878 (1969: 71); but playbills which record performances taking place in the afternoon date to the mid-nineteenth century (Armstrong 1958: 56). Barstow notes that many West End theatres followed the lead of the Savoy Theatre, where Wednesday and Saturday performances of Gilbert and Sullivan's operettas were offered in the afternoon in the 1880s. She also calculates that during the early 1890s – the 'heyday' of the matinee – afternoon performances made up nearly 60 per cent of all plays produced in London's theatres: an extraordinary figure (2001: 407). Barstow demonstrates that the matinee enabled producers to offer more performances of popular productions and provided a space to try out new work. The matinee also enjoyed huge popularity amongst female spectators. Barstow's reading of the period's theatre criticism indicates that women dominated the matinee – as spectators, actors and as protagonists – and she argues that the development of experimental theatre through scheduling as matinees in this period was due in large part to the enthusiasm of female audiences, citing matinee reviewer A. B. Walkley, who observed that 'without womankind, the modern drama would cease to exist' (quoted in Barstow 388). The relative neglect of the history of the matinee is a product, perhaps, of its continued association with the young and the old, and with women, or with distant early modern theatre practice. But examining its re-emergence in British theatre in the mid-nineteenth century and the development of lunchtime theatre in the twentieth century, discussed later, highlights the way that timing can attract and accommodate the needs of particular segments of the population.

Intervals might be considered the most unremarkable of theatrical conventions, but they have important implications for audience experience. They provide temporal markers in performance, signalling shifts in attention and opportunities for audience members to interact. Their arrival in performance practice also had a significant impact upon what was happening on stage, as well as off, as Mark Hutchings reveals in his analysis of the establishment of the interval as a theatrical convention. Hutchings connects this with the acquisition of indoor playhouses by professional companies in the early seventeenth century. He acknowledges that earlier printed texts followed classical models, which broke action up into distinct acts or scenes, but argues that this was not reflected in performance practice in the outdoor playhouses, which were performed without breaks, effectively obscuring the transitions between these segments in performance. But indoor spaces were lit with candles that could not last for entire performances and had to be tended, thus creating the need for intervals. Hutchings proposes that this generated a crucial shift to the rhythm of performance presentation, constituting a 'structurally transformative development' which became integral to the composition of performance. Intervals offered dramatists a type of 'structural punctuation', which served to highlight the beginning and ending of acts, while they gave spectators a chance to discuss what they had seen, and what was to come (2013: 263–4). For those who were seated on stage, it was an excellent opportunity to draw attention to their presence. Subsequently, intervals have been used to realize elaborate scene changes and boost the theatre's takings at the bar. They have also given critics plenty to chew on when assessing the significance of directors' decisions about where to place the interval (Dessen 2002: 94–108).

In recent years, commentators have debated whether intervals are really necessary, insisting that some shows are better without interruption, while also conceding that audience attention – and bladders – can be stretched only so far (Crompton 2017). Louis Wise, who clearly has no great love for theatre as a form, claims in 'The Joy of the Theatre Interval', an opinion piece for *The Evening Standard*, that intervals provide space for the real business of theatre-going: socializing and the consumption of ice cream (2018). When Shakespeare's Globe reopened after the Covid crisis in 2021, the theatre's announcement that they would no longer be providing intervals was greeted with dismay in some quarters, and enthusiasm in others: Lyn Gardner argued in *The Stage* that the move could accelerate broader provision of more relaxed and inclusive performances, as it made it explicit that it is acceptable for audience members to leave the auditorium when they need to (2021). At *The Daily Telegraph*, columnist Giles Brandreth spelled out his position in an article titled 'No more intervals at the theatre? But they're the best bit!' (2021). Though the interventions of Wise, Gardner and Brandreth need to be read in context, they all make important points: when it is provided, the interval makes a substantial contribution to the meaning of the event for spectators. Wise and Brandreth highlight the fact that some audience members find as much value and interest in what happens offstage at the theatre as they do in the activities which occur on the stage, while Gardner reminds us that we may all benefit from being able to take a break when we need to.

On duration

Listeners have been able to manipulate the playing speed of recorded speech and sound since the invention of the phonograph in 1877, while digital distribution now enables the viewer to make choices about the speed at which they want to consume film, video and TV. Yet, performance resists this kind of temporal manipulation. When delivered in person, theatre and performance cannot be speeded up by the audience in the ways that film, TV and audio can: productions proceed at a pace dictated by the performers. Still, there are many examples of efforts by performers, directors and producers to cut the length of plays or to increase the speed of their delivery, to ensure that there is no opportunity for an audience's attention to drift. The history of the temporal compression of Shakespeare's plays in performance (related by Peter Holland in 'Shakespeare Abbreviated') provides numerous examples of the urge to reduce and condense dramatic content (2007). As Holland notes, the ready cutting of lines, speeches, scenes and characters in modern productions of Shakespeare has many antecedents. Though 1623 is often cited as the date of the first abridgement of the playwright's work (in an amalgamated conflation of *Henry IV Part 1* and *Henry IV Part 2* created by aristocrat and theatre enthusiast Edward Dering for performance at his country house), Holland finds earlier examples. Shortened versions of many of Shakespeare's plays were presented across Europe by touring troupes of English performers from the early years of the seventeenth century (31). Holland's history stretches into the late twentieth century with an assessment of abbreviations of Shakespeare for children, and with discussion of the work of the Reduced Shakespeare Company, who first created a thirty-minute version of *Hamlet* in 1981 and went on to have global success with productions such as their one-hour *The Complete Works of William Shakespeare (Abridged)*, created for the Edinburgh Festival Fringe in 1987 (41). The works of the Reduced Shakespeare Company clearly depend upon prior audience knowledge of plot, lines or character – and Shakespeare's status as cultural touchstone – but other abbreviations of his plays do not. As Holland asserts, though some of the English performers who were using his works as material in the early seventeenth century may have been aware of his status as author, their audiences definitely were not. This is also true of the cut-down versions aimed at primary-school-age children that have proliferated in the UK during the past twenty years, which usually assume that their child audiences will not have encountered the work of the playwright before (Rokison 2013: 99–127). What they all share, however, is an interest in reducing the playing time of what is perceived to be an overly long original.

Many other texts known for their length or difficulty have been cut and condensed for staging in recent years in productions which use limited cast numbers or improvisation to highlight the creative challenge involved in the work of reduction. An adaptation of *The 39 Steps*, which combined John Buchan's 1915 novel, its 1935 screen adaptation by Alfred Hitchcock, and various other Hitchcock films, is representative of this trend. Presented by a cast of four, it enjoyed a successful run at London's Criterion theatre between 2006 and 2015. The 'Potted' series, which utilizes the talents of two BBC children's TV presenters, is based upon the same premise. Beginning with *Potted Potter* (2005), which presented J. K. Rowling's Harry Potter seven-book series in one hour, it was followed by *Potted Panto* (2010), which was advertised as presenting seventy pantomimes in one go. Their most recent production, *Potted Sherlock* (2014), referenced sixty Arthur Conan Doyle stories in seventy minutes. These efforts to provide access to works which take many hours to watch or read in full reward depth of fannish knowledge and provide a recognizable vehicle for the display of comedic talent. They are clearly designed to astonish and impress audiences through the presentation of what might seem to be impossible acts of compression, as well as showcasing the ingenuity of their creators.

The compression of literary and cinematic source texts in productions such as these may reflect the perception that the leisure time audiences have available is increasingly under pressure. It can also be read as a response to a communication culture which is defined by brevity, as Ronan Hatfull argues in his 2018 analysis of the influence of the Reduced Shakespeare Company. Yet the running times of these 'potted' productions were not unusually short. Writing in 2015, the authors of *The One-Act Play Companion* note that run times of just over an hour are now not unusual, with the result that the distinction between long one-act productions and short full-length plays has become blurred (Walford and Dolley: viii). In some cases, relative brevity is directly related to the cost of access to space, cost which can be punishing when performance space is in high demand. In the UK, this situation finds its most extreme expression at the Edinburgh Festival Fringe, where smaller venues often require practitioners to pay for rental upfront (Gardner 2015). These pressures on time and space push performers and audiences to consider the potential of unconventional sites – including cars, toilets, offices and swimming pools – but at a cost that can be unsustainably high, both financially and in terms of the health and well-being of many who participate (Putnam 2022; Harvie 2020).

There are, of course, other reasons for pursuing brevity. There are also traditions of performance that aspire to produce work that is much shorter than the fifty-five minutes that many shows at the Edinburgh Fringe clock in at. These often function to challenge audience expectations and explore the limits of the form. John Muse presents an account of this tradition in *Microdramas: Crucibles for Theatre and Time* (2017), which focuses upon performances of twenty minutes or less. Noting the relative paucity of scholarship on short-form performance, he concludes that it has often been dismissed as insignificant or frivolous, unworthy of significant consideration. Focusing upon modernist experimentation across Europe, the US and the UK in the last 125 years, he identifies several historical moments when performances defined by self-conscious brevity offer implicit metatheatrical commentary on the norms and conventions that govern theatrical performance (4–6). He points readers in the direction of playwright Michael Frayn, who has been producing short plays since 1970, and the works of Harold Pinter, whose plays grew progressively shorter over his career – with the briefest, *The New World Order* (1991), lasting only ten minutes.

Still, Muse asserts, microdramas are almost never presented as stand-alone performances, and a short performance usually appears as part of a larger whole: Pinter and Frayn, for example, have their short plays presented in publications and on the stage as collections of work (Frayn 1970: 2014; Pinter 2018; Billington 2019). Indeed, Muse's final chapter is dedicated to discussion of 'microthons', in which he provides detailed analysis of collections of short plays, including Caryl Churchill's *Love and Information* (2012), which presented fifty-seven apparently unrelated sketches which together run at 110 minutes. Churchill's work is undoubtedly challenging for audiences. It offers the briefest of glimpses into a series of unconnected lives and leaves the audience to draw out the thematic connections in their kaleidoscopic juxtaposition. Yet the work as a whole constitutes an evening or afternoon's worth of entertainment. Like other examples of short performance, it is placed in a series in order to convince audiences that the time and money expended is justified (136). Exceptions can, of course, be found. Mark Ravenhill's *Shoot Get Treasure Repeat* was initially presented a series of sixteen short twenty-minute plays as *Breakfast with Ravenhill* at the 2007 Edinburgh Festival Fringe. In his introduction to the published collection of the plays, Ravenhill invites readers and future performers to select at random, and 'shuffle' the deck of plays as they wish, but also invites them to consider the work as an 'epic in fragments' (2013: x). Nevertheless, subsequent productions of these plays have presented a selection in double or triple bills, demonstrating the commercial imperative that Muse identifies (de Waal 2017: 63). Caryl Churchill's shortest plays, which include the fifteen-minute *Ding Dong the Wicked* (2012) and the twenty-minute *What If If Only* (2021), have been programmed alongside other full-length plays when premiering at the Royal Court (Fisher 2012; Billington 2019). This strategy of collection and combination also applies when the works gathered together have been penned by a number of different writers. The Miniaturists, a group of playwrights specializing in plays with run times of less than twenty minutes, have been working together since 2005, producing and staging collections of plays every few months.

Of course, there is nothing new about the practice of presenting several performances as part of an afternoon's or an evening's entertainment. Early modern plays often concluded with music and dancing, while the proliferation of playbills in the eighteenth century makes it clear that it was customary for the main production to be accompanied by shorter comic plays. The nineteenth-century Musical Hall and Variety Theatre were based entirely on the delivery of short performances (Bratton 2004; Double 2012). For example, between 7.30 pm and midnight on Monday, 11 May 1896, London's West End Empire Theatre of Varieties offered a programme of eleven separate performances, including

> an overture lasting 5 minutes; a group of Tyrolean dancers lasting 10 minutes; a ballet divertissement [...] lasting 1 hour; a trio of jugglers lasting 15 minutes; the Lusinski's Russian dancers lasting 10 minutes followed by the celebrated juggler Paul Cinquevalli with 20 minutes;

the Schaffer acrobats 15 minutes; a French chanteuse Yvette Guilbert lasting 20 minutes; another Grand Spectacular Ballet based on Faust lasting 1 hour from 10.35 to 11.35 and concluding with 2 eccentric comedians at 11.40 p.m. (Emeljanow 2014: 56)

As Emeljanow notes, the detail provided assumed that audiences might not want to spend their whole evening at the venue, allowing them to plan accordingly.

The timing of short-form lunchtime theatre, which flourished in London during the 1960s and early 1970s, was also offered with audience convenience in mind. Matthew Morrison's history of the early years of the Soho Theatre documents the extraordinary growth of the form in the late 1960s, when venues and companies such as the Wakefield Tricycle Company, Quipu, the Basement theatre and Ed Berman's Ambiance Lunchtime Theatre were offering one-act plays, avant-garde experiments, devised and improvised performance and adaptations of scripts originally written for TV and radio. As Morrison notes, by the early 1970s lunchtime theatre was such an established part of the theatre scene in London that it had its own listings section in magazines such as *Time Out* and *Plays and Players* (2014). Looking back on the form's brief flourishing in 1980, Rosalind Asquith recalls that it was motivated by a variety of different goals. Some of these were clearly commercial and pragmatic, as lunchtime theatres provided a showcase for the work of new writers in an economically low-risk setting. Others, however, were much more radical. She notes that for some lunchtime theatre makers, the choice to present performance at an unusual time of day amounted to challenging 'one of the paradigm conventions of Western theatre'. It was hoped that the accessibility and cheapness of the offer would attract 'ordinarily disinterested audiences' and, 'by inserting entertainment into the working day, the bourgeois categorisation of time into "work" and "leisure" would be disrupted. [. . .] the old theatrical rules and petrified conventions could be discarded' (145). As Asquith acknowledges, the reality did not live up to these ambitious aspirations. She speculates that 'the average cross-section of audiences is unrepentantly theatrical: actors, agents and TV talent scouts account for most of the audience' (152). Asquith also recalls that though lunchtime theatre was attempted in other cities, it seems that it did not enjoy much success. The Pool in Edinburgh, which produced lunchtime work between 1971 and 1974, lasted longer than most. Yet there are more successful and long-lived examples. Glasgow's Òran Mór venue has been providing audiences with 'A Play, a Pie and Pint' at lunchtime since 2004, and was able to boast in 2021 that they had produced over 550 plays. With a new play being staged each week, with an average running time of forty-five minutes, and casts of no more than three, the theatre can now claim to be the most prolific producer of new drama in the UK (Brooks 2019). With such success, other venues have sought to offer their own versions, including Live Theatre in Newcastle and the West Yorkshire Playhouse in Leeds.

One-act drama is not new, of course. But the exceptional brevity of the individual performances presented in the Gi60 (Gone in Sixty Seconds) One Minute Theatre Festival established in 2004 in Harrogate – and other similar festivals that showcase extremely short works – is genuinely novel. This development could easily be interpreted (and dismissed) as an example of an established media form adopting and adapting aspects of new media to retain cultural currency, as Muse notes. He argues that the development of shorter and shorter forms of performance in the past thirty years can be considered as a response to the needs and capacities of 'a public accustomed to the rhythms of television, Internet surfing, and online or streaming video', reflecting both the 'faster perceived pace of life in a digital world but also the holistic, all-encompassing perspective of a global information age' (139). Brevity can be understood in terms of accessibility, however. Steve Ansell and Rosie Bonczek's account of the development of the Gi60 One Minute Theatre Festival does not make the connection between the brevity of the plays it contains and the increasing ubiquity of new technologies or contemporary culture's ferocious appetite for novelty. They note that the festival emerged from a desire to give more aspiring writers the chance to have their work performed, and to enable them to share it with a broader audience (2017: 2). The decision to turn to a radically short form in order to achieve these goals was clearly generated by awareness that expectations about length and duration needed to be jettisoned in order to reach this larger audience. The hybrid form of the festival, which is presented in person, with livestreamed and recorded versions available to view online, also reflects these aims. Nevertheless, though the festival's launch pre-dates the arrival of YouTube (2005), Instagram (2010) and TikTok (2016), it seems to speak directly to the apparently infinite variety of short-form video content provided on these platforms, and its hybrid form was the result of Ansell's realization that his new phone allowed him to record and upload short videos. Moreover, as Ansell and Bonczek acknowledge, the beauty of presenting one-minute plays in such quantity is the certainty that if a spectator is not enjoying one of the plays, it will be quickly replaced by another. As they observe, 'an evening of one-minute plays is practically guaranteed to engage the entire audience at some point [. . .]. With fifty different plays, there's no way there isn't a story for everyone' (5). Rather than fretting that new technologies are producing audiences with increasingly short attention spans, they accept that the festival's audience will necessarily contain a wide variety of distinct perspectives and preferences – and that one way of maintaining collective focus is the promise of variety.

> *3 May 2020. I get Tiktok on my phone. It offers the perfect distraction when I can no longer worry about other people's learning or the number of people who are dying. I become fascinated by dancing challenges. I watch video after video of people performing a routine to The Weeknd's Blinding Lights. There are families at home dancing in their gardens, builders on site, medical staff in hospitals. They all work through the same moves, apparently finding equal joy in outrageous failures as well as the moments in which they achieve perfect synchronicity.*

Meeting audiences where they are, in terms of format, location and variety, is also key to developments in recent very short-form performance. In the months before Scotland's independence referendum in 2014, the National Theatre of Scotland's *The Great Yes,*

No, Don't Know Five-Minute Theatre Show invited submissions of original, five-minute plays addressing the question of independence. Performed live over 24 hours at seven performance hubs – from the Electric Theatre Workshop in Dumfries to The Lemon Tree in Aberdeen – and broadcast on the web, the show was designed to provide an opportunity for people to express their opinions and thoughts on the choice that the referendum was offering. Co-curated by David MacLennan and David Greig, its shape and form were central to the kind of engagement it hoped to create. Greig noted, 'The show takes the Scottish Variety tradition and propels it into the internet age. [. . .] At this key moment in the nation's history it's a way for Scotland to speak to itself – not in formal political tones – but in a relaxed, rambunctious, celebratory, and personal way; and crucially, it's a chance for everyone to contribute, not just a political or artistic elite' (quoted in Nichols 2017: 280–1). Other arts organizations have also opted for very short performance in the hope of engaging audiences politically. In 2014 the Royal Court partnered with *The Guardian* to host a series of microplays on the newspaper's website, bringing together journalists with playwrights and directors to create short films that were designed to offer fast responses to current cultural and political preoccupations. These include *School Gate* by Rachel De-lahay (which explores the 'Trojan Horse' controversy in Birmingham), *Britain isn't Eating* by Laura Wade (examining food poverty), and *Death of England* by Roy Williams, with Rafe Spall as a grieving son, whose eulogy at his father's funeral descends into a diatribe about football and race. These plays run at four, seven and nine minutes, respectively. As Elaine Aston's discussion of *Britain isn't Eating* notes, they are designed to counter compassion fatigue, encouraging the newspaper's readers to connect with the lived experience or issue that is being explored in the piece (2022), while Royal Court Director Vicky Featherstone argued that the contemporaneity enabled by the speed of their creation allows them to connect with current debate (Featherstone et al. 2014). This form clearly lends itself to work that aims to engage audiences politically. Established in 2015, Climate Change Theatre Action commissions playwrights from all over the world to produce five-minute plays addressing climate change. These are designed to be presented at the same time as the biennial United Nations COP summits. The year 2022 saw contributions from UK-based playwrights and theatre makers Javaad Alipoor, Nathan Ellis, Zoë Svendsen and Chris Thorpe (Bilodeau 2022).

Watching and waiting

The examples above indicate that there have been many efforts to explore brevity in performance, to make it fit into shorter and shorter moments in time. Twenty-first-century producers are also, in the main, concerned with creating work that is delivered in a timely manner: starting, pausing and finishing at advertised or predictable times, and proceeding at a pace that meets audience expectations. Experiments with greater brevity usually address perceived audience need and exploit opportunities created by new technology. There is, however, another tradition that has developed alongside efforts to make theatre and performance shorter: the extremely long performance. Instead of fitting conveniently into a two- or three-hour slot between dinner and the last train home, these works demand a new level of audience commitment, stretching and challenging conventional standards of duration.

Jonathan Kalb's analysis of the growth in long-form late-twentieth-century theatre, *Great Lengths: Seven Works of Marathon Theater* (2011), focuses upon examples of performances with four-hour-plus running times, including discussion of the Royal Shakespeare Company's eight-and-a-half-hour adaptation of Charles Dickens' *Nicholas Nickleby* (1980) and Tony Kushner's seven-hour *Angels in America* (which played for the first time as a whole on Broadway in 1993 and was then produced at the National Theatre in 2017). He also dissects his experiences of Forced Entertainment's durational performances *Speak Bitterness* (1994) and *Quizoola!* (1996). The length of these works produces a range of effects and experiences. Forced

Entertainment's long-form performances are notoriously demanding, testing the endurance of audiences and performers alike. The length of *Angels in America* encourages spectatorial immersion in the play's dreamlike, otherworldly logic. *Nicholas Nickleby* resisted the drive to abbreviate or make Dickens' work more digestible. With forty-eight actors playing 139 characters, it preserved the novel's subplots, minor characters and digressions, as well as distributing the narratorial voice of the author across the ensemble.

Kalb places these productions in the context of a larger boom in long-form performance, a development which he notes has been enabled by the proliferation of international theatre festivals in the years following the Second World War. These attract holidaying tourists with unlimited leisure time to fill. He acknowledges that the epic productions he analyses are undoubtedly 'scandal magnets' (20), accompanied by marketing campaigns that attempt to convince audiences that they are being offered the opportunity to participate in an event which has greater worth because of its monumental temporal scale. Nevertheless, Kalb asserts that their length provides a distinct and especially valuable set of experiences. These productions, he argues, are driven by a sense that the work itself needs to sit outside of conventional temporal parameters in order to achieve its artistic aims, and they counter the modern 'hurry sickness', which afflicts audiences (2), providing a welcome alternative to the 'maddening, ubiquitous, and nearly irresistible pressure to reduce, abbreviate and trivialize' (16). He asserts that the length of time spent in the company of strangers creates 'an uncommon sense of public communion', effectively transforming 'throngs of atomized consumers into congregations of skeptical co-religionists, or at least consciously commiserating co-sufferers' (2). For Kalb, they answer the enduring spiritual need for collective communion that was supplied by events such as the City Dionysia or the Corpus Christi festivals (18).

Kalb is upfront about the fact that he took great pleasure from the seven works he selected for discussion in his book. But not all experiences of long-form performance have been produced with the aim of providing audiences with satisfying or straightforwardly enjoyable experiences. The twentieth century saw the development of theatre and performance practice that highlighted discomforting acts of endurance for audiences and performers alike, testing the strength of their connection and commitment, from the durational performance art of the 1960s onwards.

> *16 May 2021. I'm sitting on a green plastic chair, one of many carefully spaced out around the room. We are all sitting in silence, facing the front where an elderly woman – an invigilator of sorts – is engrossed in her book. We are all wearing stickers with times written on them in black marker pen. Some people are scrolling on their phones, others stare intently at the clock on the wall. I feel a trickle of blood running down my left arm and reach in my pocket for a tissue. My arm feels bruised, numb. I press the tissue to my arm and wait for the clock to match the time on my sticker. As I leave, I hear a woman in the queue arguing with a volunteer about the type of vaccine they are offering today. She says she will come back tomorrow.*

Lara Shalson notes that Samuel Beckett's *Waiting for Godot* (first performed in Britain in 1955) transformed expectations of spectatorship in contemporary performance. She argues that it demonstrated the centrality of waiting in theatre – for the audience as well as the characters, in this case (2013: 79). In recent years playwrights, directors and critics have moved to celebrate the 'magic' or 'joy' of similarly 'slow theatre', which does not offer quick returns on time invested in watching and waiting (Ravenhill 2009; Hemming 2018; Muse 2023). Productions of the work of US playwright Annie Baker *The Flick* (2013) and *John* (2015) at the National Theatre in 2016 and 2018 dispel the illusion that everyone is busy or suffering from the kind of 'hurry sickness' that Kalb and others identify. With run times of three hours-plus, they focus on the mundane minutiae of everyday lives. Characters reveal themselves gradually; pauses and stretches of silence abound; action mostly happens elsewhere; and meaning is revealed through quiet detail. Other recent productions have focused upon experiences of waiting, and banal and repetitive labour, offering glimpses of worlds and experiences that are not usually the subject of drama. Alexander Zeldin's *Beyond*

Caring (2015) and *Love* (2018) focus on the lives of cleaners on zero-hours contracts, and homeless people living in cramped temporary accommodation, while the final act of Caryl Churchill's *Here We Go* (2015) shows us the wordless world of an elderly man in a care home, where the slow, painstaking ritual of being dressed and undressed by his carer repeats again and again as the light fades. Efforts to take action in these plays are limited by physical incapacity or the pitiful systems of benefits and labour in which the characters are enmeshed. These works observe mundane, daily activities, depicting life endured in bleak circumstances. They are designed to make audiences share in the discomfort and aimlessness of the characters for the hours that they watch the production. Jason Farman's analysis of how experiences of being made to wait have shifted and changed over time, *Delayed Response* (2018), suggests that interpretations of these drawn-out twenty-first century performances will inevitably differ significantly from those which greeted the first performances of Beckett's famous work. Farman argues that we are more impatient, more unforgiving of delay, as the speed at which we now communicate and receive information means that we have become much less accustomed to waiting.

The pandemic, however, offered a corrective lesson in this regard. As Neta Alexander observes, dealing with latency was an intrinsic part of the Covid crisis (2021). We found ourselves waiting anxiously: for the government to act, for symptoms to emerge, for lockdown to flatten the curve, for computing systems to deal with the quantity of data now being loaded on to the internet, to see friends and family, to grieve. For several months we were stuck in an anxiety-inducing holding pattern, dealing with the personal and professional implications of 'The Great Pause' (Rose 2020). For theatre makers and performance practitioners, this provided time to contemplate time: to consider how we use our minutes, hours, days and lives. Post-pandemic performance reflects this process of stock-taking. The significance and form of works that highlight duration and audience interaction have been reconsidered in the light of clarified priorities, while some productions put the question of how we spend our time centre stage.

Taking the Time, created by Glasgow-based artists Gillian Jane Lees and Adam York Gregory, was initially due to be presented in March 2020 and was postponed until May 2021. A work in two parts, it offered audiences the chance to experience a sonic sculpture created by the artists over a 24-hour durational performance. The sculpture used the alarms of hundreds of digital watches to mark times of the day 'donated' by 1,440 members of the public in the Stockton area. Specific times of day, along with a brief explanation of their personal significance, were shared by completing a short form on the artists' website. These were times of meaning large and small, marking moments when a child was born, a loved one died or a life-changing decision was taken. Some offerings were clearly unique to the individual contributor, while others were likely to be widely shared: associated with a regular morning alarm, a daily commute or the end of the school day. Speaking shortly before the performance, Lees and Gregory commented on the development of the work and how its meaning had been inflected by the 'difficult time' of the pandemic, acknowledging that it provided a heightened sense of the importance of commemoration (ARC Stockton 2021).

Quarantine's *12 Last Songs*, first presented at Leeds Playhouse in 2021 as part of Transform 21-22 Festival, was first conceived before lockdown but refocused in response to the way that the crisis invited reassessment of the value of labour. While many older people decided to walk away from work after the crisis, the pandemic also generated appreciation for individuals doing jobs which might usually seem to be unremarkable: supermarket workers, delivery drivers, waste collectors. A twelve-hour durational piece, it presents itself as a work of mass portraiture. There are no actors – instead, individuals perform paid shifts of their everyday work at the event. Hairdressers braid hair, chefs cook, bricklayers build walls, as their activities invite us to recognize their skill and the steady daily rhythms of working lives. While performing, participants are asked a series of questions. As co-director Richard Gregory explains, 'across 12 hours, they move from questions about the start of a day, the start of a working day, the start of a working life, the start of life through to questions about the end of a day, the end of a working day, the end of a working life, the end of life' (quoted in Horswill 2022). The show asks audiences and participants alike to slow down and reflect on the work that we do, its place in our lives and the time that it takes.

Other works are explicitly designed to develop audience engagement with the issues that they raise far beyond the moment of encounter with their performance. Since its inception in 2015, Selina Thompson's *Race Cards* has evolved from a game, to a short theatre piece, to a 24-hour durational performance and then to an interactive installation. In the first performances, Thompson generated 1,000 questions about race that are now presented on white cards stuck to the walls of the small rooms in which the piece appears. Participants are given instructions and invited to enter and read as many of the questions as they wish, on the condition that they answer one, and take one that they cannot answer out into the world, where they can try to find an answer. This is presented by Thompson as an exchange: the intellectual and emotional labour on the part of the audience balanced against the effort that has gone into the creation of the work (Rings 2017). The shape of the piece, and Thompson's gradual withdrawal from presenting it in person, has been informed by her desire to control the dialogue and ask the questions in a conversation about race with a white liberal arts audience, rather than being required to come up with the answers (Gallagher-Ross and Makonnen 2018). This work continued to tour nationally and internationally post-pandemic, as Thompson's questions and choices around its presentation were given still greater urgency in the context of the global Black Lives Matter protests of 2020.

The way in which *Race Cards* invites audiences to take a question away with them is indicative of a more expansive understanding of the duration of performance. This usually focuses upon the running time of the performance itself from curtain-up to curtain call; but scholars have suggested that we should expand our understanding of the length of the encounter, proposing that the experience involves 'warm up' and 'cool down' periods for audiences as they prepare and then transition from the experience afterwards (Heim: 27). These analyses focus upon entry into the venue – and the way that theatre foyers function as liminal spaces – but in temporal terms, both the creation of the event and audience preparation for it begins much earlier than the moment when audience and performers cross this spatial threshold. Performances may be years in creative preparation while audiences may know weeks or even months ahead of time that they will be attending a particular show. In terms of audience experience, performances do not end when we leave the building. Interviews with theatre makers and audience members indicate that memories of theatre-going and encounters with performance can last for years, if not a lifetime (Reinelt 2014; Johnson 2015; Faull 2022).

> *27 April 2022. I'd forgotten about the gig until I get a text from my brother reminding me the day before. I really don't want to go. I don't think I'm ready to be back in large crowd. But it's a band we both loved as teenagers. So we go. When we arrive I fight the urge to leave immediately. No one is wearing a mask. Gradually I start to look at the people around us. Almost everyone is our age, but there are a few younger people. Do they wonder what it was like to be there 30 years ago when the album was first released? Half-way through the set I suddenly relax. I close my eyes and dance. I'm still here, still me. I still know the words.*

Performance can appear to have a complex and paradoxical relationship with time. It is understood as transient and enduring, unique and endlessly repeated, offering us opportunities to connect with contemporary debates and concerns, but also providing access to 'time out of time'. In contrast to these conceptual tensions, the conventions which determine the temporal aspects of the relationship between performance and audience can appear ingrained: so unremarkable as to be unworthy of commentary. Traditions and norms shift and change slowly, with attachments to seasonal and weekly patterns of behaviour more deeply embedded than we might imagine. Yet, returning to the historical record indicates that expectations surrounding performance's place in time have been subject to significant variation across time and that these variations can help make performance more – or less – accessible to particular types of spectator. Some traditions (such as the interval) may not usually attract much attention, but when change is proposed, it becomes clear that their presence or absence matters.

The dark festival time of the Covid crisis demonstrated that norms of duration and timing can be broken. It suggests that we need to look again at why events happen when they do, providing further evidence to support the findings of studies that argue that arts organizations could benefit from moving away from basing event start times upon tradition, and open themselves to consideration of the kind of scheduling that suits their audiences instead (Rhine and Murnin 2018). The pausing of business as usual during the pandemic also gave us all cause – if not time – to reflect upon how we spend our days, and on the widely varying experiences of time. Bree Hadley and others have insisted that a genuinely inclusive theatre-making culture needs to look not only at the logistical issues that must be addressed in order to make spaces and events accessible to all practitioners. It also needs to adapt methodologically, acknowledging that collaborators with different disabilities will need to work at different speeds. It is possible to apply their insights about the connection between the creation of 'quick trust' and the provision of 'slow time' to the audience/ performance dynamic, too (Hadley, Paterson and Little 2022). Recent years have seen performers push performance to extremes in terms of pace, brevity and longevity, suggesting that we should reconsider assumptions about the duration of the spectatorial encounter with individual performances, and with the form as a whole. Instead of celebrating the transience of the event, we should perhaps think of the relationship between performance and audience as a long-term commitment.

2

Spatial relationships
Exclusivity and inclusivity

23 October 2020. It's 1.00 am. I creep downstairs to the living room in the pitch black. I open my laptop and click the booking link for Live Action Relay *by choreographer Sue Healey. It is about to start on a live stream as part of 'Live on the Line' – the 2020 online iteration of Liveworks Festival, from Performance Space, Sydney. I am transported to a vast Australian landscape in the midday sun, where drones capture dancers moving gracefully with the elements. The drone cameras shift between offering wide-angled, all-encompassing views and intricate close-up images of dancers interacting with objects and each other. The landscape is extraordinary – sand, rocks, the ocean and rough-looking grasslands. I feel as if this is a dream – and that I am part of something much bigger than myself. I'm aware that I am one of many others around the world tuning into this extraordinary experiment. When the performance ends, I look up from my screen and stare back into the darkness of my living room, where the moonlight picks out the details of my suburban reality. I close my laptop and clap.*

The Covid crisis provided new perspectives on the use of space and created a blurring between public and private realms. During the first phase of the pandemic, the 'stay at home' order went from guidance to legally enforceable requirement in a matter of days. Adherence necessitated a radical reordering of our understanding of the potential uses of the home, and the meanings and activities associated with it. Some found themselves using domestic space as a workplace – and as a site for full-time education – for the first time. Instead of being an occasional site of labour, education, childcare and leisure, for many it became the only location for these activities. For those with access to adequate technology and a good broadband connection, the boundaries between private and public worlds were redrawn as the domestic interior became an everyday backdrop to online interactions. Many were given unprecedented access to glimpses of the home lives of others, while also sharing – or deliberately obscuring – views of their own bedrooms, kitchens and living rooms. This extended time of confinement not only highlighted inequalities in housing provision across the nation, between those with gardens and spare rooms, and those without. It also heightened awareness that although home is experienced by many as a place of shelter, rest, security and comfort, for others it is a place of constraint, fear and danger.

The crisis also changed our relationship with the spaces beyond our homes, as the background hum of traffic noise in our cities was silenced and the skies emptied of planes. Locations which the luxury of air travel had made more accessible were suddenly impossible to reach, while the everyday rhythms of movement between spaces in cities and towns, which had given structure to many lives, were abruptly curtailed. The three national lockdowns and the 'tiered' regional restrictions on social interactions, travel and leisure choices across 2020 and 2021 overturned commonly held assumptions about access to spaces previously thought of as being open to all – streets, parks, beaches, moors – while public amenities such as 'non-essential' shops, libraries and pubs had to close. Instructions were issued about access to public outdoor space, the distances deemed acceptable to travel by car to take exercise, and the permissibility of travel to and from particular zones of the country in ways that would have previously been unimaginable (UK Government, 2020; Barber, Brown and Ferguson 2021).

Images of ghost lights on bare stages provided a poignant visual summary of the emptying of previously busy venues and the devastating impact of the crisis on the theatre industry, while also seeming to promise a return to these spaces (Staples 2021: 551). While the ghost lights burned, however, artists and companies were finding other locations and platforms to present their work, challenging assumptions about the necessity of bringing audiences and performers into close physical proximity, and pushing performance into spaces where it had rarely been seen before. In the midst of the fear, boredom and frustration of the first national lockdown (from March to June 2020), practitioners and companies small and large began to provide access to video footage of past work online. Perhaps the most visible of these large-scale initiatives, National Theatre at Home, used YouTube to livestream sixteen productions which had originally been filmed for cinema screening as part of the NT Live project (first initiated in 2009). Major European companies began to make similar offerings, providing theatre enthusiasts based in the UK with the opportunity to view work which had previously been inaccessible to them. Rarely seen recordings of famous historical performances surfaced, too, providing a glut of viewing opportunities which challenged even the most voracious and dedicated of cultural consumers (Aesbischer 2022: 22). These moves to make streamed footage of previously recorded performance available to audiences at home presented a significant shift in understanding of where theatre can and should take place, and challenged assumptions about the necessity of bringing audiences and performers into close physical proximity. It also made performance accessible to many who would previously have had no opportunity to view it.

As it became clear that lockdown was going to last for months rather than weeks, practitioners began to offer work online, which represented creative responses to the constraints of the situation. Live online productions which invited audience participation and curated interactions between audience members drew on some of the tropes and traditions of participatory performance, but also provided another level of intimacy and insight as a result of connecting with audience members viewing from their homes. Some theatre makers found themselves creating work from home for audiences in their homes, exploring new levels of intimacy and exposure at a distance. As well as heightening the sense that divisions between public and private realms were becoming blurred – through offering small but sometimes highly revealing insights into the domestic lives of other audience members – these productions also challenged the assumption that copresence and shared space are an integral and intrinsic part of the theatrical experience.

As the severe constraints of 'stay at home' spring were gradually relaxed in the summer of 2020, existing open-air venues suddenly found themselves with a new appeal, and spaces which had never been previously considered as possible sites for theatrical performance – such as the car park outside Scottish Opera's production studio in Glasgow – were repurposed as performance venues. Some companies, such as Newcastle's Unfolding Theatre and Liverpool's 20 Stories High, offered literal 'doorstep theatre', bringing small-scale work to the street or garden outside people's homes. When some cultural venues were permitted to reopen in July 2020, many struggled to manage the implementation of social distancing guidelines. Those responsible for the assessment of enclosed spaces, designed to bring people together in close proximity, often concluded that it was impossible to accommodate audiences in ways that were both safe and financially sustainable. Elsewhere, innovations sought to find ways of bringing people together safely and addressing differing audience perceptions of risk. Some companies found themselves attempting to cater for a variety of audience needs in relation to social distancing practices as a result of heightened awareness of the range of access needs amongst audiences.

The crisis also provided a renewal of critical perspectives on the spaces being regularly used for the presentation of performance pre-Covid, not all positive. It highlighted deep tensions within the theatre industry about the relationship between buildings, practitioners and audiences. The distribution of emergency government funding designed to help the sector survive the pandemic was focused upon large organizations with big buildings to maintain (Banks and O'Connor 2021: 8). Many staff, suddenly deemed non-essential, were made redundant, joining thousands of freelance artists who were abruptly without income. This decision to focus funds upon large organizations highlighted the sector's problematic, long-term dependence upon a precarious workforce. It also gave the impression that buildings were being protected and preserved, rather than people. In 2021, many practitioners were questioning whether conventional theatres were going to be fit for the purpose in the future. Having been forced to look beyond buildings, to reconsider the potential of performing outside and to explore online interaction with audiences, some questioned what these buildings were really for.

This chapter uses these new understandings of place, space and performance to provide critical perspectives on some of the most commonly held ideas about the configuration of space in historic theatres. It explores how these ideas are connected to earlier attempts to change relationships with audiences, and what the issues have been with these efforts. It argues that we should reconsider how we think about privacy and publicness, transparency and exposure, distance and proximity, and distinctions between different types of space. Finally, it reflects upon how we deal with buildings which represent problematic past practices, and the extent to which they can be repurposed.

Exclusion, division and hierarchy

Rethinking the conventions that govern and protect theatres as specific kinds of spatial institutions represents a major challenge. Spaces which regularly host theatrical performance are often set apart or concealed from everyday life and the natural world. David Wiles traces the significance of these qualities of separation and enclosure back to the Romans, whose theatres were contained by high walls and covered by awnings, shielding the auditoria from the sun and effectively 'insulating the tragic or festive world of the play from the natural world and from everyday life' (2003: 40). Boštjan Vuga's comments on modern theatres and 'publicness' make a similar point in relation to the fundamental character of theatre architecture, as he notes that performance venues are usually 'introverted buildings', in which performances – the main purpose of the building – are delivered 'in the core of the building [. . .] far from the perimeter and the outer walls', effectively secluded and hidden from the outside world (2021: 17). Vuga attributes this structural introversion to 'technical, acoustic, accessibility and visibility concerns' (17), but it clearly serves other purposes, too. Enclosure and introversion go hand in hand with exclusivity, enabling institutions to control who has access to the event. Architectural design features enable institutions to carry out discrete checks for payment or to ensure that only guests or members of a select group get in. Sometimes these features are immediately apparent, such as high encircling walls or narrow doorways to auditoria. Others, such as unmarked entrances, are deliberately obscure: ensuring that only those 'in the know' will make it across the threshold (White 2012: 224; Carlson 1989: 127).

Some of the architectural features of Britain's oldest theatres also serve to remind today's audiences that theatres have functioned to embody and perpetuate class distinctions and social hierarchies through elaborate systems of social segregation. Amongst the most visible reminders of these systems are the boxes which appear to the side of the stage in older theatres, such as the Theatre Royal Haymarket in central London, or the Palace Theatre, Manchester. These may seem curious, outmoded excrescences to twenty-first-century theatregoers, most interested in securing the best possible view of the stage, but their inclusion in the design of these theatres served to enable the display of the social order, and reminds us that theatre-going has, at times, been just as much about watching other members of the audience as it has been about viewing performances. These boxes are also unabashed in their celebration of hierarchy and power, with the right to privacy being central to this expression. The relationship between those seated in the 'first boxes' and those seated elsewhere in the auditorium was marked by the fact that the boxes – which were often provided with anterooms – gave the occupants the luxury of deciding how and when they wanted to be seen by the rest of the audience. For the most privileged – such as the Duke of Bedford (who owned the grounds on which the

Drury Lane Theatre Royal was rebuilt in 1794) – they supplied private entrances, toilets and staircases as well (Carlson 1989: 143).

Royal boxes remind twenty-first-century audiences that the behaviours and priorities of theatregoers in earlier periods may have differed significantly from their own. Yet, these boxes are only the most visible reminders of the complex systems of audience segregation that have determined past theatre design. London theatres of the nineteenth century have frequently been listed as the epitome of social segregation expressed in theatre design (Mackintosh 1993: 23; Carlson 1989: 151; McAuley 1999: 61; McWilliam 2020: 182–5). The large public theatres of this period provided a range of seating options, catering to all levels of social aspirations and budget, with the middle classes seated in the stalls, higher prices creating a space of greater exclusivity in the middle level and the cheapest seats in the galleries at the top of the theatre: systems of separation via pricing that will be familiar to the twenty-first-century theatregoer. Less familiar, however, will be the way that this spatial categorization extended to the entrances and passageways to the galleries. Entirely separate, they provided access to the building on side streets rather than the main entrance at the front of the building, ensuring that those purchasing a more exclusive experience were not required to brush up against those who occupied the cheaper seats. These systems of differentiation were clearly visible to the theatregoers of the day, who marked their development. Drawings of audiences in this period often focus on the distinctions between these different levels in the theatre and the way that their behaviour reflects the social hierarchy (Davis 2017). These images are reminders of the ways in which the spatial layout of theatres have served to reify and perpetuate social hierarchies. Almost all of the surviving stock of nineteenth- and early twentieth-century theatres retain clear divisions in comfort (and pricing) between their stalls, circles and uppermost balconies. Markers of processes of social segregation and exclusion are everywhere in the theatre estate. The innovations in theatre design and use of space in twentieth- and twenty-first-century theatre can be read as a response to this oppressive legacy, as alternative methods of organizing the spatial relationships in performance venues – and beyond them – were pursued in the hope of creating greater opportunities for interaction between audiences and performers, or greater unification of the audience as a whole. Theatre designs emerged that highlighted inclusivity rather than exclusivity, and that made a point of being welcoming and accessible to the public. These innovations were often framed as returns to earlier – better – moments in theatre history, however, as architects, theatre makers and critics looked to the more distant past for theatre designs which appear to express and enable these kinds of relationships.

Many of what Iain Mackintosh refers to as 'the purifiers' of the modern movement (1993: 41) took inspiration from the form of ancient Greek auditoria, which have long been idealized as enabling more egalitarian viewing experiences, and a more meaningful connection between state and culture. The remains of ancient Greek amphitheatres still visible today make it clear how their design suggests an experience characterized by equality and unity. Sited as part of the landscape, there appears to be no significant distinction or separation between seating tiers. These flowing, symmetrical spaces seem to resist differentiation between classes or categories of spectators, offering a more democratic viewing experience. The way that the siting and design of Greek amphitheatres frequently enabled spectators to view both performance and the environment beyond the theatre is cited by Marvin Carlson as representative of their connection with the city and the natural world. He argues, 'In many cities, including Corinth, Priene and Epheseus, the spectator in the theatre sees before him [*sic*] not only the performance space, but a magnificent perspective of the lower city, the ramparts, and beyond them, the plain or the sea.' He notes that as well as being major cultural monuments, they were also 'mechanisms for presenting to their users a striking panorama of artificial and natural space' (1989: 61). Carlson also contrasts the marginal, precarious location and status of the early modern public theatres of London – positioned outside the city proper, beyond the reach of the authorities – with that of the highly visible public performance venues of Greece and Rome: 'major civic monuments, which held prominent positions in the urban text' (1989: 68).

The twentieth century saw the creation of auditoria designed to echo the spatial organization of Greek amphitheatres through the lowering of the stage and provision of a single sweep of seats in a steeply raked auditorium. The Olivier in the National Theatre (which opened in 1976) has surely received the most scholarly attention, but they also include The Mermaid (converted from a City of London warehouse in 1959), the Leicester Haymarket (1973) and the Quarry Theatre of the West Yorkshire Playhouse (1990) (Hewison 1995: 60). The use of this design in outdoor spaces being used for performance is now widespread, from the Minack Theatre, cut into the cliffside in Porthcurno, Cornwall (1931), to more recent additions, such as the Sheffield Amphitheatre (2011), the BOAT (Brighton Open Air Theatre, 2015), the Ballycarry Amphitheatre (in County Antrim, Northern Ireland, 2015) and Thorington Theatre, constructed in a Second World War bomb crater in woods near Southwold in Suffolk in 2020. Publicity for these spaces often highlights their status as part of civic regeneration projects, their inclusivity, environmental sustainability of their construction or the way that they are maintained by the collective goodwill of volunteers.

Scholarship on audiences for theatre has followed and bolstered this valorization of ancient Greek theatre, arguing that ancient Greece offers a compelling model of the interrelationship between active citizenship and theatrical spectatorship. As Simon Goldhill asserts in his regularly cited discussion of the audiences for Athenian tragedy, 'in Greek culture [. . .] to be in an audience is above all *to play the role of democratic citizen*' (1997: 54 [italics in original]). Elsewhere, David Wiles acknowledges that his reading of Western performance space is rooted in classical antiquity (2003: 19), while Susan Bennett begins *Theatre Audiences: A Theory of Production and Reception* with a brief historical narrative which sketches out a long-term cultural shift from active audience engagement to passive consumption. Ancient Greek theatre functions here as an ideal, characterized by Bennett as closely linked to, and supported by, the economic and political systems of the period. For Bennett, the close relationship between society and theatre is expressed through the proximity and interaction between performance and audience. She quotes Peter Walcot on the unification of stage, orchestra and auditorium:

> [N]o physical barrier separated performance from audience; the presence among the spectators of the cult statue of a god [Dionysus] who might also be active on the stage further reveals that the absence of a physical barrier was matched by the absence of any 'spiritual' barrier. Stage, orchestra and auditorium formed a single unit and so too did actors, chorus and spectators, all of whom were sharing in a common act of devotion. (1976: 4–5, cited in Bennett 1997: 2)

Indeed, the attachment to the layout of the Greek amphitheatre appears to remain just as powerful today as it has ever been. When Dan Hutton turns to historical examples to illustrate his ideal in *Towards a Civic Theatre*, the theatre of ancient Greece is first up, as he highlights the scale of the event as key to the mass participation it was able to achieve (2021: 28).

The other historical architectural form which is strongly associated with broad public engagement and exceptional levels of active participation is that of the purpose-built theatres in London which emerged at the end of the sixteenth century. These large public amphitheatres, such as The Swan, The Globe and The Hope (built between 1576 and 1614), are often celebrated as extraordinary innovations, the product of exceptional cultural creativity and entrepreneurial energy, and certainly represent a significant moment in the development of British theatre. Holding approximately 2,000 to 3,000 spectators, they were commercial, secular and professional institutions, marking a move away from the practices of locally dispersed touring troupes, the non-profit religious ritual traditions which were created by and for the townsfolk across the UK, and private performances at court and in the households of the nobility. These new spaces are renowned for the heterogeneity of their audiences, which included lords, ladies, knights, foreign visitors and officials, merchants, soldiers, sailors, trades and craftsmen and their wives, watermen, labourers, household servants, apprentices and students. Also present were those making their living from this diverse assembly: hawkers, prostitutes and pickpockets (Gurr 2004). These audiences were markedly different to earlier ones in significant ways. London's population had grown significantly during the reign of Elizabeth I, creating potential for interactions with unfamiliar strangers in the crowds of the capital (Griffiths 2008). As a consequence, as Jane Milling notes, these playgoers were no longer subject to the self-discipline imposed by 'hierarchical structures of household obligation or the presence of civic and guild dignitaries, patrons or employers' (2004: 171). These audiences, freed by the relative anonymity of the crowd, their elevated status as customers rather than guests, and the liberty of movement enabled in the Yard, have become renowned for their exuberant, demanding and sometimes disruptive behaviour.

Shakespeare's status as cultural icon and popular association with these buildings have fuelled fascination with what their reconstruction can tell us about the performances that originally took place on early modern stages and the kinds of interaction they enabled between audiences and performers. This has resulted in numerous permanent and pop-up versions of early modern playhouses in the UK and many other locations across the world since the end of the nineteenth century (O'Connor 2002). Active and rumbustious audience response has become something of a feature – and possibly an attraction – at what is, perhaps, the most well known of these reconstructions, Shakespeare's Globe (1997). This space appears to provide twenty-first-century audiences with the same sense of license and disinhibition that Milling describes amongst the crowds in early modern London.

The design of many other twentieth-century British auditoria evidence the interest in using the principles governing the organization of space in early modern theatres, even where there is no attempt to reconstruct their form exactly. One of the most celebrated of these is the thrust stage configuration promoted by director Tyrone Guthrie across the 1940s and 1960s, which seats audience members around three sides of the stage. Guthrie sums up what this was attempting to achieve in his description of the staging of *The Three Estates* in The Assembly Hall at the second Edinburgh International Festival in 1948:

> One of the most pleasing effects of the performance was the physical relation of the audience to the stage. The audience did not look at the actors against a background of pictorial and illusionary scenery. Seated around three sides of the stage they focussed upon the actors in the brightly lit acting area, but the background was of the dimly lit rows of people similarly focussed on the actors. All the time, but unemphatically and by influence, each member of the audience was being ceaselessly reminded that he was not lost in an illusion [. . .] but was in fact a member of a large audience taking part, 'assisting at', as the French very properly express it, a performance, a participant in a ritual. (cited in Mackintosh 1993: 54).

Today, versions of this can be seen at the Chichester Festival Theatre (1962) and The Crucible in Sheffield (1971). This idea was pushed still further by the introduction of an 'in the round' theatre in space above a public library in Scarborough by Stephen Joseph in 1955, followed by the Victoria Theatre in Stoke-on-Trent in 1962 and the Royal Exchange Theatre in Manchester in 1976.

The building of these stages was part of a major building boom in British theatre. This was supported by significant changes in the funding streams available to regional theatre companies. As Alistair Fair demonstrates in his history of the twentieth-century playhouse, subsidy from the newly formed Arts Council and the 1948 Local Government Act – which permitted local authorities to fund art – underpinned the creation of many new repertory and university theatres across the regions between the 1950s and the 1980s. As Fair notes, this transformed theatre's status, and the creation of numerous 'civic theatres', 'not only illustrates the role of local authorities as the landlords and funders of these theatres, but also implies a sense of citizenship' (2018: 12).

The architecture and layout of many of the more conventional theatre buildings constructed during the mid-twentieth century also speaks directly to an aspiration to connect with the communities they were designed to serve. The provision of expansive foyer spaces, cafes, restaurants and exhibition spaces, which were open to all, often all day, represented a new emphasis upon inclusion rather than segregation and exclusivity. They also included adequate toileting facilities for men and women alike, unlike nineteenth-century theatres, which have become notorious for the limited number of women's toilets they contain (Snow 2019). The exterior design of many of these theatres is also indicative of the desire to communicate the welcoming and accessible nature of the interior through the use of glass in entrances and facades. Buildings such as the Belgrade Theatre, Coventry (1958) and the Key Theatre, Peterborough (1973) make bold declarations about their openness to the outside world. This trend continues. The design of CAST in Doncaster (2013), for example, makes a visual statement through the generous use of glass in its facade. Fair notes the way in which the details of this design – which included specialized glass that maximizes transparency – combined modernist concerns to expose the workings of a building with a desire to demystify its contents and hopefully tempt new audiences to cross its threshold. For Fair, this is an example of 'modern monumentality', in which the presence of users humanizes the building (2019: 88). Other twenty-first-century updates to older theatres have also adopted this approach, as can be seen in the all-glass frontage to the Festival Theatre in Edinburgh, which houses a 1911 auditorium at its core, and the addition of glass to the eighteenth-century York Theatre Royal's colonnade in 2016. As discussed in what follows, this kind of exposure does not always succeed in making audiences want to cross the threshold – or making those inside feel at home.

The problem(s) with buildings: reconfiguring the spatial relationship

Not all of these architectural interventions have been a success: the long timescales of building and renovation projects, and the numbers of people involved in the most expensive, can militate against the realization of a coherent vision (Mackintosh 1993: 89–90). Even the most carefully planned spaces have been the subject of fierce critique. The National Theatre has been slated for its external appearance and the limitations of its main stages (Hall 2019). Richard Eyre, Artistic Director between 1987 and 1997, argued that the Olivier had too much volume for too little capacity, with the result that the 'acoustically unfriendly' concrete sections of walls and balcony left those unlucky enough to be seated at the edges of the stalls or at the back of the circle 'disenfranchised – remote, detached and unable to hear properly' – at least until the installation of a sound enhancement system at the end of his tenure in 1997 (Eyre in Short, Barrett and Fair 2011: xxii). Yet, for some critics and practitioners, the issue is not that some building projects fail to deliver the audience experience promised. They believe that large, resource-heavy buildings are simply incompatible with a thriving and diverse performance culture, and that theatre buildings are bastions of privilege and conservatism, inculcating mental alongside physical passivity, political quietism alongside cultural conservatism. Director Michael Elliott offered a sharp critique of the limitations of large, expensive buildings in a talk broadcast in 1973, for example. Discussing the National Theatre (under construction at the time), he argued that it reminded him more of a battleship than a theatre. He asserted, 'We are not only building huge, inflexible, hard-to-demolish buildings, but huge, inflexible, hard-to-demolish institutions' (1995: 19). He argued that we should 'stop building for posterity', and 'lumbering our grandchildren with our mistakes'. Instead, he observed, 'Don't we need something less daunting, less expressive of civic or national pride, more reflective of changing taste – something perhaps less permanent? In future shouldn't we try to retain a certain lightness and sense of improvisation, and sometimes build in materials that do not require a bomb to move them?' (1995: 17).

By the end of the twentieth century – while public funding continued to flow into capital projects via the National Lottery – critics and performance practitioners were voicing concerns not only about the inflexibility and expense of major new buildings but also about the political limitations of building-based work. Writing in 1998, director and academic Mike Pearson articulates the perception that sitting still while watching performance is an inherently disempowering convention, at the service of a conservative and increasingly anachronistic institution. He noted,

> I can no longer sit passively in the dark watching a hole in the wall, pretending that the auditorium is a neutral vessel of representation. It is a spatial machine that distances us from the spectacle that allies subsidy, theatre orthodoxy and political conservatism, under the guise of nobility of purpose, in a way that literally 'keeps us in our place'. (1998: 9)

Many other practitioners have felt Pearson's unease and frustration with the distanced perspective and physical constraints that are an unavoidable part of the theatre-going experience in large buildings crammed with row after row of fixed seating. In 1999, Baz Kershaw offered an unequivocal rejection of theatre buildings, concluding that they were

> not so much the empty space of the creative artist, nor a democratic institution of free speech, but rather a kind of social engine that helps to drive an unfair system of privilege [. . . by] ensnaring every kind of audience in a web of mostly unacknowledged values, tacit commitments to forces that are beyond their control, and mechanisms of exclusion that ensure most people stay away. (1999: 31)

Evidence that the suspicion, distaste and frustration represented here by the interventions of Elliott, Pearson and Kershaw has been shared by many practitioners can be found in the range of approaches to the use of theatre buildings, auditoria and stages in the recent past. Many practitioners have sought to treat traditional theatre spaces in new ways, creating work which questions the notion that theatre audiences need to be kept in their place, seated passively in the dark of the auditorium. From the 1960s onwards, theatre and performance practitioners have made work which has challenged and exploited the understanding that theatres should be divided spatially into 'them and us', with audiences occupying foyers, bars and their seats in auditoria, while performers belong on stage or behind the scenes. Productions from Peter Shaffer's *Equus* at the Old Vic in 1973 to James Graham's *This House* (which premiered in the Cottesloe at the National Theatre in 2012) have seated spectators on stage in order to draw out parallels with other situations which require groups to observe, listen and judge: from the banks of seating in the House of Commons to the 'tiers of seats in the fashion of a dissecting theatre' called for by Shaffer ([1973] 2005: 4). Other works have offered audience members a place on the stage in more radical explorations of what it might mean to position spectators in this space. *Lifegame* (which draws upon the improvisation strategies developed by Keith Johnstone) presents the biography of a different non-performing guest on stage in each performance. First staged in 2004 by Improbable, this is part improvisation game, part chat show, in which an interviewer asks the guest about their life, in order for the cast – who have never met the guest before – to turn the details of people, places and events into theatre. At the end of the show audiences are invited to volunteer to star in future performances.

The idea that audience members are themselves worthy of elevation to the stage was pushed further by the conclusion to Forkbeard Fantasy's 2006 *Rough Magyck*, which brought the whole audience up onto the stage of the Royal Shakespeare Theatre in Stratford in order to experience a curtain call. This inversion of the usual performer/audience position encouraged audience members to consider the role that they perform at the theatre (Kirwan 2007: 99). Conventional spaces have also been reconfigured, removing seats and requiring audiences to take to their feet. Promenade productions such as the premiere of Jim Cartwright's *Road* at the Royal Court Upstairs in 1986, in which the narrator moved the audience around the space, allowing them to visit the homes of the disenfranchised characters, sought to address the passivity so often associated with being seated throughout a performance. Pushing further into the spaces which are traditionally considered to be the preserve of cast and crew, artists and companies such as Uninvited Guests (*It Is Like It Ought To Be: A Pastoral*, 2006; *Love Letters Straight From Your*

Heart, 2007), Tania El Khoury (*The Search for Power*, 2019) and Kate McIntosh (*In Many Hands*, 2016) have presented productions that have merged boundaries, taking audiences onstage and/or backstage. Each of these works blurred the boundaries of the playing space, and required visceral, sensory task-based participation from audience members (such as apple bobbing, eating, staring into a stranger's eyes, smelling and touching unknown objects). By bringing audiences onstage or by requiring audience members to take a path incorporating backstage areas as they arrive in the playing space, audiences were being prepared for the experience and level of participation that was to unfold. The artists in these examples simultaneously established intrigue and curiosity by providing access to spaces that usually exclude the audience, while also attempting to develop cohesion, intimacy and a sense of inclusion by blurring these lines. Before Covid, many theatres offered backstage tours, which aimed to provide a glimpse behind the curtain into dressing rooms, workshops, green rooms and lighting boxes, highlighting the venue's history while often playing up the exclusivity of the opportunity. Companies also use social media to provide glimpses 'behind the scenes' during performance. Performance has also moved into spaces which are traditionally considered to be the preserve of the audience, such as the foyer. Kneehigh Theatre Company (1980–2021) often utilized foyer space before performances, with productions such as *Nights at the Circus* (2005) having performers in character putting on make-up at a row of dressing-room tables in the bar before the show.

For some critics, however, the theatre building has remained something to escape from, rather than a container which can be explored, exploited or played with. Greater availability of subsidy for touring resulted in many small- to medium-scale companies across the 1960s, 1970s and 1980s leaving traditional, purpose-built theatres behind them in order to bring their work to audiences, effectively establishing a network of performance venues across the country (Saunders and Bull 2015: viii–ix). For some companies this innovation was clearly driven by a desire to meet communities where they were, culturally and geographically, rather than expecting them to travel to the theatre. In Newcastle, 1973 saw the formation of Live Theatre Company: a group of actors, folk musicians and comedians touring variety shows and plays to local community halls, working-men's clubs and schools around the city. As Rosalind Haslett notes, their plays were designed to reflect the kinds of cultural participation valued by their audiences. C. P. Taylor's *Some Enchanted Evening* (1978), for example, included a 'Bingo break', so the audience could fit in a game of Bingo as usual (2019).

Theatre makers also began to appreciate the exciting creative potentials of spaces which had no prior association with the presentation of performance during this period. The development of site-specific work which emerged across the 1980s and 1990s has been characterized as a refusal and repudiation of 'all the expectations that are attached to the proscenium arch of the realist stage and its requisite passive audiences' (Bennett and Polito 2014: 2). It can be seen to have influenced theatre-making at all levels: both the National Theatre of Scotland (NTS, established 2006) and the English-language National Theatre Wales (NTW, established 2009) are peripatetic. Rather than occupying flagship venues dedicated to the presentation of their work, they highlight their active engagement with a wide range of communities and use of unconventional spaces across Scotland and Wales. NTS labels itself a 'theatre without walls', while NTW asserts that 'the nation of Wales is our stage'. Both stress commitments to working with communities 'within their own localities and landscapes' and taking 'work to wherever audiences are to be found' (NTW 2022; NTS 2022). This approach was clear from the start of both companies. NTS's opening production, *Home* (2006), involved the simultaneous staging of ten site-specific shows in a wide variety of non-theatre spaces across the country, including an eighteen-storey block of flats, a forest, an old glass factory and the deck of a car ferry. NTW's opening production, *A Good Night Out in the Valleys* (2010) was staged in a series of Miners' Institutes across south Wales, with the rest of the company's productions in their first year ranging from a house in Penygroes in the north (*The*

Weather Factory), to the beach at Barmouth (*For Mountain, Sand & Sea*), to the Old Library in Swansea (*Shelf Life*). For both companies, the decision to eschew connection with – and containment within – a single building is explicitly framed as a way of forging relationships with communities across the nations they serve.

Immersive theatre experiences emerging across the early years of the twenty-first century have also aimed to provide a new kind of relationship with audiences through exploitation – or creation – of non-conventional spaces, removing the audience 'from the "usual" set of rules and conventions expected from "traditional" theatrical performances' (Machon 2013: 26). These works occupy a distinct (or perhaps just more marketable) genre than earlier site-specific works that took place in abandoned spaces, such as *Gododdin* by Brith Gof (which premiered in a disused car factory in Cardiff in 1989) and *Hotel* by Geraldine Pilgrim (2000), staged in the empty Midland Hotel on the sea front at Morecambe. Taking promenade to a new level, works such Punchdrunk's *Faust* (2006) and dreamthinkspeak's *Before I Sleep* (2010) have created events which leave audiences to work their own way through elaborately staged and often labyrinthine installations, offering opportunities to interact with individual performers or tantalizing glimpses of larger-scale spectacle. Spectators for this kind of theatrical experience are actively rewarded for moving independently around the space, subjecting the carefully curated contents of each room to detailed inspection. In these kinds of immersive works, discussed in further detail in Chapter 3, it is the spectators' responsibility to access the viewing experience and to piece together the fragments of the whole in order to make meaning.

This interest in using unconventional spaces has also been enhanced and, at times, exaggerated by the emergence and growth of festival culture since the end of the Second World War. As discussed in Chapter 1, pressure on space and time during festivals has resulted in the siting of performance events in spaces which are not usually associated with theatre or performance, as demand from audiences and performers exceeds the capacity of a city's regular venues. There is, as Johansson sets out in her discussion of large-scale theatre festivals, considerable power in the way in which festivals make use of everyday urban space: space which is often considered unremarkable and unchanging. Johansson argues that festivals 'have the potential to disrupt this taken-for-grantedness and present us with an alternative reality' (2020: 62).

Sites of mythologized origin

The dark festival of Covid forced new approaches to where theatre is made and viewed: most prominently and notably in the increase in work shared and made to be experienced online, as discussed in Chapter 3. It also provided new perspectives on past performance's use of physical spaces old and new, traditional and unconventional, purpose-built and found. The crisis has made it more important than ever to avoid romanticizing the use of spaces created in both the near and the distant past. Instead, we need to acknowledge the past's complexity in order to encourage more critical reflection on what we want to take into the future. Recent scholarship on ancient Greek theatre, for example, encourages reconsideration of the enduring attachment to the notion that it was a site of unified response and purpose. David Kawalko Roselli's *Theater of the People: Spectators and Society in Ancient Athens* concludes that participation in the festivals of ancient Greece was not limited to male citizens, equal in status. His research indicates that their audiences included not only women but also non-citizens: foreigners, *metics* (non-citizen residents) and slaves (2011: 118–58). He also reminds readers that this audience was not unified but subject to categorization by class, status and ethnicity, with special seats set aside for the policy-making executive council, war orphans and priests. Areas were also reserved for particular tribes and foreigners. Kawalko Roselli also cites evidence of occasionally violent disagreement and dispute over seats (122), and systems of fines and ejection designed to deal with unruly spectators (152), revealing that the design of these sites did not necessarily achieve the idealized experiences of audience unity and equality that they have come to be associated with. His work suggests, instead, that this is a projection, a utopic ideal, associated with a site of mythologized origin.

Greater engagement with the broader cultural context that The Globe and the other large public amphitheatres were operating within in the late sixteenth and early seventeenth century may also temper the urge to read these spaces as especially egalitarian or libertarian. The entrepreneurial energy which clearly underwrote the building of these new theatres may seem, for example, to signal a new level of independence from court and Church support. Yet, the companies which occupied these venues were still heavily reliant upon the patronage of the court. Before the emergence of the London amphitheatres, travelling theatre companies were sponsored by noblemen, and carried their name, attending court at the invitation of Queen Elizabeth I to offer 'command performances'. This arrangement continued after the emergence of the public theatres. It is also important to remember that systems of social segregation via pricing operated in these venues. A range of entry prices enabled the distribution of social groups across the theatre, from the 'groundlings' standing in the Yard immediately below the stage, to the next level up seated on benches in the upstairs galleries, to the most wealthy, housed in private boxes. Moreover, though the audience may have been diverse, this form of performance still shut some out. Enclosed within a high-walled, gated building which you had to pay to enter, access was dependent upon having some disposable income. Though standing in the Yard cost only one penny, this still would have excluded the city's poor. Though these buildings have been celebrated for the heterogeneity of their audiences, they remained fundamentally exclusive institutions, whose spatial organization served to reflect and consolidate the social hierarchy.

2 May 2021. I am walking home from BALTIC Centre for Contemporary Art in Gateshead, where I have just spent three full days alone in the building apart from a security guard. I have been leading an event over Zoom, connecting with people who are spread all over the world, sharing questions and concerns, issues that we believe to be pressing in this moment. As I walk home, I grow aware that there are teenagers everywhere. Some are clustered in groups, sitting on pavements, lounging around down by the river drinking. Others weave past me on bright orange electric scooters, bottles in their hands, crashing into each other, screaming with laughter. I think about what this last year has meant for them. I wonder if they'd care about the things I have been discussing online over the past three days.

Privacy, transparency and exposure

Reviewing past practice may require us to set aside ingrained beliefs about some historical theatre structures and spaces. It also pushes us to think again about the assumption that purpose-built theatre buildings are inherently culturally and politically conservative, as Pearson and Kershaw argue. And it is important – if disquieting – to acknowledge that private spaces have hosted and enabled highly influential experimentation in theatre practice, while some of the most significant developments in performance have been underwritten by patronage associated with exclusive performance. For example, the second indoor theatre to be established at Blackfriars in 1609 – which provided a private space for courtly audiences – is credited with bringing about a profound shift in audience experience through its use of candlelight (Collins 2018). The experiments with perspective built into the extravagant scenography of the court masques designed by Inigo Jones and staged between 1604 and 1640 represented a significant shift towards elaborate visual spectacle, supported at massive expense by James I and Charles I (Lindley 2004: 383). Private spaces have also enabled the continued development of performance practice in periods where public performance was banned or severely constrained. When public theatres were closed following the Civil War and Interregnum (1642–60), private homes provided spaces for select gatherings

(Milling 2004: 176). The private theatre clubs which emerged in the late nineteenth century, such as the Independent Theatre Society, also enabled the sheltered sharing of theatre practice deemed too challenging by the official censor, the Lord Chamberlain (Thomas, Carlton and Etienne 2007: 112–22). Privacy can provide a shelter and a safe space, as well as being exclusive.

We also need to reconsider the ways in which the architectural expression of transparency impacts the audience experience. Transparency as a value or concept is usually celebrated without demur. But though we might imagine that the idea that what happens inside a building or institution should be made clear to those outside of it is to be promoted, it can have negative as well as positive aspects when it is applied to the architectural design of the buildings that house arts organizations. Buildings which allow audiences to see inside before they enter, through banks of ground-to-ceiling windows at street level, glass doors or even uninterrupted glass frontages, may provide a compellingly attractive glimpse of their interiors. The 'preview' of the space the venue supplies may reassure audiences about the scale and likely feel of the space that they'll be entering, should they choose to cross the threshold. But it may also serve to intimidate, revealing a scene which makes it clear to those outside the building that it is not for them. Equally, transparency also has an impact on those using buildings which feature this kind of facade. Their design means that the activities of the people inside are on display, whether they are comfortable with this or not. As Alistair Fair notes in his discussion of the frontage of CAST in Doncaster, this effect is particularly notable at night, when the inside of the building is lit up in a way that creates a quasi-theatrical display (2019: 88). It is unlikely that all of the users of buildings such as this will welcome being put on view in this way. Indeed, some of the theatres which have had most success in attracting the public to use their foyer spaces are those which do not provide a clear view from the outside. The inside of the Barbican is all but invisible from the street, but the internal spaces which connect its stages, restaurants and bookshops contain numerous banks of seating and quiet corners, providing a measure of privacy which encourages people to gather, talk or work – together or alone. This is a space which is all the more welcoming and user-friendly because it is not available to view from the outside.

We also need to reflect on the forms of discipline which determine the delivery of performance in public space outdoors, rather than clinging to the idea that leaving theatre behind, and going outside, necessarily amounts to ideological liberation. Some of the forms of processional performance dominant in the medieval period were clearly designed to reach the broadest possible audience, and their movement through public space was often about the assertion of power. Monarchical processions through cities, and the Corpus Christi cycles taking place on the streets of towns including York, Coventry and Chester from the 1200s through to the mid-1500s evidently intended to reach the population at large, all the better to impress upon them the power of religion and the monarchy through their delivery in locations which were usually secular and mundane. The employment of 'whifflers' – officials who cleared a path and maintained order in the crowd – indicates the way in which public interaction with these events was managed (Easterling 2022: 39) and their ultimate aim of ensuring public acquiescence and support for the authority they celebrated.

31 July 2021. I go to watch Tim Crouch perform I, Malvolio *outside on a trailer in Leazes Park. The last time I saw this was at Northern Stage in 2012. That time, Tim got me up on stage for the show's piece of carefully managed audience-member humiliation, getting me to bend down to tie Malvolio's shoelaces. This time, it's a young boy up on stage with Tim. He plays along, puzzled but compliant. But it feels like a different show. We are sitting in bubbles, little groups of plastic chairs on concrete, exposed to the curious gaze of dog walkers and the sound of sirens as well as Malvolio's furiously bitter rants. We are the spectacle.*

Performers looking to work outdoors following Covid also found that there are many rules and regulations governing the use of what we might have imagined to be public space. Securing permissions, licenses and access to sites for outdoor performances often requires a complex series of conversations and requests between councils, private landlords and private companies: a skill set normally reserved for outdoor producers and production managers. Sometimes navigating permissions from local councils to gain access to public space, only to discover it is, in fact, privately owned, can present obstacles for theatre makers that make working in this way insurmountable.

Theatre as home

The pandemic has also encouraged us to reflect on the relationship between the private domestic realm and the space of performance. In the past, some performance spaces have attempted to make themselves welcoming and accessible through mimicking the interior design of a comfortable and fashionable middle-class home. Manchester's HOME (established in 2015 following the merger of the Cornerhouse and the Library Theatre Company) makes this aspiration literal in its name, as well as in its interiors, which are designed to be warm and intimate, evocative of 'an urban living room' (Mecanoo 2022). The impulse to provide middle-class audiences with a sense of reassurance and security through the recreation of a luxurious but familiar design aesthetic has been around since Marie Wilton and Squire Bancroft refurbished the tiny Prince of Wales' theatre as a 'home from home' in 1867 (Maguire 2000). Nina Auerbach cites the judgement of a delighted playgoer, who observed, 'It was the prettiest, most charming little house imaginable, for it was . . . all upholstered in palest blue, and there were little antimacassars over the backs of the chairs in the stalls, boxes, and dress circle'. They go on to note that this may not seem 'artistic to modern ears' but 'they were the fashion then [and . . .] very clean, lacy and pretty they looked in the theatre' (1987: 169). HOME uses 'rugged concrete floors' and 'warm oak' (Mecanoo 2022), rather than dainty seat-covers and pale blue upholstery, but the principle is the same: a culturally coded welcome to those who recognize the style.

Covid, however, unsettled commonly held understandings of what 'home' represents, even for the most securely and comfortably housed. Instead of attending the theatre to peep into the imagined lives of others in plays which seek to make our hidden private lives public, we could view the domestic interiors of our friends, family, colleagues, clients and strangers through the magic of Zoom and Teams, and find our own domestic world on partial display, too, as the crisis put aspects of our private lives on public view (at least until we worked out how to change the appearance of the background). During lockdown, artists who decided to make work from home often used it to establish connection and commonality with audiences. Yet the pandemic also provided more disturbing insights into what goes on in homes across the country. Reports from charities such as Women's Aid, Safelives and Refuge noted that the pandemic restrictions had made the home an inescapable site of terror and entrapment for victims of domestic abuse. If home is somewhere to escape from, rather than a restful retreat, then what are the implications for venues which model themselves upon the concept, or performances which imply home is refuge or comfort?

Proximity and intimacy

The crisis also raised other unsettling questions, requiring the reconsideration of commonly held assumptions about proximity between performers and audiences. Distance between the two has often been seen as a problem: an obstacle or a barrier to be overcome in the interests of enabling greater and more meaningful interaction (Bennett 1997: 3). This belief has been shared by many twentieth- and twenty-first-century practitioners who have found ingenious ways to bring audiences and performers into closer contact. The emergence of very small theatres, such as the London pub theatres The Old Red Lion and The Finborough (established in 1979 and 1980, and seating sixty and fifty, respectively), placed audiences in close proximity with the performers and each other. The development of one-to-one performance as a genre – and performances which involve direct physical contact between performers and audiences – appeared to eliminate the gap between the two altogether (Heddon, Iball and Zerihan 2012). Some commentators have emphasized spectatorial perceptions of risk inherent in these encounters (Gomme 2015: 289), but others have highlighted the ways in which immersive theatre rewards 'presumptive intimacy' on the part of spectators, producing 'narcissistic spectatorship' that encourages the transgression of conventional behavioural boundaries in the interests of securing fuller access to the world of the performance (Zaiontz 2014: 425), as discussed in Chapter 3. The conventions of the sixteenth and seventeenth centuries reveal that this is not a new phenomenon. Proximity to performers has often been a position of privilege and power. Sitting on the stage, immediately next to the performance, was the preserve of the monied and influential until the eighteenth century. Jane Milling detects the frustrations of performers attempting to deliver their lines in close proximity to 'self-aggrandising gallants' in the work of several seventeenth-century playwrights (2004: 171). These include Ben Jonson, whose prologue to *The Devil is an Ass* (1616) berates the onstage 'grandees' whose 'presumptions' allow them to 'thrust and spurn/ And knock us o' the elbows, and bid turn' (lines 3, 7, 11–12). Sadly, on stage, as elsewhere – and now, as then – close physical proximity is not always accompanied by mutual respect. Conversely, Covid required us all to 'socially distance', teaching us that distance is not necessarily inimical to intimacy.

30 March 2020. I do the same walk with the children every day, a fifteen-minute loop around the smarter streets with wide pavements and large front gardens near our home. We pretend that we are visiting particular trees and plants: the delicate crab apple massed with blossom, a mullein with furry grey leaves growing – improbably but vigorously – out of a wall. Without the usual traffic thrum, the streets are incredibly peaceful. But negotiating other people becomes a curious dance of politeness and fear. Some take pre-emptive action, crossing the road before we reach them. When we get home I insist we all wash our hands. The children ask me why we are doing it. I don't have a good answer.

The powerful and painful disruption wrought by Covid reinvigorated debate about the form and function of theatre buildings, past and present. There can be no doubt that many old theatres retain disquieting markers of past and present systems of social segregation and exclusion. Parts of the theatre estate can appear to be perfectly designed to evidence Henri Lefebvre's observation that 'Space commands bodies', determining the kinds of behaviour and relations which are possible within it (Lefebvre 1974 [1991]: 143). Indeed, in the surviving stock of nineteenth- and early twentieth-century theatres, the past can often feel very present, not least because they have a long association with ghosts and haunting in popular culture (Shillito and Walsh 2007; Ogden 2009; Hindson 2014). The traces of wear and tear which accumulate on their surfaces can also serve to remind present-day users of all those who have passed through the space before them, functioning as an expression of their use by the audience over time (Bowler 2016: 128). With their clear distinctions between stalls, circles and balconies, they seem to confirm that space commands behaviour: dictating how audiences are able to move around within a building, their relationship to the performers, to each other and to the theatrical event itself. But behaviour can also be generated by powerful myths that dictate expectations and current understandings of past practices. As we have argued elsewhere, the loud, boisterous behaviour that audiences have become known for at Shakespeare's Globe may be just as much a product of the representation and descriptions of Shakespearean audiences provided in tourist guidebooks, in films and on television, as the building itself (Freshwater 2022: 45). Those seeking guidance about appropriate behaviour at the venue, for example, will find that the theatre website tells potential audience members that groundlings in the past did not sit in well-mannered silence but were vocal in their responses, good and bad. The venue's description of the behaviour of audiences past suggests that active participation is legitimated by historical precedent.

As discussed earlier, rewriting the narratives which govern our understanding of the appropriate use of historical space can free up even the most traditional and restrictive theatre venue, and demonstrate that it is capable of being repurposed and used in ways that invite critical reflection, rather than serving the perpetuation of the social norms which determined its original organization. Audiences can be invited on stage and behind the scenes, while performers can step off the stage, into the stalls and into the world at large. Nevertheless, there are limits to how much 'repurposing' can erase or obscure the earlier use of a building. Site-specific and site-responsive work is able to play with and evoke the histories and atmospheres of non-theatre spaces because of the longevity of the affective associations that cling to them. Audiences can also demonstrate resistance to the repurposing of theatres themselves, as the management of the Birmingham Rep theatre found when they decided to allow the building's use as a 'Nightingale court' – a temporary court designed to increase capacity in the legal system to address the backlog caused by the Covid crisis – in 2020 (Snow 2021). Social media recorded the impact of this decision on perceptions of the Rep's cultural and political integrity. Assertions that the decision represented a 'breaking of trust', and accusations that the venue was alienating audiences, staff and the broader cultural community, were made (Paxton 2020). Theatre companies and arts organizations who had been working in partnership with the Rep argued that the decision to house the operation of an institutionally racist justice system with a history of enabling the criminalization of LGBT+ people risked undermining the work they were doing to bring Black and LGBT+ audiences to the theatre (Hughes 2021). This affair demonstrates the limits of the ability to 'overwrite' earlier cultural associations, or the idea that a space can ever be 'empty'. The controversy was one of the many ways in which the 'teachable moment' of Covid invited us to reconsider how we think about space, audience and performance. The crisis upended assumptions about privacy and publicness, transparency and exposure, distance and proximity, and distinctions between different types of spatial arrangements in venues and other sites of performance. As memories of the crisis fade, we surely need to recall the new perspectives that it provided as we continue to meet to experience performance in spaces old and new.

3

Technologies, connection and copresence

29 November 2022. I'm in Scotland, visiting an old friend. The city is beautiful, a grid of grand buildings surrounded by hills – but it has seen better days. In between the cracks disturbing things are growing. We visit a repurposed shop, which houses an art installation by Rachel Maclean. It's full of boxes of identical toy dolls. At the back of the shop a tiny room houses a giant phone. Its screen shows us a video animation of the doll – Mimi – obsessing over her digitally alterable image, haunted by the fear of aging. It's compelling but horrific. Back on the streets outside, an anti-vax demonstration stops traffic. Protestors shout about hoaxes and leave copies of their newspaper, The Light, in their wake. We duck inside a charity shop and watch them pass. I wonder about these people's lives. Where have they come from? What has led them here? What needs are being met by their beliefs?

In the early months of the pandemic, laptops, mobiles, tablets and connection to the internet had a significant role to play in enabling the continuation of activity across all areas of our lives. They facilitated health care, business, education, social interaction and the consumption of culture. Those that could work from home did, making use of software which most were only vaguely aware of before March 2020. Many children began to access lessons online. Businesses focused on facilitating remote access to their services. Relationships with loved ones were maintained via video conferencing services such as FaceTime or Whereby, increasing traffic to already familiar platforms and encouraging the use of new ones. Systems of digital surveillance and data-gathering designed to trace and curtail the spread of the virus were launched. Biotechnology brought effective treatments and vaccines more quickly than anyone had initially dared to hope. The crisis has been described as 'the great accelerator', as the speed of innovation, adaptation and adoption of new technology during 2020 and 2021 has been celebrated as one of the few benefits of the pandemic. And yet, the crisis also revealed the inadequacies of many of these technologies, their shortcomings and their side effects. It demonstrated that the effectiveness of a technological solution can be determined by the limitations of scientific knowledge and common understanding, and our collective commitment to its use. Early interventions designed to prevent the spread of the virus were hampered by a lack of appreciation of the role of air-borne transmission and, as the pandemic progressed, it became clear that even the most well-informed interventions were only of value if people were both prepared to co-operate and able to do so. This was true of sophisticated and basic technologies alike. In the UK, it became apparent that information about potential exposure provided by digital tracing systems was only of use if those being identified as at risk were willing to act upon the information, while vaccines were only effective if people could be persuaded to receive them. It became clear that masks did, in fact, have a significant role to play in limiting the spread of the virus, but many refused to wear them. Towards the end of the period of mandated mask use in shops and public transport, use was often tokenistic, with many people wearing their face coverings in ways which would have provided little or no benefit.

It also became obvious that technology was not able to provide satisfactory substitutes for certain kinds of experience. Perhaps the most compelling evidence of the limitations of technological responses to the challenge of the pandemic were the poignant images of families visiting elderly relatives, pressing hands to windows in a desperate symbol of the urge to touch and physically comfort one another (Kanem 2020). For those working from home, the limits of videoconferencing quickly became evident, with many reporting 'Zoom Fatigue': the peculiar exhaustion experienced after extended and frequent online meetings (Nesher Shoshan and Wehrt 2022). And, though technology enabled the continuation of life and business during the periods of national lockdown, the swift returns to football stadia, cinemas and nightclubs once restrictions were lifted across the UK in the summer of 2021 indicated the continued strength of the urge to gather in person, despite the extra risks now associated with these activities.

The pandemic also highlighted significant levels of distrust of new technologies and demonstrated that effective deployment of technology and scientific knowledge can be derailed by fear. Many refused to get vaccinated, exposing deep levels of anxiety about the safety of the intervention. The spread of disinformation on social media about vaccines and alternative methods of treatment illustrated the challenges of the rapid development of communication technology as well as revealing a huge public appetite for conspiracy theories about the pandemic and efforts to control it. Wearing a mask was also presented by some as an affront to personal liberty. In the early months of the pandemic, the new mobile phone 5G masts – and the teams installing them – were subject to attacks, the product of beliefs that the 5G system was the source of the virus (Jolley and Paterson 2020). These responses were not, of course, simply a product of the pressures of the pandemic. They were underpinned by deep-rooted reservations about the change that new technologies create and symbolize. The benefits that technological innovation has delivered in terms of speed and ease of communication, information exchange and travel, improvements in health care, efficiencies in food production and domestic convenience in the developed world have been accompanied by resistance and anxiety from the Industrial Revolution onwards (Bauer 1995). Energetic adoption and celebration of the affordances of new machines, medicines and methods of communication have been supplemented by fears – founded and unfounded – about human labour being replaced by machines, detrimental side effects and the perception that technology may come to control us. The speed of development in personal computing and digital interconnectivity over the last thirty years has generated deep ambivalence about increasing social isolation and the erosion of trust between individuals and organizations, underwritten by powerful technophobia (Brosnan 2002; Turkle 2011; Botsman 2017).

This complex and apparently contradictory mixture of attitudes towards new technology – with energetic innovation and enthusiastic adoption sitting alongside deeply embedded distrust – can also be detected amongst people who are invested in theatre and performance, as makers, scholars and audience members. The pandemic highlighted the tension between the two positions. During the first weeks of lockdown, with gathering indoors and outdoors outlawed and movement severely constrained, many theatre makers felt they had little choice but to use online platforms if they wished to continue to connect with audiences. The pandemic forced speedy adoption of new technologies, pushing artists and audience members alike to get to grips with the potentials – and limitations – of unfamiliar digital tools, while extending our understanding of what constitutes copresence: the quality that is now, arguably, of greater significance for the relationship between audiences and theatre makers than liveness (Sullivan 2022: 36–7). This chapter examines these distinct approaches to the use of technology in relation to the potential connections between audience and performance. It sets out key examples of theatre's past use of technology to assess the way in which it shapes this relationship, and is shaped by it. It suggests that closer engagement with the detail of the use of technology – historical and recent – might help us overcome deep-seated instinctive concerns about its impact.

Before we begin, however, it is essential to acknowledge that technology is not just fibre-optic cable, genetically engineered crops or VR headsets. The wheel, the printing press and steel are technologies, too. Theatre technologies include acting, writing and architecture as well as the latest developments in live-feed video, algorithms and smart phone apps – as W. B. Worthen argues in *Shakespeare, Technicity, Theatre* (2020). There is also a vast and ever-increasing wealth of scholarship on the relationship between theatre and technology, including many alarmingly weighty tomes on the subject (Grobe 2012: 145). We are sharply and rather uneasily aware of the impossibility of doing justice to the range and nuance of practice and scholarship on the topic in this chapter. Yet, the centrality of the issue for contemporary theatre makers and for audiences during the first lockdown phase of the crisis demands that we weigh up the implications for the relationship between them, and engage with debates over whether technology creates greater audience isolation, enables access and inclusivity or enhances copresence. But before we reflect upon the ways in which theatre makers and audiences explored the virtual spaces available to them during this period, we turn to consider how technology has shaped the relationship between audiences and performance in the past.

Awe, novelty and power: the attraction of technology

British performers and theatre makers have always been enthusiastic early adopters of new technologies. They have been quick to exploit and celebrate new materials and machines to attract and retain audiences, providing opportunities for spectators to marvel at extraordinary spectacles and enjoy the cultural capital of being able to say that they have experienced the next big thing. Technology has often been used to create spectacle which is designed to astonish, amaze and impress audiences. Medieval performance made full use of the technologies available at the time in order to highlight human ingenuity, represent heavenly power and to honour secular authority when it came to call. Records detail the construction of 'exquisite devices', elaborate semi-automata in pageants marking the visits of monarchs and local dignitaries (Butterworth 2017: 218–25). The visual and sonic power of fireworks was employed to illustrate awe-inspiring encounters with divinity, or the terror of hell fire. Flame was manipulated through water-filled glass spheres, angled mirrors and polished metal surfaces in order to create intense, shimmering light; pyrotechnic salts, oils, resins and combustible alcohols were mixed to make explosions, flashes and smoke, simulating thunderbolts accompanying messages from heaven and to illustrate the mischief and danger of devils (Butterworth and Harrop 2022). The medieval period pageant wagons used in the Corpus Christi play cycles functioned, on one level, to highlight the skills and specialisms of the guilds which sponsored and staffed them. The props, costumes and special effects they deployed were designed to encourage audiences to appreciate and admire the technical prowess of local craftsmen, as well as their moral respectability and status in the community (Higgins 1995).

The early modern period saw the development of sumptuous scenography enabled by increasingly sophisticated stage machinery. Architect and designer Inigo Jones brought perspectival scenery to the British stage through his contribution to the staging of lavish, exorbitantly costly masques at the courts of James I (1603–25) and Charles I (1625–49). Inspired by Italian innovations, Jones introduced moveable painted flats which slid along grooves in the floor, while ropes were used to lift gauzes and backcloths in and out of scenes, and flying devices moved objects and people through the air. These spectacles served to celebrate the quasi-divine authority of the king. The masques functioned to make his power visible through illusions which evoked divinity and the sublime grandeur of the natural world, and honoured his status as patron and primary spectator by seating him in the optimal position to enjoy the perspectival spectacle. Designed to create wonder amongst spectators, these complex spatial spectacles were purposefully assembled to convey the extraordinary scope of the monarch's power, his position as the unifying centre of the court and country, and his exclusive access to a perfect view of the world before him (West 2002: 59–60).

Theatre has often sought to exploit the novelty value of new developments in technology, using stages and auditoria for the display of technological innovation which is not yet readily available elsewhere. The nineteenth century provides many examples of the inventive deployment of technology in theatre buildings and on stage, reflecting broader cultural fascination with the affordances and issues raised by new technology. The early years of the century saw the major London theatres advertising the introduction of gas lighting to audiences who did not yet have access to this technology at home (Nield 2017: 215). Photography and photographers made regular appearances on the

British stage from the middle to the end of the nineteenth century, highlighting the process of taking and making photographs as theatre negotiated its relationship to this new medium (Novak 2016: 36).

The late nineteenth century saw special effects being deployed at a new scale and level of sophistication, as producers exploited the power of steam and electricity. Treadmills and revolves were used to deliver convincing and spectacular illusions, recreating chariot races and speeding trains, earthquakes and avalanches, sinking ships and hot air balloons. At Drury Lane, the installation of hydraulic stage machinery in 1894 enabled the company to break new ground in terms of what could be visually represented on stage, and the speed at which these spectacles could be delivered and replaced (Bradley 2012). As Nicholas Daly notes in his discussion of the extraordinary number of productions featuring realistic train crashes, the public seemed to have an insatiable appetite for seeing the artefacts of modernity on stage (1999: 50). This fascination continued throughout the twentieth century, and on into the twenty-first, as theatre made use of film, computing technology and the internet. Microphones, speaker systems, headphones, binaural sound, video projections, live-feed video, LED lighting, motorized and automated rigging systems, communication headsets, social media platforms, mobile phone apps, VR: all have been set to work in creation of theatre and performance. As Christopher Balme argues, theatre is, and always has been, hypermedial: in as much as it adopts, incorporates and represents other media (90). These developments have always been driven by a desire to attract and retain audiences.

Fear of the dark: shared light and the soul of theatre

A parallel tradition runs alongside this enthusiastic exploitation of new forms of technology, however. The belief that technology demeans and debases theatre – making it somehow less itself – has been expressed at various moments across theatre history. Concern often focuses upon the notion that theatre's use of technology impairs the relationship between practitioners and audiences, and between audience members. Sometimes these reservations are expressed by theatre makers who have long experience of the full potentials of technological innovation. Playwright Ben Jonson, who produced the scripts for many of the masques which Inigo Jones designed, eventually fell out with Jones because he concluded that the scale of the spectacle created by the designer was overpowering his contribution as poet, for example. Ellen Mackay highlights Jonson's positioning of spectacle versus script in the preface to *Hymenaei* (1606), where he argued that his writing was the 'soule' of the masque while the scenography was the 'body' or 'outward celebration' (2017: 301), which was obscuring the script's deeper meaning. In this treatise, as elsewhere, Jonson asserted that audiences were being overwhelmed by the scale of magnificent but forgettable experiences, leaving them dumbfounded rather than meaningfully enlightened.

The concern that theatre's use of technology risks undermining the contributions being made by writers and performers, and detracts from the essence of theatrical communion between audiences and performers, can also be found in the work of a range of twentieth-century theatre directors who sought to minimize theatre's use of advanced electronic technology and to separate theatre from film and TV by stripping theatre back to a pristine state, unadulterated by technological intervention in the intimate, immediate interrelationship between performer and audience. During the twentieth century this impulse animated the work of many theatre companies that sought to emulate the stripped-back aesthetic of Jerzy Grotowski's 'Poor Theatre', which made minimal use of costume, scenery and artificial lighting effects, instead focusing upon the physical and vocal resources of the performer. The Polish director's emphasis upon the encounter between actor and spectator was based upon a conviction that the way in which 'Rich Theatre' assimilated other artistic disciplines was generating a degraded, hybrid spectacle, lacking integrity or 'backbone' (Grotowski, Wiewiorowski and Morris 1967: 62). As Pablo Pakula demonstrates, Grotowski's work had a significant influence upon British theatre, evident both in the work of directors and companies across the 1960s and 1970s – including Peter Brook, Triple Action Theatre and Freehold – and through the widespread use of his book *Towards a Poor Theatre* in theatre education following its publication in 1968 (2011).

Given the ready use of technology in twenty-first-century theatre practice, we might imagine that attachment to 'poor theatre' is a thing of the past. Yet, writing in 2008 Balme convincingly argues that there remains an enduring attachment to the logic of 'media specificity', which understands every medium as having its own distinct character or essence that distinguishes it from others (82). In what follows, we offer a review of recent scholarship on the impact and use of new technologies that evidences the kinds of attachment that Balme describes. It demonstrates that concerns about the ways in which the introduction and integration of new lighting technology affects the relationship between audience and performance have dominated public debate and scholarship.

The transition through novel forms of lighting in the modern theatres of the nineteenth century – from gas, limelight and, eventually, electric lighting – has been identified as one of the moments in theatre history which has received a huge, even disproportionate, amount of scholarly and critical attention (Sauter 2010: 135). This attention, however, is often grounded in ambivalence about the implications of this development and the changes in audience experience it created. These developments are frequently presented as harbingers of greater audience passivity, detachment and atomization. For example, Susan Bennett's short history of the development of the relationship between audiences and performers (discussed in Chapter 2), moves from celebration of the ideal represented by the active audience engagement in the festivals of ancient Greece to a critique of the total separation of audience and performers in the darkened auditoria which emerged at the end of the nineteenth century. Bennett presents the moment in which the pit was replaced by stalls in the mid-nineteenth century, which effectively made the footlights situated at the edge of the stage into a hard barrier, as a key moment in the apparently inexorable slide towards the separation and pacification of the audience. Lighting comes to signal an uncrossable barrier between audiences and performers, determining the nature of their relationship (1997: 3).

Caroline Heim also focuses upon the disempowerment of the audience created by the introduction of lighting technology in her work, *Audience as Performer* (2016). Heim claims that exuberant, expressive audiences effectively ruled the theatre and dictated to actors until the first half of the nineteenth century, but the arrival of electric lighting, which enabled the dimming of the house lights, together with a new focus upon theatre etiquette, effectively functioned to subdue their behaviour, removing their ability to communicate with performers, and with each other (76). For Heim, the combination of darkened auditoria and a new preoccupation with decorum amounts to nothing less than the anaesthetization of effusive audience interaction.

Nicholas Ridout asks readers to consider the impact that electric light – and the deep darkness it creates in the auditorium – may have had upon performers' perception of their position in relation to the audience. He argues that it is a key component in the mix of social, economic and cultural factors which are responsible for the emergence of stage fright as an immobilizing affliction. Facing a mysterious and threatening darkness – an 'awful hole' – rather than a visible gathering, the actor is frozen in the spotlight in a position of horrific exposure (2006: 35). Ridout's account points to the concern which animates this area of scholarship more broadly: the possibility of connection and reciprocity between audience and performers (29). Lighting technology is seen to have had a profoundly damaging effect on the connection, and the possibility of face-to-face interaction.

Sophie Nield also offers an analysis of the interrelationship of power and the gaze in the theatre during this period, arguing that we should attend to nineteenth-century theatre's invention and use of artificial darkness, rather than artificial light (2017: 205). Nield traces this back to Henry Irving's introduction of adjustable lighting into the Lyceum (221) and argues that the darkness created in the auditoria of the period serves to occlude the audience's connection to each other, and to the space they occupy. In this historical moment audience members became invisible: both to others in the audience and to the performers. For Nield, the artificial darkness of the nineteenth-century theatre can be seen as reducing its audiences to disembodied floating eyes, ghostly in their separation from the illuminated theatrical illusion that appears inside the picture frame before them (223–5). It also serves to obscure and conceal the sources and mechanics of illusion, and the labour involved in the creation of theatrical spectacle (205). This body of scholarship reveals deep-seated fears that theatre's use of lighting technology destroys copresence and hides the realities of systems of theatrical production from audiences, making theatre less ethical and less democratic.

These concerns about the implications of the use of artificial lighting in the theatre do not only preoccupy scholars, however. In 2016 they became a matter of high-profile public debate in one of the few spaces where contemporary performance, practice-led scholarship, literary celebrity and debates over theatre lighting meet: Shakespeare's Globe. In October 2016, seven short months after taking up the role of Artistic Director of the Globe, Emma Rice's departure was announced by the theatre's board, who stated that her interest in the use of electric light and sound was inimical to its commitment to the principle of offering 'shared light' productions. The decision made headlines, was reported on BBC2's *Newsnight* and Radio 4's *Today* programme, and generated a huge amount of commentary and passionate criticism across the media (Cornford 2017). Pascale Aebischer provides an account of the affair in her introduction to *Shakespeare, Spectatorship and the Technologies of Performance* (2020), arguing that Rice's removal can be read against the backdrop of a long period of economic decline in Britain and the isolationist sentiments that found form in the 2016 Brexit referendum. In this context, Shakespeare comes to symbolize national traditions and a simpler past characterized by more direct human interaction: values and qualities which require stout defence against the destructive acceleration of technological innovation and globalization (2). Though Aebischer avoids taking sides with Rice or The Globe in her opening discussion of the director's dismissal, she does offer a strong critique of the notion that theatre was ever 'technology-free'. She notes that although some might like to indulge in purist fantasies about theatres in which audiences and performers meet each other without mediation of any kind, we need to be clear that such a theatre has never existed. The idea that the early modern period, with its candles and bare wooden boards, was free of technology is simply a 'nostalgic fallacy' (13). Nevertheless, the conviction that theatre can offer a form of unmediated communion between audiences and performers, if only conditions are right, continues to compel commitment to 'shared light' at The Globe. And concerns about the impact of technology can be found even where practitioners, critics and scholars are most aware of its potential.

> 21 April 2020. I press 'leave meeting' on my Zoom screen, where I have been in back-to-back meetings for most of the afternoon. I go to see how my five-year-old is getting on with the home school activities I gave him. He is watching TV, transfixed. It looks like he's on Netflix – but we don't have Netflix anymore. He explains he managed to get it back again. He's worked out how to re-subscribe.

Immersion, interactivity and digital culture

W. B. Worthen's interrogation of the claims that are made for immersive theatre set out in 'Designing the Spectator' indicate that these concerns do not just focus on the use of technology during performance. His analysis reflects disquiet about how the broader digital sphere has influenced understanding of the ways in which we might participate as spectators at a theatrical performance – and in other areas of our lives. Worthen offers a sharp critique of the form of twenty-first-century immersive theatre, arguing that the freedoms that this kind of work appears to offer spectators are illusory. He mostly surveys shows created in the United States, but also includes discussion of work created by UK-based companies, including *You Me Bum Bum Train* (2004) and *Sleep No More* (2011), spending a good deal of time considering responses to Punchdrunk's work, taking the specifics of their approach as representative of the form as a whole.

Worthen does acknowledge that spectators do enjoy much greater mobility in these works – being free to explore the vast, intricately decorated spaces in which they take place rather than being contained within fixed seating. But he argues that far from empowering the audience, the form provides it with no meaningful agency. He measures the opportunities for interaction provided by these productions against the criteria for two-way exchange developed by early researchers into human–computer interaction at MIT, recorded by Roseanne Allucquère Stone (157). These criteria include '*mutual interruptibility*', '*no-default*' and '*limited look-ahead*'. Together they indicate that each participant should be able to change the course of the interaction; that there should be no automatic reversion to a pre-selected option; and that there should be constraints on the extent to which the shape of the exchange or conversation can be anticipated or predetermined by either party (Stone 1996: 10–11). Worthen argues that these immersive theatre productions fail against these criteria for interaction. The work is tightly scripted and choreographed, and is not designed to accommodate interruption, as it always defers to default, predetermined actions. He detects no significant improvisation on the part of the performers, beyond responses which are designed to manage unwelcome acts of spectatorial intervention. Moreover, no space is made for creative contributions on the part of spectators: they cannot alter the course of the show in any significant way.

Worthen's discussion of the function of the mask in Punchdrunk's work makes the extent of his sense of the limitations of the form in terms of interactivity clear. The identical white masks which spectators are required to wear during the show not only signal the distinction between performer and spectator – identifying them to the production's crew, and to each other – but also constrain the kinds of contributions that spectators can make. The masks prevent speech, and position the spectator as an isolated, anonymous voyeur (169). Though they signal an individual's status as part of the audience, they militate against communication or collaboration with fellow spectators. As a result, as Worthen and other critics have noted, behaviour at these shows does not respect standard norms governing conduct in public space. Anonymity lowers inhibitions and encourages selfish and even aggressive behaviour on the part of spectators, whose actions seem to suggest that they view other audience members as an inconvenience or as a barrier to the full realization of their own experience (Zaiontz 2014: 414; Sherman 2016: 74).

Nevertheless, there seems to be a divergence between this competitive in-person conduct and the collaborative community which has developed around the shows online. These works are surrounded by huge volumes of online commentary. Fans discuss the show in minute detail, sharing information which may unlock particular types of experience for future visits in a fannish form of mutual aid. For Worthen, however, there is no discrepancy between the two modes of interaction, as he argues that the form of immersive theatre is indicative of the transfer of expectations from digital culture: expectations which reflect a profoundly limited understanding of the potentials of participative culture. He equates digital production cultures with ineluctable systems of surveillance, discipline and corporate exploitation, arguing that immersive theatre mirrors the logic of the digital culture on which it is modelled (150–4). In both, the spectator – or user – becomes a prosumer: a producer of content as well as a consumer. For Worthen, there is no agency to be found in this position, as he equates the unpaid labour of fans – whose online activity serves as valuable marketing material – with the theatre industry's broader dependence upon young, unpaid volunteers. He argues that the form may assume and reward a level of active engagement, but the forms of participation it provides are 'deferred, mediated, distant' (150). He goes on to assert that the kind of relationships that are fostered in the immersive theatre experience are no more meaningful than those on Facebook, expressing a deep sense of the limitations of online activity (173). On social media platforms, as in immersive theatre, he notes that the 'spectator is part of the machine' (158).

There are, of course, other – more positive – ways of viewing the growth of fan-generated content, as the work of Kirsty Sedgman (2022) and Matt Hills (2021) indicates. But Worthen's critique resonates with broader concerns about technology's deleterious impact upon the quality and strength of copresence at performance expressed by other scholars. Worthen argues that these shows hide their 'productive apparatus' – how they work and are produced – from their audience in ways that chime with Nield's observations about the masking effect of the introduction of artificial darkness (153). His concern about the pacification of audiences through their inculcation to the conventions of a relatively new technology parallels Heim's reading of the impact of electric lighting, while his argument about the deep divisions created by the anonymous mask shares Ridout's understanding of the significance and importance of the face-to-face encounter between performer and spectator. In sum, Worthen's critique of the limitations of interaction in immersive performance is representative of a deeper shared ambivalence about the ways in which technology has influenced the development of twenty-first-century theatre and the relationship between audiences and performance.

Alone together: creating copresence

Responses to the difficult choices facing performance practitioners during the pandemic reflected the division in attitudes towards the use of new technology described previously. This tension was evident in commentary and practice in the first months of the crisis, which saw an extraordinary explosion in the amount of theatre and performance available online. Theatre makers already producing work for audiences to view online found they had a vast new audience, while many practitioners moved their work into digital space for the first time as the dark festival of Covid made its disruptive force felt. These forms of theatre were not universally welcomed, however, with debate about the status of digital theatre taking place across the theatre-making world.

Some cultural commentators were happy to pass definitive judgement on digital offerings. One of the most high-profile, Laura Collins-Hughes' article for *The New York Times*, 'Digital Theater Isn't Theater: It's a Way to Mourn Its Absence' (2020) summed up objections to the form.

Most practitioners expressed their reservations in less contentious terms, however. As Balme noted in 2008, contemporary performance practitioners tend not to view the relationship between live and mediated forms in the confrontational way that some scholars and critics have (85). Moreover, digital theatre and mediated performance have been developing alongside in-person performance presentation since the late 1990s (Dixon 1999a; Giesekam 2007). Though Allred and Broadribb argue that the digital space was seen as the 'Wild West' by some practitioners – which they equate with an exciting frontier, inviting exploration and cultivation (2022: 5) – most theatre makers will surely have been aware that the digital space was already well populated, with a sophisticated culture and history of its own. The rich period of development that new media and digital art had experienced prior to the Covid crisis was acknowledged as part of Fusebox Festival's virtual edition (April 2020), when the festival directors asked the established new media artist Angela Washko to offer a keynote address as part of the festival's programme. In the talk, *Feminism, Intervention and Digital Culture* (2020), Washko referenced a wealth of existing practice in this area and supplied a 'reading list' to help ground audiences in existing digital performance practice. In this context, the 'Wild West' metaphor can be read as a useful if disingenuous fiction. As histories of colonialism teach us, it is surely easier to move into and occupy a territory if you present it as empty (Hendlin 2014).

Nevertheless, though there are many examples of practitioners deciding to explore online work in a way that was new to them – as Allred and Broadribb's survey of the work produced during the fourteen months in which theatre was closed indicates – some practitioners decided that online and digital forms were not for them, putting their energies into other ways to reach audiences in person as soon as the initial phase of lockdown lifted, as discussed in Chapter 2. Others experimented with different ways of connecting with audiences from a distance – through postcards, podcasts and audio experiences (Fuchs 2022: 143–82). Some of the organizations and artists who did decide to go online clearly viewed it as a last resort. Many were not keen on the move to digital, with some scholars concluding that it amounted to a 'forced marriage' between theatre and the digital realm (Chatzichristodoulou et al. 2022: 2).

This ambivalence can be seen in some of the work being made. Fintan Walsh engages with this in an article which examines the way that some online offerings seemed to be mourning for touch, gathering and physical presence. He notes that the work that was made during the months of lockdown failed to evidence the much-rehearsed argument that digital and physical performance practice have a vibrant and synergetic relationship. Instead, as performance makers shifted to sharing work online, and then began to create pieces specifically for digital dissemination, the distinctions between the two formats became more apparent (365). In part, Walsh notes, this was because Covid inverted the sets of assumptions which accompany digital and physical theatre-making. Suddenly the 'living theatre' – previously considered to be a place of vital, in-person connection – became associated with contagion, disease and death. In contrast, the digital realm took on new meaning as it became the vessel through which new currents of professional and personal experience flowed (396). This reversal of traditional associations can, as we discuss in Chapter 4, be seen as characteristic of dark festival.

Moreover, as Walsh notes, much of the work being made for experiencing online during the period was clearly preoccupied with the limitations of mediatized experience, acknowledging the inadequacy of digital communication as a substitute for physical touch and gathering in person. He focuses on a series of examples of mediatized performance projects that seem, he argues, to be grieving for the live, shared experience. In these works – which were either livestreamed or disseminated online across 2020 – performers cuddle Ipads, webcams capture empty stages and actors use direct address to call out to the distanced, dispersed audience.

> 10 March 2021. I make an arrangement on WhatsApp to meet an old school friend who is up from London visiting his parents in Northumberland. His wife died less than a month ago. He said he wanted to see me. He has been through two years of hell. I finish my Zoom call and I leave my house to walk to meet him at Jesmond Dene, a park where we spent a lot of our teenage years. It is pouring with rain. When I see him, I have no words. Instead I hug him. As I do, I realize this is the first real hug with somebody outside of my household that I have experienced in a year. We cry.

Some practitioners, however, moved beyond registering and mourning the loss of copresence to thinking about how to provide equivalents online. Works such as Varjack Lowry's hybrid *iMelania* (first developed at the Barbican in March 2020, and then offered at festivals including GIFT in 2022) incorporated access to gather, a creative online meeting platform intended by the designers to make online meetings 'more human'. This was used by the artists as a pre- and post-performance 'venue', where you could greet and message others watching the performance. The concept of the pre- and post-show 'virtual bar' became a regular feature across online performances in an effort to bring audiences together in a conceptually familiar space. Following the streaming of a pre-recorded version of *It Don't Worry Me* by Barcelona-based theatre company Atresbandes (created in collaboration with theatre makers Bertrand Lesca and Nasi Voutsas) audience members were invited to join a post-show cocktail bar in Zoom as part of GIFT's online edition in 2020. Individuals were sent into different break-out rooms, each hosted by a member of the cast, who were spread between Kent, Paris and Barcelona. Cocktails and conversations flowed, and shared actions were encouraged. In one particularly anarchic moment, a performer instructed everyone to get into their bath or shower: audience members clambered in, holding their devices in their hands. As with all great house parties, many audience members joined from their kitchens, and a DJ set encouraged a mass Zoom disco as everyone was reunited in the main Zoom room. Levels of natural light and darkness in the background of the Zoom windows indicated the breadth of time zones of participating audience members, dancing together in a shared Zoom call.

In the opening of *Telephone* by Coney (2020), a performance about the history of telecommunications that also took place on Zoom, audience members were welcomed by performer Tassos Stevens to a very low-key 'Coney Bar'. The bar here served as a unifying concept or as a signal to audience members to relax and settle into the show. Towards the end of *Telephone*, audience members were invited to share stories and personal memories about telecommunications with each other, which enabled the creation of a strong sense of copresence. For Glasgow's 'Take Me Somewhere' festival's virtual edition in 2020, audiences 'arrived' via the festival's homepage that was also the virtual festival bar, where audiences gathered prior to and in between festival events. The 'bar' came complete with DJ and AV sets, and a chat room that enabled audience members to communicate and greet each other on arrival at the festival website, functioning as a space to converse about the works experienced at the festival.

Social media also played a distinctive role in establishing copresence online around events, especially in festival contexts during Covid. It became online etiquette for chat functions that were built into platforms being used for performances to be switched off for the duration of a performance. So, while performances took place, audiences moved their conversation and comments to social media platforms, instead. 'In the moment' reactions were shared between audience members on Twitter, as festivals promoted the use of specific hashtags for performances, leading to exchanges in real-time about performances. The inclusion of performance-specific hashtags allowed for audience members – however dispersed – to find each other, and engage with one another while watching. Facebook Watch Parties also became a regular feature, where audience groups would come together to watch along online. Watch Parties were often initiated by one person and shared amongst their own networks, making the experience more exclusive, akin to a private theatre club. Public or private, these gatherings demonstrate how audience copresence can be experienced online. As Erin Sullivan notes in her careful articulation of our understanding of what it means to experience 'liveness' in performance, this quality is no longer dependent upon audiences coming together with performers in shared space and time. She argues that we should focus our attention on internal rather than external factors, noting that 'the feeling of meaningful connection to others' is more significant for twenty-first-century audiences than physically sitting alongside one another (2022: 36). Collective experience and community is key to this understanding of what 'liveness' means in performance, but can be detected in 'a particular kind of phenomenological experience that foregrounds interactivity, collectivity, and a sense of eventful connectedness', rather than the space or time a piece of performance is made in (37).

Access and inclusion

Clearly, Zoom theatre and other forms of online performance are so much more than a way to mourn the absence of 'real' theatre, contra Collins-Hughes. A negative and dismissive position towards the use of digital platforms reflects failure to appreciate their potential to provide experiences of copresence and to develop and sustain relationships between practitioners and spectators. The theatre of lockdown also highlighted the benefits that new technology can deliver in terms of greater accessibility. British theatre companies had been experimenting with broadcasting to cinemas since 2009 when the National Theatre launched NT Live, following the lead of New York's Metropolitan Opera and the Berlin Philharmonic. Martin Barker's study of audiences for this 'alternative content' – as it was first referred to by the industry – found that many were deeply appreciative of the opportunity to view these works at venues closer to home (2013: 67). Large-scale studies of audience behaviour carried out in the early years of this emergent form indicated that, far from 'cannibalizing' local theatre – with audiences choosing to watch broadcasts from distant 'centres of excellence' rather than attending local theatres in person – they had no negative impact on attendance at local theatres and actually appeared to increase the amount of theatre-going overall (Bahkshi et al, 'Beyond Live' 2010; Arts Council England 'From Live-to-Digital' 2016). 'Event cinema' quickly became an established part of the cultural landscape despite the misgivings of some playwrights and directors, who voiced concerns about its impact on theatre in the regions and the ecology of touring theatre (Youngs 2014; Freestone 2014).

Until Covid, however, the rise of the parallel practice of livestreaming performance to the computers, tablets, phones or smart TVs of individual spectators – rather than the screens of publicly accessible venues – received much less attention, despite the fact that it predated the arrival of event cinema, having been going on since the early 2000s (Sullivan 2020: 93). But the practice of using technology to give individuals access to live performance in their own homes has a much longer history. John Wyver argues that the NT Live experiments were continuing a tradition which dated back to 1938, when the BBC first produced an outside television broadcast of J. B. Priestley's successful comedy *When We Are Married* direct from London's St Martin's Theatre (2011). There are still earlier examples of new technology being used to bring live theatre into people's homes, however. In the late nineteenth century, before the invention of radio, entrepreneurs in several European cities set up a service that provided subscribers with access to the sound of live theatre productions at home – as well as concerts, lectures and church services – exploiting the potential of newly installed telephone lines. Relatively short-lived in comparison to the Parisian original, the theatrophone (which was in use between 1881 and 1936), the London Electrophone provided subscribers with access to theatre between 1893 and 1925 (Van Drie 2020; Liedke 2022). Still, while these experiments indicate awareness of the potential of providing access to theatre at home, they did not represent major contributions to the broader accessibility of performance. In 1938 television ownership was for the few, with approximately 20,000 sets in homes across the country

(Goodhart 2020), while the cost of subscription to the Electrophone also made it a toy for the wealthy (Kitcher 2020).

In contrast, event cinema and online livestreaming present a significant expansion in accessibility, making the works available to people who are not able to travel to the venues in which the productions were staged. Those who enjoyed the privilege of being able to journey across the world to experience performances of their choice prior to Covid may choose to pass over the benefits of increased access swiftly (Carlson 2022), but it is worth considering the kind of audience members who stand to gain most from this innovation. They include – but are surely not limited to – those who cannot afford the time and costs of travel and accommodation; those who have caring responsibilities, disabilities, physical or mental health issues, which make travel impossible or extremely challenging; the neurodiverse who find large venues overwhelming; and people of colour who have been made to feel unwelcome in spaces which are dominated by white practitioners, staff and audiences.

> *12 November 2020. I watch* The End *by Bert and Nasi on a livestream from HOME in Manchester, lying in bed. In the corner of the platform there's a counter which tells you how many others are watching. I become fascinated by this tiny visual measure which tells me that I'm not alone in my viewing. I've seen the show before, with Kate, in Edinburgh. She told me I'd cry then, and I do again now. This time though, instead of stumbling out into the courtyard at Summerhall, I sit and watch the equivalent of the credits. They show a Google Earth image of the venue from above, which slowly but steadily pans out – first the streets, then the city, region, country, continent, then the world. The Human League's plaintive 'Together in Electric Dreams' plays. I can imagine Bert and Nasi laughing as they chose the song. How ridiculously perfect it is.*

Many have greeted experiments in digital delivery during the pandemic as a significant step forward in terms of access for audiences with disabilities, celebrating the increasingly widespread provision of captions and audio-description (Webster 2021; Walmsley et al. 2022; Allred and Broadribb 2022: 6). This use of assistive technology builds on foundations laid over the past forty years, however. Screened surtitles were first deployed by opera companies looking to provide translations of foreign-language productions before being used to provide captioning and subtitling for D/deaf and hard of hearing audiences (Alland 2018). The history of captioning in the UK dates back to 2000, with the establishment of Stagetext, a deaf-led charity that initially worked to make theatre productions accessible through the use of captioning, and now offers services to a wide range of arts and heritage organizations. The year 2007 saw the launch of a captioning service in Scotland, while Northern Ireland has had a dedicated service since 2011 (Zárate 2021: 86). Stagetext's annual reports indicate the rapid growth of demand for their work (Moores 2020: 180).

This period also saw increasing technological experimentation in this area. Stagetext primarily works with 'open' captioning systems provided on screens which all in the auditorium can view. 'Closed' captioning systems have also been developed, providing information directly to individual mobiles or other handheld devices, giving audience members greater control over when and whether they wished to read the information being supplied (Zárate 2021: 91). Some innovations sought to provide a more integrated visual experience, as advances in wearable Augmented Reality technologies (AR), and especially mobile AR, encouraged attempts to do away with the awkward and tiring work of switching back and forth between information provided on screens and the performance itself. In 2017, the National Theatre announced that they were working on provision of smart caption glasses, which display a transcript of the play's dialogue and descriptions of the production's sound on their lenses (Secară 2018). Spectators were now able to watch the stage (or the audience) at the same time as viewing the extra information provided by their glasses – or even move around the space in immersive productions. Audio description designed to provide access to blind and partially sighted audience members also advanced significantly during this period, as practitioners sought to develop shared standards and guidelines (Neves 2018).

As we discuss in the following chapters, there is clearly more to access than technology. But technological solutions have enabled companies to ensure that their work is more available to audience members who have access needs relating to their sight or hearing. Nevertheless, these advances should not be allowed to mask the fact that many issues and problems remain, as indicated by a study led by Jo Robinson (Mével, Robinson and Tennent 2023). Captions and audio-descriptions are usually an afterthought, created after the production is finalized, rather than being considered during its development. Exceptions exist, such as Rosa Postlethwaite's *Composed* (2018), developed with an audio description advisor and incorporating a live palantypist into the presentation of all performances of the work. But these are, as yet, rare. Access provision continues to be partial and patchy, with specific dates being made accessible rather than full runs. Users report that the smart glasses are uncomfortable, can cause headaches and eye strain and have the unwanted effect of marking out the person wearing them as 'different', while also still requiring users to switch their focus between the text and the stage, which are sited at different focal distances. The use of auto-captioning tools by many companies when shifting productions from stage to screen during the pandemic has also been critiqued as an inadequate response to the needs of the d/Deaf community. Even when companies address inaccuracies in speech recognition, irresolvable problems remain with positioning, as well as lack of sound description, paralinguistic features and speaker identification. Yet research and innovation continue to develop at speed in this area. Companies are experimenting with creative captioning and collaborating with academics to address these problems, and to devise and trial methods of integrating access considerations from the initial stages of creative development (Mével, Robinson and Tennent 2022). Handbooks offering guidance on how to factor in the experience of disabled audience members earlier in the creative process are appearing (Fryer and Cavallo 2022), while the concept and application of Universal Design – which takes the needs of all audience members into account – are also being explored (Conroy 2019; Hadley

2022). The work of Unlimited, an arts commissioning body founded in 2012 to support, fund and promote new work by disabled artists for UK and international audiences, indicates the range of issues that require negotiation, from parking to the provision of information about what you can expect to happen on entering a venue (Giraud and Miles-Waldin 2018): issues which receive further discussion in Chapter 4. Some coverage of technology's potentials and limitations when it comes to dealing with access problems for audiences with disabilities demonstrates the tendency to think that it can provide a powerful, straightforward solution (Biggs 2021). Closer interrogation, however, reveals a more complex reality.

Reassessing the value of shadow and failure

Returning to the historical record with an awareness of the common themes that run through critical coverage of the historical use of technology also provides a more nuanced understanding of the way in which it has determined relationships between audiences and performance. Looking again at debates over technology's impact upon this relationship with an awareness of our propensity to approach the issue from polarized perspectives may enable us to think again about the ways in which technology can support and enable the things that we value most about theatre, rather than allowing ourselves to be governed by a residual and instinctive distrust. Here, Scott Palmer's assessment of the historiographies which have come to dominate the interpretation of technological innovation in theatre lighting provides a valuable perspective. He argues that these are sometimes inaccurate and often reductive, and that they fail to capture the creative potential of darkness and shadow. First, however, Palmer suggests that we need to acknowledge the influence of the powerful set of associations which frame our understanding of the relationship between darkness and light. As he notes, atavistic instincts associate light with safety, and dark with the threatening unknown, and may even serve to remind audiences of their own mortality. Religion has also taught us to align light with good, and darkness with evil. In the theatre, the tradition of the ghost light – left burning in empty auditoria – provides an evocative symbol of this set of associations. Originally designed to operate as a piece of basic safety equipment, preventing falls from the stage, it has taken on a symbolic or even mystical quality as a guard against threats from the supernatural realm (40). Its dual function is indicative of the way in which darkness in theatres comes with a high conceptual charge. It registers the strength of our fear of the dark. Palmer also asserts that the darkened auditorium – the source of so much critical concern – is rarely quite as dark as some accounts might suggest. Indeed, both historical and contemporary directors have found that the creation of a total blackout is extremely hard to achieve. Even powerful and responsive gas burners need pilot lights, which are never extinguished. Working alongside constraints determined by venue license-holders and fire regulations means that it is extremely difficult to remove light entirely from auditoria in the twenty-first century. Unless you can negotiate the reinterpretation of health and safety legislation – as Battersea Arts Centre did for their 1998 'Playing in the Dark' season (Welton 2020) – Emergency Exit signs inevitably intrude. As Palmer notes, complete darkness is often more convention than observable phenomenon (41).

Palmer goes on to challenge the claim that shared light gave way to separate spheres of brightly illuminated stage and darkened auditoria as part of the emergence of naturalist theatres in the late nineteenth century (41). Instead, he reminds readers of numerous examples of earlier uses of deliberately dark auditoria, which in Britain date back to the performances at court in the Elizabethan era and private indoor theatres such as the second Blackfriars playhouse (1596–1642). These spaces were lit by candles and oil lamps but were also equipped with manually operated shutters that could be opened and closed, allowing daylight to illuminate the space, or to create night-time scenes (2017: 45). Decoupling the deliberate darkening of performance spaces from a moment in theatre history which has come to be associated with an undesirable shift towards audience passivity allows us to consider the implications of these practices in new ways. Palmer highlights the practical benefits and dramaturgical uses of darkness and shadow on stages and in auditoria, rather than presenting the increasing sophistication of lighting technology as a fundamentally deleterious development. From this perspective, though the moment when the house lights go down may now function as a signal to audiences that they need to transition from chatter to silence, movement to stillness, and concentrate their gaze upon the stage – the problematic passivity deplored by Heim, Bennett et al. – the differential in light between stage and auditoria also allows directors to 'harness shadows', to use light and dark as part of a symbolic and expressive scenography (56).

Palmer focuses upon what darkness achieves on stage, but we argue that the kinds of experience it enables when it envelops the audience are worthy of further consideration. Accounts such as those provided by Heim, Ridout and Nield draw up a long charge sheet as they detail the downsides of dark auditoria: the silence and passivity that they are presumed to produce; the removal of the ethical impulse associated with the face-to-face encounter and the act of collective witnessing; the creation of an 'awful hole' of dark disconnection between performers and their audiences; the elision of the labour which creates the spectacle. Worthen also picks up the problematic lack of inhibition enabled by the combination of darkness and anonymity provided by masks in more recent immersive performance. Yet, moments of blackout can clearly be used to create a range of heightened experiences for audiences, from the moments of suspenseful blackout in the long-running Agatha Christie adaptation *The Mouse Trap* (Dalrymple 2019) to the 'sonic spectatorship' enabled through long periods of immersion in darkness in the work of companies such as Sound & Fury (Alston and Welton 2017).

Here, though, we want to register that the anonymizing cloak of darkness can benefit audiences in performances which are not specifically looking to generate a jump-scare or to experiment with placing audiences in pitch-black conditions. While scholars such as

Heim are undoubtedly correct to observe that theatre lighting and design have enabled audiences to perform for each other, drawing attention to their presence in spaces which encourage and enable self-display, we need to question the idea that audiences necessarily want to be seen. The experience of being watched, and our ease – or lack of it – with this kind of public exposure is informed by our relation to power, and the kinds of gaze that the bodies we inhabit invite. The bodies of certain types of spectators, as Sedgman argues in *The Reasonable Audience*, are 'marked' by their difference and are subject to heightened scrutiny as their behaviour is measured up against a series of implicit conventions (Sedgman 2018). Scholarship which returns to nineteenth-century images of theatre audiences shows us how female spectators were subject to the spectatorial male gaze as they watched – a situation in which being positioned as a performer involves the negotiation of the constraining conventions of gender (Meier 2018). Bree Hadley's *Disability, Public Space Performance and Spectatorship: Unconscious Performers* (2014) asserts that, for people with disabilities, everyday social interactions can feel like a series of performances, in which their idiosyncrasies are interpreted as spectacle, as they are subjected to embarrassing, unwelcome and often painfully intrusive curiosity (1–2). The question of what it means to be a Black spectator in the theatre – a space which is all too often dominated by whiteness – is only just beginning to receive the attention it deserves in theatre studies (Sörgel 2020; Snyder-Young 2020; Syler 2022). Taken as a whole, this scholarship should help remind us that not everyone gets to enjoy the privilege of being entirely at ease in a public gathering, and that being visible should not be equated with being in control.

The question of audience visibility took on new significance during Covid, as theatre makers and audiences came together to explore the potential of online platforms as performance spaces in greater numbers than ever before. Many of these early experiments were, inevitably, fraught with bloopers and blunders, as well as fear of being targeted by hackers or being 'Zoom bombed' (Shaw 2020). During the first months of the pandemic, as anyone who spent any time on Zoom or other video meeting platforms will recall, even the most confident users could find themselves caught out: inadvertently leaving camera and audio on, forgetting they were on mute or being found to be AFK – away from keyboard – when they were supposed to be present. As artists became more familiar with the space in which they now found themselves, they tended to make a distinctive choice between presenting their work in 'meeting mode' or in 'webinar mode'. In meeting mode audience members could choose to switch their cameras on, and become visible to one another. Alternatively, in webinar mode, performances functioned as broadcasts, as audience members remained invisible to one another. Meeting mode had the potential to give audiences the freedom to create their own audience experience, as the platform allowed individuals to decide which Zoom square to focus on through to 'pinning' or 'spotlighting' other people on the call. Though this provided a greater level of audience agency, it also enabled voyeuristic viewing of other audience members who could have no way of knowing that they were the subject of this form of observation. Though the meeting's 'hosts' – the artists or company who had set up the call – could limit audience access to these functions through engagement with the detail of the platform's settings, it became clear that audiences could tailor their own viewing experience in ways that other audience members, and those making the work, might not have initially anticipated. As practitioners became more familiar with the full range of the platforms' affordances, it became increasingly common for works to be framed by clear instructions about whether audiences should be watching with cameras switched on or off, in amongst other instructions and information, such as content notes or age guidance. While Zoom Webinar offered artists more control over how their works were experienced by audiences (as a broadcast), many artists reported deep dissatisfaction with performing in this mode. Without having the audience visible or available to them, they struggled to have any sense of performing to anyone at all. Webinar mode did, however, allow artists to perform online with many of the equivalents to performing in person, with a pre-broadcast mode allowing for a sense of 'backstage' to be established prior to the 'house opening' and the performance beginning. As audiences and practitioners became increasingly familiar with the platform, it became clear that it had the potential to amplify anxiety about exposure as well as providing greater control over how and when individuals might choose to become visible in their role as audience.

> *2 May 2020. I'm back at my laptop with my ice cube in my hand, just in time to see the first few audience members appear on screen who have used the 'raise hand' function to indicate they want to become visible. I'm watching* Elision *by Gudrun Soley Sigurdardottir as part of GIFT 2020, and Gudrun is performing from her living room in Glasgow. Behind the scenes, I know that the tech team are frantically switching more and more people into panellist mode as more hands are raised – a lot more people want to join in than we'd ever anticipated. Face after face appears on screen, each with an outstretched hand holding an ice cube. Most are on their own, but some are couples, households even, and then I spot whole families with young children watching along together. Our ice cubes are melting in our hands, slowly. It's magical. But it's at this point I remember that we'd added an age guidance of 16+ for this performance.*

Palmer's assessment of the histories of theatre lighting reminds us that technology is rarely as efficient or effective as we might hope or fear. His professional experience as a lighting designer no doubt informs his appreciation of what can be achieved with light in the theatre, as well as his observation that we need to acknowledge its limitations. At a global level, the pandemic experience has demonstrated that we should avoid overstating technological achievements, acknowledging their limitations rather than their omnipotence. Vaccines, treatments and testing are imperfect, and even the most effectively administered systems of testing and contact tracing will eventually meet human resistance (Hill 2022; Tan 2022). Technological failures have received relatively little discussion in theatre and performance studies, however. There are many accounts of the importance of a wide range of creative failure (O'Gorman and Werry 2012), but technological failure only makes fleeting appearances in theatre history as anecdote and asides: the misfiring pistol which kills a mother and a child in the crowd, reported in a letter in 1587; unconvincing train crashes which are greeted with laughter and derision by nineteenth-century audiences; delays and interruptions as an unremarkable but unavoidable aspect of viewing online performance (MacKay 2011: 2; Daly 1999: 2; Ptacek 2003: 185). These kinds of mishaps and malfunctions are not usually deemed worthy of significant scholarly attention. Yet, audiences and performers both know that there is always the possibility that the theatre-machine will break down, and, as theatre makers attempting to produce work online during the pandemic had to acknowledge, glitches and crashes are all part of the online experience. Reflecting on her experience of working on the digital iteration of *The Evidence Chamber* (2020), Rachel Briscoe, one of the lead artists at Fast Familiar, argues that rather than worrying about whether something will go wrong it is better to assume that there will be a new technical challenge to deal with daily (2022). Though these kinds of interruption are undoubtedly frustrating and challenging for audiences and performers alike, they provide reassuring evidence of human and technological vulnerability and limitations, revealing the hidden workings of the system (Alexander 2017b). Rather than showing our devices as tools in smoothly manipulative disciplinary processes, they serve to remind us of the labour involved behind the scenes, and the determination required to maintain the connection between audience and performance from both parties.

Though Covid generated significant technological and scientific innovation in areas of research and development, which received major investment during this period, it is important to remember that the technologies being used to present performance during the pandemic were not new in and of themselves. Yet the scale of the engagement with performance online in the first months of the crisis did represent something genuinely novel. Prior to the pandemic, the use of technology in theatre was often thought of as something supplemental: evidence of the form's eclectic-ness and use of wide range of media (Balme 2008). But for a moment during the early days of the crisis, the use of technology to facilitate viewing at a distance was no longer niche or experimental: it was the only way to do it. The experience of encountering performance online, mediated by our screens, challenged conventional understandings of copresence but also demonstrated the depth of attachment to the experience of gathering in shared time and space. Indeed, the use of digital technology to continue to provide access to performance during the pandemic was never a straightforwardly celebratory affair. The new work being made was inevitably inflected by the deep fear and anxiety caused by the pandemic. It was also, as Walsh reveals, often expressing a deep sense of loss and melancholia – as performances explicitly referenced longing for the bodily copresence usually associated with gathering to witness theatrical work (2021).

Taking the long view and setting aside the urge to condemn or champion the use of technology makes it easier to see that technology is not a panacea for the challenges facing theatre in terms of concerns around access and inequalities. Theatre has never been an inherently democratic medium – and it did not suddenly become more so when so much of it moved online during the early months of the Covid crisis. But we need to ensure that the value of diverse methods of access, and the insights provided by the experimentation during Covid are not lost by a return to 'normal' underwritten by unacknowledged resistance to technology's benefits and the notion that 'real' theatre must always be physically copresent. Instead, we need to consider what constitutes copresence – and how it can best be created.

4

Honesty, secrets and lies

How theatre communicates with audiences

12 March 2020. Over the last few years I've started trying to avoid hearing politicians speak. I want to know what they are saying but I don't want to hear them say it. But in the last few days I've started listening to Boris Johnson's speeches. I don't want to wait for the digested version. I want to hear exactly what he says and how he says it – as if assessing the form will help me gauge how serious things are. I watch the latest on my laptop sitting at the kitchen table. He tells us that it's not like the flu, that it's not just a seasonal thing. He says he has to level with us. That many more families are going to lose loved ones before their time. I feel sick. Sick that this is happening, sick that he gets to tell us.

Covid can be interpreted as a crisis in communication as well as health. Responses to the crisis exemplified and exacerbated existing problems with communication at all levels. National authorities and international institutions struggled from the start over when and how to communicate the details of the virus and its implications. China initially attempted to silence doctors and journalists when people first started to succumb to an unknown disease in late 2019 (Hegarty 2020). The World Health Organization was criticized for not labelling the outbreak a 'public health emergency of international concern' – its highest category of alarm – until 30 January 2020. Yet, when they did, few countries heeded the warning and launched the testing, tracing and systems of social distancing required until it was too late (Maxmen 2021). Once underway, efforts to communicate the changes in behaviour required met with a range of success in the UK. At first, directives from the country's political centre seemed surprisingly effective. The majority of the British population responded to the order 'Stay at Home, Protect the NHS, Save Lives' with a level of compliance that surprised some (Reicher and Drury 2021). Daily televised press briefings from 10 Downing Street gave updates and information, while their format evidenced the government's desire to demonstrate that their response was being driven by scientific expertise and medical advice: with the Chief Medical Officer for England, Professor Chris Whitty, and the UK's Chief Scientific Adviser, Sir Patrick Vallance, standing alongside Prime Minister Boris Johnson. The limitations of the press briefing format quickly became apparent, however. The lack of a British Sign Language interpreter was immediately noted, and it also became obvious that the format was not going to reach some communities and individuals from culturally diverse backgrounds which were, as the government's own advisory committee pointed out, most in need of this advice (Mathers 2020; SPI-B 2021). In early May, the four nations of the UK announced differing approaches to reopening. In England the advice was changed to 'Stay Alert, Control the Virus, Save Lives' to mark a gradual easing of lockdown measures, while Scotland remained in lockdown. Memes ridiculing the slogan being used in England and the idea that staying alert would be sufficient to control the virus circulated on social media (Handley 2020). By June 2020 the clarity of communication in the press briefings was clouded by questions focused upon the latest political scandal, and the lies that may or may not have been told by politicians and their advisors, rather than updates on the progress of the virus (Siddique and Campbell 2020). Local authorities struggled to keep people informed of the latest guidance as the country then moved to a 'three-tier' range of local lockdown restrictions. The official report issued by the House of Commons Health and Social Care, and Science and Technology Committees which outlines the lessons learned from the crisis acknowledges that the move from a unified to a divergent approach caused confusion, and ultimately eroded trust in the government's actions (2021: 55). Disinformation about the pandemic's sources and treatments for the virus proliferated, as Covid's dark festival created deep uncertainty about who, and what, could be trusted (Freeman et al. 2022). The term 'infodemic' was readily – and problematically – adopted to describe the swift growth and spread of information and data about the virus, as concerns grew that populations were threatened both by too little and too much communication about the crisis (Simon and Camargo 2021).

> *16 March 2020. I have never considered myself to be a numbers person. But in the first few weeks of the crisis I become obsessed with the tallies of people who have tested positive for Covid in cities and regions across the UK provided on The Guardian website. I check it compulsively every day, trying to work out how bad it is. The numbers do not make me feel better – they creep upwards slowly, then begin to jump higher and higher each day. This, I learn, is an example of exponential growth. I know it's not helping. But I can't stop looking. I need to know.*

Other aspects of the pandemic impacted communication in ways that were both banal and deeply affecting. For those obliged to observe the 'stay at home' order issued on 23 March 2020, opportunities for embodied interaction with others shrank dramatically. Many found the social isolation during the lockdown phase of the pandemic acutely distressing, contributing to the perception that the 'modern epidemic' of loneliness – already viewed as enough of a concern to justify the creation of a Minister for Loneliness in 2018 – was reported to be growing at an alarming rate (Alberti 2019: 2; Groarke et al. 2020). Though others could still easily be reached on phones and screens during lockdown, the coming months demonstrated that communication is about so much more than what we write and say, or what our faces may express. The whole body speaks, not just the parts of it that are easily captured on Zoom or the screen of a smart phone; and it is not only infants that desperately need touch to comfort and reassure (Vallee 2021). The use of face coverings – mandated in shops and on public transport as lockdown eased in July 2020 – had a negative impact upon communication. Studies have confirmed that they reduce sound transmission and the visibility of movements of mouth and lips, which enable speechreading, posing a particular challenge for people with hearing loss and for dementia sufferers (Saunders, Jackson and Visram 2021). They make emotion harder to perceive, reducing interpersonal connection and increasing misunderstanding as communication becomes embarrassing, tiring, stressful and frustrating (Jeong et al. 2021). Isolation also had a markedly negative effect on the development of language in young children. Studies indicate that there has been a significant growth in demand for speech and language support since the pandemic for children whose early years learning was interrupted by lockdown (Clarke 2022).

Theatre is sometimes presented as a panacea for challenges in communication, sharing experience in ways that are deemed to be more direct, more effective and more democratic than other media. James Moran argues that the theatre is especially well placed to puncture the smooth, slippery patina of fake news (2022). The continuing interest in documentary and verbatim theatre suggests that it is perceived to communicate more effectively than other media, countering the challenges of the post-truth era (Stuart Fisher 2020: 180). Others highlight theatre's potential to tackle social isolation and loneliness (Salman 2016; Batsleer and Duggan 2020: 147–60; Booth 2022). This conviction that theatre and performance are especially effective forms of communication has also been shared and amplified by those who have been most convinced of its potential to cause harm. Censors old and new fear that theatre spreads performed behaviour virally – that its influence works its way unseen from stage to audience (Freshwater 2009b: 104). Of course, theatre and performance, at their best, can provide experiences which can seem to confirm the worst fears of the censor: they can be deeply moving, outraging, uplifting, thought provoking, horrifying and energizing, bringing audiences together in powerful collective expressions of emotion. They can make audiences laugh, cry and cheer, unifying crowds in acts of celebration, song and dance. This is, of course, what theatre and performance are designed to do. Their purpose, if nothing else, is to communicate with the public. Practitioners have deployed all of the media at their disposal in the hope of achieving this aim. Words and voices; bodies and movement; light, dark and shadow; music, sound, noise and silence; space, objects, costume, colour: the stage has used every art form, material, resource and technology available to craft experiences, to tell stories and to capture the attention of audiences. The sites and buildings that performance appears within also communicate in their own way. Signage, posters, the design of entrances and their location, and the organization of space within buildings, in auditoria and in online platforms – all provide audiences with information about what kinds of experience are being made available within. Programmes and websites provide details about the show's contents, the cast and creative team, and the kinds of institutional support that the production has received. They also include advertisements which position the work within a broader landscape of consumption and reflect judgements about the kind of goods and services that the people who read them are likely to buy.

Theatre and performance are haunted, however, by the possibility – or probability – of communication failure. As all practitioners know, this is an unavoidable occupational hazard: audiences can remain unmoved, unamused or unimpressed despite the best efforts of everyone who has contributed to the delivery, design and construction of the experience. As we have described elsewhere, a thread of deep frustration and ambivalence about audiences can be detected in theatre makers across history (Freshwater 2009a: 42–55). Given the regular experience of rejection and critique, and the occasional ridicule which performers are subjected to at the hands of audiences, it is hardly surprising that they may approach the audience with trepidation at times. Moreover, the theatre is built around spatial and narratological structures which withhold information as well as presenting it, preventing certain types of communication as well as facilitating others. Theatres and performance practices are often deliberately designed to enable concealment in order to provide a more satisfying moment of exposure, from the sumptuous spectacle that greeted the court at the dropping of a curtain in Greenwich in 1527 (Dillon 2006: 37), to the aerial performers ripping through the false paper ceiling above the heads of the audience in De La Guarda's *Villa Villa* (first performed in the UK in 1997, and evocatively described by designer Tom Pye in 2017). The moment of 'reveal', when secrets are divulged, truths discovered or realities exposed can also be found in the plot or narrative structure of almost all forms of theatre and performance. In the UK, cast lists occasionally include 'Walter Plinge' (a close relation of A. N. Other, and North Americans George and Georgina Spelvin). The pseudonym serves to disguise the identity of the performer and conceal casting details that would give away doubling and spoil a later moment of dramatic surprise (Martin 2017). Purpose-built theatres and performance venues are structured to shield or screen certain areas from the public, with the notable exception of the Curve in Leicester, which was conceived as a flexible, porous space with no traditional backstage area (Short 2011). From workshop and rehearsal spaces, dressing and green rooms, modern theatres usually contain spaces which separate performers from spectators, giving the former shelter and privacy as they prepare for the moment of public presentation. In most theatres, the stage cannot be seen from the street. Though some are now built in order to highlight their transparency, as discussed in Chapter 2, this is a relatively new development – and a glass frontage does not, of course, provide a view of the stage. These architectural, scenographic and creative structures do not indicate that theatre makers and performance practitioners do not want to communicate directly with audiences or build relationships with them, of course. But they do suggest that the kinds of relationships which are formed within these structures and conventions are likely to be determined by the careful management of where, when and how contact between the two parties takes place. They also imply that some aspects of theatre-making are fundamentally private rather than public.

This chapter focuses upon the forms of communication that performers and organizations have used to create, develop and maintain relationships with audiences in the past. It reflects on the strategies used to attract audiences and engages with how theatres approach the establishment of contracts, conventions and boundaries with audiences, considering how explicit statements about audience behaviour may facilitate communication and better relationships, as well as creating barriers. It provides critical discussion of the use of relationship marketing, exploring how theatres and performance practitioners have sought to develop relationships which move beyond superficial engagement with this model. It touches upon moments when theatres have been less than honest and direct with audiences, as well as models of clarity and transparency. It closes by contemplating the parallels between the relationships that can develop between an organization and its audience, and those that we foster and value elsewhere in our lives, before returning to the question of what the dark festival of Covid has had to teach us about communication.

Addressing the audience

Many performances manage the beginnings and ends of the work through acknowledgement of the nature of the relationship between audiences and performers, marking the transition in and out of theatrical time with a moment of direct address. These liminal moments often make the hopes and fears inherent in the act of theatrical communication explicit. Puck's final 'Give me your hands if we be friends' sign-off in *A Midsummer Night's Dream* directs the audience to applaud, and evokes an easy and familiar relationship between performer and audience, while being undercut by the doubt of the conditional 'if'. The insecurity and vulnerability inherent in all acts of public performance – hinted at in Puck's final lines – have been negotiated in a range of different ways. The appeal to the audience written by Samuel Johnson for actor-manager David Garrick at the opening of the theatre in Drury Lane in 1747 insists that the 'voice' of the stage reflects the preoccupations and preferences of its patrons, suggesting a relationship which is defined by complex co-dependence:

> Hard is his lot, that here by Fortune plac'd
> Must watch the wild vicissitudes of taste;

> With ev'ry meteor of caprice must play,
> And chase the new-blown bubbles of the day.
> Ah! Let not censure term our fate our choice,
> The stage but echoes back the public voice.
> The drama's laws the drama's patrons give,
> For we that live to please, must please to live. (1763: 202)

Actors and managers have not always dealt with the challenge of managing audience expectations by adopting a deferential tone in these moments of direct address. Caroline Heim cites theatre critic Clement Scott's assessment of the shift in power that occurred in the late nineteenth century. Comparing earlier periods, when the 'public dictated to the manager, who was the servant, not the master of the audience', Scott notes that the average theatre manager was now more likely to be seen 'grandiloquently speechifying to the public, dictating terms, protesting against fair criticism, and airing views and theories to his patrons' (1899 Vol I: 12, quoted in Heim: 66).

Theatre managers no longer address the audience directly from the stage as a matter of course. Post-curtain call, performers may invite the audience to stay for a post-show discussion or encourage them to tell their friends if they enjoyed the show. In the event of an accident or emergency, Front of House Managers will appear in order to inform the audience that they will need to wait, or leave. But today's equivalent of the theatre manager – the company's Artistic Director or CEO – does not usually take to the stage to lecture audiences on what they can expect or how they should behave in person. A great deal of communication happens before and after the event, however. From playbills to targeted mailshots, building facades to banner adverts, new technologies are deployed as enthusiastically offstage as they are onstage. Theatre makers and performance practitioners past and present have used all the forms of communication available to them to pique audience interest and provide information about what they are offering. Many of these forms of communication appear to be one-way, as Christopher Balme has noted (2014: 48). Playbills, programmes, posters and websites address audiences but do not usually invite or enable dialogue. In what follows we reflect on what these forms of theatrical communication reveal about the relationship between audiences and performance.

Reaching out: playbills, programmes and online platforms

From a historian's perspective, old playbills and posters occupy a curious position as documents which anticipate events which are yet to come. Their existence does not guarantee that the performance listed actually happened. They are also unreliable guides to the performances they advertise or list. They describe and detail the work but also function to hype and plug. They do, however, provide a good indication of how institutions were attempting to position themselves with the public and tell us a great deal about how theatre and performance makers have conceptualized their relationship with audiences as they address readers (Balme 2014: 50).

Playbills that provided details about place, time and prices in the hope of converting readers into audiences first began to appear in public spaces in the early seventeenth century. Very few playbills have survived from this period, but contemporary references to them provide clues as to how they were viewed and the assumptions about audiences that they contain. Tiffany Stern's analysis of the evidence that remains from this period reveals that playbills were a ubiquitous part of the cityscape, pasted on buildings and posts alongside legal bills and official announcements (Stern 2006: 77). As Balme notes, the vigorous Puritan anti-theatrical prejudice of the late sixteenth and early seventeenth centuries extended to the playbill, finding its omnipresence enraging. He cites George Wither's *Abuses Stript and Whipt* (1614), which presents the cautionary tale of a gentleman who happens to catch sight of a playbill on his way to listen to a sermon. The allure of the theatre is such that the glimpse of the playbill compels him to leave the narrow path of the righteous and head off to the playhouse. Wither opines: '[B]y the way a Bill he doth espie, Which showes there's acted some new Comedie; Then thither he is full and wholly bent, There's nothing that shall hinder his intent' (quoted in Balme 2014: 52). This parable registers both the pervasiveness of the playbill and its perceived power as a form of communication.

Millions of playbills have survived from the eighteenth and nineteenth centuries, presenting a gift and a challenge to scholars and archivists. As librarians at Harvard – which holds one of the largest collections – note, 'So Many Playbills, So Little Time' (Hoggatt, Capobianco and Pyzynski 2014). Some of these bills contain vast quantities of information and had developed into documents of considerable complexity by the nineteenth century. They supply the basic informational necessities, detailing the different items of performance to be presented, timings and cost of tickets, but they also function to situate the theatre in the civic life of the city and to regulate audience behaviour, as well as promoting the event through claims about positive audience responses to the work. Balme's reading of a playbill issued by the New Theatre Royal in Glasgow in 1840 exemplifies its many different functions. The playbill attempts to exclude certain types of audience, and to dictate the way that they behave ('children in arms are not admitted and no smoking allowed in the galleries'). It gives audiences information about the experience they can expect inside the building. Having recently reopened following renovation, the playbill notes the safety regulations which the building conforms to, and the latest technical innovations that provide better air circulation in the theatre's boxes. It promotes the work of the tradesmen involved in renovation of the theatre, and advertises for doormen. Tone of address is all. The renovations are 'respectfully submitted to public approval', as the theatre's proprietor informs readers that his work is 'in the service of that Public who have so frequently honoured his exertions with patronage and support' (quoted in Balme 2014: 58–60). As Balme observes, the playbill informs, but it also employs a large number of different strategies as it attempts to attract audiences: it directs and asserts, but it also pleads, coaxes and flatters.

The visual form and style of the playbill contributed to this active courtship, as technical innovations in print and typography added to its appeal. In the early nineteenth century, the appearance of the playbill – and many other forms of ephemeral print – changed significantly as bigger and bolder typefaces were introduced, increasing their visibility from a distance. Gillian Russell describes the way in which the impact of this change registered at the time, quoting an 1823 report in *Theatrical Examiner* which observed, 'how the large type staggers under the weight of so much gorgeous announcement', while in 1851 one of the writers for *Tait's Edinburgh Magazine* recalled seeing posters for entertainments at Vauxhall in London as a child which struck him as 'colossal words of fire . . . oracular announcements' that 'flamed from a background of the blackest wood' (quoted in Russell 2020: 162).

Over time, as David Gowen sets out in his history of the playbill, the form evolved into what we would now recognize as a programme. The 1850s saw the modification of the playbill from a long single sheet, printed on one side, to folded documents with several pages, which could be easily held in the hand (Gowen 1998: 7). In this form, programmes are designed as silent guides and companions, available for consultation immediately before the performance, and serving as souvenirs and aide memoires long after the event. Like the playbill, they have multiple communicative functions. As Susan Bennett has noted, the content and the design of the programme provides an 'interpretative framework', contributing to the mood and atmosphere of a production before it begins (1997: 145). They provide information about the venue and set the scene, as well as containing idiosyncratic editorials from theatre managers that aim to communicate with audiences directly and personally, positioning and scripting audience experience (Gowen 253). They also carry advertisements which situate the event as part of a wider landscape of consumption. Initially, they listed products available for sale in the theatre: coffee, chocolate, ices. Drinks lists appeared in the programmes of Victorian music halls. They also contained adverts which suggested that other businesses might like to make use of their pages. This invitation was quickly taken up, to the extent that commentators began to grumble about the quantity of adverts that were appearing in programmes. In 1890 S. J. Adair Fitz-Gerald observed:

> On the first page you are most likely informed where you can purchase coffins on the hire system, tooth powder, basinettes and brandy; on the second, third and fourth you are confronted with a perfect encyclopaedia of toilette requisites. [. . .] The cast of the play is supposed to be on it somewhere, but very few are equal to the task of discovering the exact spot. (308–9, quoted in Gowen 52)

As the nineteenth century became the twentieth, programmes became glossier and more expensive. The adverts that appear in their pages helped position the theatregoer as a monied consumer and situate the experience they had purchased in the context of other luxury goods.

Playbills and programmes also direct audience behaviour in other ways. They seek to establish contracts, conventions and boundaries with audiences, setting out behavioural norms. Caroline Heim identifies the second half of the nineteenth century as the moment when the policing of loud and expressive audience behaviour began to take hold. Linking this to the dimming of lights in auditoria, she notes that rules proscribing demonstrative response were 'printed in playbills, on placards, handbills, notices on the backs of seats and outlined in lectures by theatre managers before performances' (2016: 67). In fact, theatre managers had been using playbills to dictate behavioural norms to audiences since the late seventeenth century. Gowen lists a playbill from 1697 for a revival of Robert Howard's *The Committee* at the New Theatre, Little Lincoln's Inn Fields, as the earliest example of a playbill seeking to admonish audience behaviour. Under the title of the play, it asserts, 'NO PERSON TO STAND ON THE STAGE' (1998: 131). When Garrick took to the stage in 1747 to present *An Ode to Drury Lane* (cited earlier), the playbill advertising the evening told patrons that since 'the Admission of Persons behind the Scenes has occasioned a general Complaint on Account of the frequent interruptions in the Performance, 'tis hop'd Gentlemen won't be offended, that no Money will be taken there in the future' (quoted in Nicoll 1981: 79). Though the tone mirrors that of Garrick's deferential prologue, this detail represented a significant change in convention. Until this point, 'Gentlemen' had been able to pay to wander around backstage, with access to the green room and the sides of the stage. Garrick was telling them that they would no longer be able to do so.

Negotiating with audiences about appropriate or desirable behaviour is an enduring part and parcel of performance-making. Heim notes that several instances of calls for audience silence can be found in medieval plays, while the playbills and programmes of the eighteenth and nineteenth centuries often informed audiences what was expected of them. There are many more recent examples of attempts to tell audiences how they should behave, as John Wyver's account of the BBC's 1938 broadcast of J. B. Priestley's *When We Are Married*, discussed in Chapter 3, makes clear. Wyver notes that the broadcast was carefully constructed in order to evoke the experience of attending the theatre. The first shots displayed the theatre's exterior, before moving to images of the pages of a theatre programme turning. The presenter announced the characters and cast, then offered several suggestions about how the audience at home might want to behave during the play's two ten-minute intervals. This included leaving their chairs, putting the lights on, and discussing the play. After these intervals, the television recalled its audience to their seats in front of their screens at home with a 'theatre bell effect' (2011). We might assume that attempts to dictate audience behaviour when watching from home would no longer occur in the twenty-first century. Indeed, some livestreamed productions have explicitly acknowledged that audience members could be anywhere – including on the toilet – when watching the show (Walsh 2021: 395). But the urge to try to shape reception remains, however politely expressed. Actor Gillian Anderson took to Twitter in May 2020 to tell spectators to stay away from their phones during the stream of the Young Vic's production of *A Streetcar Named Desire*, in which she starred (Jacobson 2020).

Recent scholarship has most often concentrated upon past efforts to curtail and constrain expressive audience responses. But there is another historical tradition which seeks to produce and amplify visceral and emotional engagement rather than repressing it. Gowen demonstrates that puffs and promotion have long depended upon descriptions of enthusiastic audience response: claims that performances had received 'universal Applause' and 'unanimous approbation' made common appearances on playbills for touring productions in the late eighteenth and early nineteenth centuries (213), becoming increasingly detailed and exuberant. An 1824 playbill for John Home's *Douglas* included an extended depiction of audience response to previous performances. The playbill noted that the new musical drama had been 'received with unqualified delight by an audience at once superlatively brilliant and overflowing – scarcely a scene but received three distinct rounds of applause, and at the close, the Whole House, as if electrified, rose and with shouts that rent [. . .] the Air' (quoted in Ward 1973: 31). These hyperbolic portraits became the subject of satire. A parody of English 'Theatre Puffing' printed in an American newspaper in 1816 envisaged the audience response to the much anticipated appearance of a 'Mrs _____', 'queen and princess of tears', at an unidentified Theatre Royal:

> The house was crowded with hundreds more than it could hold, with thousands of admiring spectators. [. . .] Several fainted before the curtain drew up – the very fiddlers in the orchestra blubbered like hungry children for their bread and butter; 109 ladies fainted; 46 went into fits, and 95 had strong hysterics. The world will hardly credit the assertion, that fourteen children, five old women, a one handed sailor, and six common council men were actually drowned in the inundation of tears that flowed from the galleries and boxes. (quoted in Gowen 212)

This satire did not, of course, put paid to puffing. The late nineteenth century saw playbills morph into posters that privileged compelling images over text (Smyth 2010), and theatre posters, flyers and their online equivalents are now frequently adorned with ratings from reviews and the briefest of quotations, which vouch for the quality and impact of the work. The brevity of the textual content invites inventive and potentially misleading use of words and phrases from reviewers, as discovered by journalist John Barber in 1982 when taking a closer look at the promotion of R. D. MacDonald's *Summit Conference* at the Lyric Theatre in London. This used single word quotes from *The Times*, *The Observer* and *The Guardian*, which appeared to judge the production 'Dazzling', 'Stunning' and 'Impressive', respectively. Returning to the original reviews revealed, however, that the reviewer from *The Times* was referring to another production of the same play; *The Guardian* was praising the set (which was judged impressive in comparison to the show itself); and *The Observer* was using the term 'stunning' ironically (Barber, quoted in Gowen 214). This expose does not, perhaps, reveal anything particularly surprising about the insincerity and artificiality of some forms of promotion. But it does indicate that publicity often attempts to script and predetermine audience response and behaviour, whether it tells audiences that they should find themselves stunned, dazzled or impressed, shouting with delight, or drenched in tears. Whether the emphasis is upon the creation of visible and audible approbation, genteel restraint, or putting away your phone, the urge to tell audiences how to behave and how they should respond clearly has a long pedigree.

> *23 April 2020. I'm in the bedroom at the back of our house one evening when I hear the noise: an indistinct clattering, cheering. I open the window and lean out. The sound of people clapping and bashing pots and pans becomes clearer. For a moment, I'm totally nonplussed. Then I remember, I know what this is: this is for the NHS. The sound goes on and on, the need to witness and hear each other's gratitude and relief echoing across the terraced buildings and backyards.*

Behind the scenes: intimacy, personalization and papering

There are, of course, other approaches to audiences which eschew the issuing of explicit or implicit directions in favour of emphasizing connection and exchange. Relationship marketing emerged as a concept in the 1980s, encouraging businesses and organizations to foster dialogue and connection with their customers (Berry 1983). This approach encourages businesses to conceptualize their interactions with customers as part of an ongoing relationship: moving from attraction, maintenance, development, and enhancement (Ritter and Geersbro 2010). This represents a shift from previous more transaction-focused marketing approaches, which focused upon the '4Ps' – the four core elements of product, place, price and promotion – and was driven by the realization that it is more cost-effective to retain existing customers than acquire new ones, as strong, trusting relationships with loyal customers provide a sustainable competitive advantage. The concept has found wide application, particularly with organizations which are offering a service rather than simply selling a product, and it is now actively used by a range of theatre companies (Dunnett 2017; Anderson 2019). Efforts to personalize promotion, and to create a sense of greater trust, intimacy and commitment can be viewed as a product of thinking of audiences in terms of relationships.

Not all of these efforts can be seen as wholly successful, however. 'Behind the scenes' video footage of rehearsals, shots of actors making up in dressing rooms and detailed rehearsal diaries may be trying to foster a sense of intimacy and trust by giving audiences a glimpse of what goes on backstage, but they can also serve to maintain and bolster the exclusivity of these spaces. For example, 'Behind the Scenes at the Palace Theatre', a promotional video for *Harry Potter and the Cursed Child* (2016), both promises a privileged view of the building and also reminds audiences of its exclusivity. Producers Sonia Friedman and Colin Callender welcome watching fans to 'come inside with us', as they pass through the stage door. The camera pans up to rest upon the inscription carved into the mantel which lies above. It reads, 'THE WORLD'S GREATEST ARTISTES [sic] HAVE PASSED AND WILL PASS THROUGH THESE DOORS.' The producers enthuse about the Gothic grandeur of the theatre, as shots of chandeliers and marble staircases aim to impress the atmospheric quality of the building upon viewers. The RSC's Open Rehearsals project exhibits a similar tension between access and exclusivity. The project provided livestream online access to the company's rehearsals for a production of *Henry VI Part I* over three weeks in 2021, and was then made available in shortform film on YouTube in 2022. In this recording, members of the creative team speak warmly to the camera, inviting viewers at home to join in physical warm-ups and vocal exercises. Everyone is dressed informally, chatting to each other about the liberation inherent in showing the 'rough bits'. The Ashcroft Room in which they are filming, however, is extraordinary: an enormous, round space, with a high, vaulted cathedral-like ceiling, panelled from top to bottom with warm, glowing wood. We are also shown performers taking a break on the balcony immediately outside of the space, with glimpses of swans on the grassy banks of the River Avon as a backdrop. Only the most privileged of viewers would find the world the footage depicts easy to relate to.

Other attempts to approach audiences more personally and directly can also be seen as problematic. Reciprocal marketing of events, for example, is now a common strategy used across the UK performance sector. Organizations and artists request support from one another in the promotion of upcoming shows and events with the intention of reaching new and wider audiences than the individual organization could alone. Requests arrive from practitioners and organizations in the form of an email containing pre-prepared social media posts and images, ready to share, or a DM on Twitter with a request to re-tweet or add a personal shout-out. The pre-prepared content often contains a message with a very personal tone, designed to give the impression that the person or organization promoting the event is genuinely excited about it, and will be attending themselves. Clearly, this approach is disingenuous at best. Individuals and organizations are often putting their names to the promotion of works they may know little or nothing about, and the result is often a welter of very similarly worded social media posts about the same event. Cascading information in this way risks overwhelming audiences and diminishing trust in the sender. It is clear to see that the connection being strengthened in these campaigns is that between artists and organizations, rather than between practitioners and audiences.

> 13 June 2020. I read on Twitter that there is going to be a Black Lives Matter protest happening in Newcastle city centre. I want to go. I want to show up. But on the actual day, I can't bring myself to. The idea of being in a crowd is stopping me. Later on, I hear that there were counter-protesters who were violent towards peaceful protestors. Lots of people were injured. I feel relieved that I wasn't there but ashamed too.

Sadly, there is plenty of evidence that parts of the British theatre sector are now only really interested in building transactional relationships with audiences. This is most apparent in the use of dynamic ticket pricing. This approach was well established in British theatres by 2015 and operates along similar lines to the systems which determine the cost of a budget airline flight. Demand determines pricing: when a ticket is much in demand, its cost rises; when there is little interest, it falls (Jones 2015). It is possible to argue that this development represents greater personalization, allowing audiences to make choices which best suit their budget. Yet, this system has seen a great deal of criticism – not least for the extremely high prices that the most popular shows can now command. Interviewed on BBC Radio 4's Front Row in 2017, director Robert Icke voiced frustration about the long-term impact of rising prices. He declared that the high price of tickets 'makes me really angry [. . .] we have to address this, because otherwise, in fifty or sixty years' time, there will be no audience' (quoted in Armstrong 2017: 18). Here, the relationship between producers and consumers is purely transactional.

Nevertheless, the purpose of dynamic pricing is clear, at least. Not all pricing and ticket sales strategies are as transparent. The offering of a number of different ticket types, including 'early bird' offers and membership discounts may be designed to encourage advance bookings and to make tickets more affordable for students, seniors or the unemployed, but the number of options can serve to confuse. Other pricing and sales tactics are more obviously problematic. Sections of the house can be withdrawn from sale or withheld initially to create the illusion of demand (Katz 1992). The practice of 'papering the house' – giving away tickets for free in order to fill auditoria – is a long-standing ruse (Corry 1980). In recent years, seat filling clubs have proliferated, making this 'below-the-radar' practice increasingly visible, although those who use them are still directed not to discuss the club or their use of it at the venue or on any type of media (Linford 2018). These clubs clearly benefit producers, performers and the seat-fillers themselves. Time-rich cultural omnivores get the chance to see new shows which have yet to attract a paying audience, often for nothing more than the price of a booking fee. Performers play to fuller houses, and the production looks as if it is finding an audience. But the practice has been shrouded in secrecy for a reason: it suggests that theatres are not being honest with audiences. Unsurprisingly, theatregoers paying full price take a dim view of the practice, as revealed in the reporting of the papering of the 2020 stage adaptation of *Grandpa's Great Escape* by comedian and children's novelist David Walliams (Duffin).

Dialogue and decision-making

Personalized promotion practices, dynamic pricing and papering can be interpreted as the product of a superficial application of the concept of relationship marketing. Companies that offer glimpses behind the scenes may be interested in promoting the exclusivity of the experiences they offer, rather than building genuine connections with audiences. But not all attempts to create and maintain relationships with audiences are as disingenuous. Some theatres have tried to develop more meaningful dialogue with audiences by giving opportunities to provide feedback to theatre makers and a more active role in creative processes. Battersea Arts Centre first began to experiment with 'Scratch' performances in 1996 (Battersea Arts Centre 2015). The practice of showing work which is considered unfinished has now become a regular part of the development process at many venues.

It clearly has the potential to offer emerging artists and companies valuable exposure – often with the hope and aspiration on the side of the artist that this will lead to subsequent opportunities with the host venue, or a commission – but concerns have been raised about whether it is as fruitful and beneficial as initially hoped. Questions have been asked about whether artists presenting work in this format are receiving appropriate levels of support, and whether audiences are getting enough information to contextualize the work they are seeing or guidance on the kinds of feedback that is being sought (GETINTHEBACKOFTHEVAN 2013). Over time, artists and companies have been refining their approach to the sharing of unfinished performances in order to ensure that it is a rewarding and worthwhile experience for both parties, often concluding that it is better to share work when it is still at an early stage of development, when ideas are fresh and flexible, and audience input can be more meaningful. When a show is close to completion, new ideas or significant critiques are less likely to be acted upon, and the exchange risks being bruising for artists and frustrating for those who have offered feedback. Thought has been given to how questions can best be framed to enable generous reflection, and how the spaces in which these conversations take place can be made more supportive, relaxed and informal. There is also acknowledgement that the experience needs to be enjoyable and rewarding for audiences in its own right. As part of the 'Little GIFT' strand for young audiences at GIFT 2018, for example, children were invited to provide feedback in a creative workshop appropriate to their age group. This enabled the artists to gain insight into what the children had understood, while the children were entertained. Seeking out this kind of insight and feedback is particularly important when some members of the creative team do not have first-hand knowledge of the lived experience or perspective that they are exploring. For example, Nicky Hatton details the work undertaken to join up audiences with dementia and performances made about the experience of the condition at Every Third Minute: a Festival of Theatre of Dementia and Hope, which took place at the Leeds Playhouse in 2018 (2021: 54). Featuring twelve productions, the festival worked with five people with dementia as curators, who offered their thoughts on programming as well as rehearsals, the design of marketing material and workshops accompanying the shows. This included 'This Is Us', an evening of scratch performance for artists living with dementia, which invited encouragement and suggestions for development from the audience in an open forum.

Feedback and dialogue are always more meaningful when it is clear that decisions will be taken as a result of the exchange. In recent years, some theatre and performance companies have taken this on board and used a range of different methods to give the communities they serve much greater involvement in programming decisions. York Theatre Royal established a 'TakeOver' festival in 2009, programmed and produced by young people; in 2010 Theatre Royal Stratford East worked with fifty volunteers to interview over 1,000 local residents about what they would like to see programmed at the theatre (Walmsley and Franks 2011: 13; Glow 2012: 131–43). The Arts Council England Creative People and Places programme, launched in 2013, enabled several programmes with even more ambitious aims. Focused upon increasing participation in the arts by changing decision-making processes, the fund has supported community programming projects such as 'Go & See' in South East Northumberland and Home Slough (Lawson 2017; Nicholson 2023: 24). These projects encourage audiences to contribute to the programme creatively as well as making decisions about which activities are programmed and funded. ARC in Stockton has been running regular 'Pizza and Pitches' events since 2019, in which local members of the community have an opportunity to 'pitch' a creative project idea to other audience members. The audience then votes on which project they want to support, and ARC seed fund the project with £1,000. The practice is becoming increasingly well known: The Lowry in Salford was nominated for 'Community Project of the Year' in *The Stage* 2023 awards for its 'show selectors' initiative. Some organizations have taken audience involvement in decision-making a step further, looking to include representatives of the communities they hope to reach on their boards in order to give them a voice in high-level organizational decision-making. Contact Theatre in

Manchester places the participation of young people at the centre of its operation and gives them access to the institution's governance structures and decision-making by providing two spaces on the board for young people (Fenton and Williams 2017).

Dynamic pricing can be seen as a particularly invidious interpretation of personalization. There are, however, many other pricing models which suggest an entirely different kind of relationship between performance makers and audiences. In the early 1990s the Battersea Arts Centre in South London pioneered the 'Pay What You Can' approach on Tuesday evenings (Lister 1993). In recent years, the terminology has shifted, from 'Pay What You Can' to 'Pay What You Decide' or 'Pay What You Feel', moving away from assumptions about affordability towards an emphasis upon audience agency, making it clear that judgements about the value of the work are firmly in the hands of the audience (Turpin 2015; Richards 2019). These are clearly powerful methods of renegotiating audience expectations about how the value of their experience might be expressed.

Spelling it out: access and honesty

The last ten years have also seen fresh thinking about what audiences might need from theatres, and the ways in which performance venues communicate about the kinds of experiences that audiences can expect when they visit. Making audiences feel comfortable and relaxed is now seen as being worthy of recognition across the industry: since 2011 UK Theatre has offered an award for the most welcoming theatre amongst their other categories (2022). Covid highlighted care and access needs, creating greater awareness, which can now be felt across the industry. Many venues now offer regular relaxed performance and dementia-friendly events (Hall and Wilshaw 2022); some offer a free ticket if a companion is needed for access reasons (Dundee Rep, 2023). Theatres such as Wyndham's in London offer access hosts, dedicated booking lines and videos which provide social stories explaining the sequence of events, signage and social interactions that can be expected during a visit to the theatre (Delfont Mackintosh 2023). Instead of assuming knowledge of theatre's behavioural conventions and spatial set-up, theatres are working on the basis that visitors would like to know more about the venue before they visit, rather than less. The websites of theatre and performance spaces such as Dance City in Newcastle not only give full details about access and facilities for disabled visitors, they also provide 3D plans of the building and walk-through video tours so that visitors can familiarize themselves with the space before they attend in person (2023). Some venues manage to achieve an impressive level of clarity and honesty about what they can and cannot offer audiences, and what audiences – and staff – have a right to expect. The Young Vic in London includes details on age guidance and getting the cheapest tickets, and titles its FAQ section 'How Can We Help You?'. These might seem like unnecessary details, but they are produced by thinking through theatre attendance from the perspective of the uninitiated. They also cater for audience members who may not have English as their first language. They unearth and explain the unspoken assumptions, rituals and ruses which will be familiar to regular attendees – and the meaning of the acronym which appears on the websites of many other venues. The Young Vic website also includes a statement about 'Audience values in practice' under 'What to Expect'. This states:

> There are things you can expect from your visit to the Young Vic and things we ask of you too. We believe everyone belongs here. We want our space to feel informal and welcoming. We want everyone to have an equally enjoyable experience and will do our best to adapt to your access requirements. We prioritise kindness. Please respect one another and our staff. If a visitor treats our staff or others in a way we feel is unacceptable, they will be asked to leave. We believe in being accountable. Give your feedback with kindness, and we will listen and follow up with you. (2023)

They then provide email and phone contact details. There is a radical directness and transparency to this statement. It does not flatter, coax or plead. There is no suggestion that the audience is responsible for what the theatre provides, or that performers and audiences are 'friends'. The statement makes it clear that the theatre's staff also deserve to be treated well, setting out a model for a more equitable, mutually beneficial and respectful relationship.

Some theatres are also reinstating the tradition of direct address from theatre managers or directors. At the start of every show at Alphabetti Theatre in Newcastle, Artistic Director Ali Pritchard – or whoever is in charge at the venue that day – explains how to behave in the space, making it clear that the audience should feel at home. This introduction covers what to do if you want to leave the space and come back in, that noise travels between the performance space and the bar, and how the doors need to be closed one after the other to avoid disturbances. Far from lecturing audiences, this in-person instruction is designed to help them relax in the knowledge that there is a shared understanding of what is acceptable, as well as providing an introduction to the person to whom questions and feedback can be directed. It provides a genuinely personal touch. This introduction invariably ends with a round of applause from the audience, marking the end of the venue's welcome, and the start of the performance, heightening both the anticipation and the sense of collective experience before the performance has even begun.

Thinking about the ways in which audiences interact with the organizations and individuals who create performance as a relationship is not unproblematic. Concerns have been voiced about the notion that business–customer interactions are analogous to other human relationships (Tynan 1997), while John Harker and John Egan propose that in many organizations relationship marketing is simply 'a technique for trapping and imprisoning customers' (2006: 228). Some find the whole idea of 'relationship marketing' highly distasteful, and resistance to the concept of customer relationship management – the application of the relationship marketing approach – is particularly deeply embedded in the arts (Walmsley 2019: 34). Yet, the shift to focus upon relationships between producers and consumers – or theatres and their audiences – does provide some valuable insights, particularly when reflecting upon the broad range of different forms of relationship that are evoked in these exchanges (Gummesson 2011), and the kinds of emotional and psychological responses that may be at play (Palmatier et al. 2009). This approach reminds us that relationships come in many different forms. They can be familial or collegial, short-lived or long-lasting, casual or formal. Considering what makes each of these different forms of relationship successful can help us describe and recognize a good relationship between audiences and performance. It also helps us expand our sense of the potential duration of this relationship. Audiences will usually experience performance on multiple occasions across their life. It is rarely a one-off encounter. Their relationship with theatre and performance may build upon experiences and norms laid down in childhood, but it can be shaped and fostered in later life, too. Deep attachments can be formed, encouraging audience members to dedicate time, energy and money to support work they value. Trust can be won, but also lost. Maintaining a long-term relationship with an audience requires ongoing commitment. Equally, engagement with a single performance work may be fleeting, but no less meaningful for the brevity of the experience. Thinking about the principles which underpin successful communication in relationships also helps clarify the practices which we might want to transfer into the relationship between audiences and performance-making. Successful relationships depend upon dialogue, active listening and responses which indicate that each party has been heard. Relationships where one party informs the other about what the other should think or feel, or in which only one side of the party gets to speak, are either short-lived, or long and abusive. Consideration of relationships with audiences in these terms can provide us with greater understanding of the meaning and potential of the interactions that are created by and through performance, as well as their limitations.

The dark festival of Covid illustrated extremes of communication success and failure, testing the strength and quality of relationships between friends, families and neighbours; local, regional and national authorities; states and global power blocs. Widespread access to communication technology produced a collective, global experience quite unlike anything witnessed before, unprecedented in the way in which it preoccupied people across the world simultaneously. Though the novelty of the virus meant that it was able to spread ahead of scientific knowledge and reporting in the first weeks following its emergence, global communication and reportage quickly caught up, bringing the latest information on the crisis to communities living at vast distances from one another. Yet, the collective experience being enabled by this technological interconnection was one characterized by physical isolation and separation from others. We were being brought together in our collective concern about the spread of Covid, while also being held apart: locally as well as globally. This was a public, collective event often taking place in private spaces or at carefully managed distances from others.

In part, perhaps, the experience of enforced isolation, and the way that encounters with others in the public realm became synonymous with risk, accounts for some of the failures in communication which were so apparent during the crisis. Covid's dark festival was characterized by fear about the threat posed by invisible contagion, and suspicion about deception and deceit, as it compelled us all to see other people as potential sources of infection. The trustworthiness of communication between the authorities and the people that they are supposed to represent, protect and govern was also called into doubt. The crisis showed us how badly communication can dysfunction but also how profoundly needed effective and direct forms of public communication are. It created an environment where the need for transparency, honesty and trust in public life became acute.

Perhaps the darkest side to the pandemic, however, was the way that it did not reflect the inversions of power which are usually considered central to the licensed misrule of festival and its close relation, carnival. The crisis served to illustrate and entrench inequality in all its forms, as it revealed stark disparities in the vulnerability of the rich and poor; the securely housed and the homeless; the country's white majority and its ethnic minorities; the healthy and those in need of care and support. In the theatre industry, it exposed the gulf in working conditions between the vast numbers of self-employed freelance artists in the sector and the salaried few, almost overnight. In the political realm, the revelations which emerged in late 2021 about the multiple parties and social gatherings held at 10 Downing Street during the crisis – in clear contravention of the legislation produced by the government – cemented the impression of profound inequality between the powerful and the powerless, as well as representing a degradation of the terms of the social contract between legislators and populace.

Yet, this was not all that was revealed by the crisis. We should not forget that alongside the fear and uncertainty that dominated the first weeks of lockdown, there was a strong sense that the pandemic was a reckoning or an opportunity: a portal through which we could pass and emerge changed for the better, as evoked by Arundhati Roy (2020). As Kate discusses in the following chapter, the potential for profound change in professional practice preoccupied many contemporary performance makers in the first months of the crisis. Of course, critics have long been divided over the progressive political potential of festival, or carnival. These events can be viewed as social 'safety valves' – enabling people to transgress standard boundaries and enjoy a period of licensed indulgence before the inevitable return to the mundane status quo – or alternatively, as rehearsals for revolution (Humphrey 2000). Considering Covid as a period of dark festival highlights the way that the crisis demonstrated that long-standing cultural traditions and conventions relating to time, space, technology and communication are capable of change: just as the innovations and otherness associated with festivals old and new do. It revealed that things could – and often should – be done differently. Covid, like the periods of license and disruption enabled by festival, allowed all of us to experience new ways of being in the world and with each other, as well as giving us the chance to reimagine the form of our relationship to theatre and performance.

5

On the present and future needs of audiences

Care, access and sustainability

Curators and creative practitioners are always thinking about the future. We imagine events to come, happening in a time that we have not yet experienced, that often take place in contexts and media that we are not yet familiar with. We dream up new uses for old technology and try to work out how we can use new tools to connect with the people we work with. In my own creative and curatorial practice as festival director of GIFT, I (Kate) reimagine how the festival will manifest each year to best support the needs of the programmed artists and to satisfy my own creativity, but also out of necessity. If I want the festival to survive, I have to think about the future almost all of the time. The Covid crisis amplified and expanded this aspect of my work, however. Between April 2020 and May 2022, I was invited to speak on numerous occasions online about the future of theatre and the future of festivals – as part of Fusebox Festival's virtual edition from Austin (April 2020), Copenhagen's CPH STAGE (June 2020), Identidades Festival in Chile's Atacama Desert (October 2020), Nexus #1: In/Action hosted by The Royal Conservatoire of Scotland in Glasgow (December 2020) and for Australia Performing Arts Market (May 2022) – to name just a few. These panel invitations were generated, in part, by interest in learning from my experience of moving GIFT online at short notice in early May 2020 in response to the first UK lockdown, which I have written about elsewhere (Craddock 2021). Each invitation presented a new opportunity to reflect on what a possible future might look like for performance and its audiences, as discussion at each event was inflected by the latest legislative and creative developments. There were phases during the dark festival of the Covid crisis when the future for theatre felt completely unknown – when venues were closed, gathering was illegal and the industry was in turmoil. Writing now, in the winter of 2022, the depth of our shared fear and uncertainty is difficult to fully recall or grasp.

Within this destabilized reality, the various visions for the future of theatre that I shared alongside panellists and colleagues from across the globe varied wildly at different points in the development of the pandemic. I recall provocations that suggested theatre, as conventionally conceived until now, was (really, finally) dead. Speakers declared that we would not be returning to sit alongside one another in venues and instead performance would only be experienced outdoors, or in drive-ins, or online, or in individual pods, or on your phone, or experienced via a DIY kit that arrived through the post. Others asserted that theatre was something that we could not live without, and that when we could 'return', performance would reunite with audiences with an energy that we had never witnessed before. Venues would sell out and the industry would experience a spectacular resurgence. Neither extreme, it would seem, has turned out to be true.

These conversations were, of course, haunted by unease and anxiety about the future. Despite this, the opportunities for reflection created by this unexpected pause also seemed to open up the potential for meaningful transformation to occur across the industry as we re-emerged. It is important to acknowledge that this was not a time when practitioners were necessarily preoccupied with the development of technological innovations. Instead, the inequalities laid bare by the pandemic experience rightly commanded attention. Discussion focused upon how future experiences should respond to the stark inequities that the crisis had exposed. In the UK, discussions revolved around disability, race, employment status, caring responsibilities and so on, highlighting that changes needed to be made and activated quickly. Such inequities were of course also very much apparent pre-Covid, but the crisis highlighted them to such an extent that increased levels of expression of solidarity grew across the live performance sector.

Contributors agreed that it was time to notice, to imagine and, ultimately, to activate change: to re-prioritize resources and energies and to support the emergence of a new future for theatre and its audiences. Participation in these conversations allowed for a kind of collective optimism to grow and provided a space to think about what could change in our approach, in our practices, and in the sector. For me, and many others, it offered a chance to consider what a more inclusive and more equitable future might look like for theatre and its audiences.

Alongside these opportunities to muse and reflect, those who were attempting to reinstate in-person performance after the initial period of lockdown faced the challenge of painstakingly producing and un-producing events in response to government restrictions, as they attempted to work out when and how theatre could (possibly, safely) meet audiences in the future. This was an excruciating and at times paralyzing process for those working in theatre and performance, planning events in response to what was legally possible one week, to find themselves having to unplan and start again as legislation changed or as Covid surged again, the next. Yet, the labour of setting aside assumptions about when, where and how audiences and performers gather, and then working through the logistics of new configurations, also offered an opportunity to consider what the future relationship between the two might look like in a more philosophical way.

The experience of being separated from each other, and of seeing that other ways of operating are possible, has brought a distinct new vision for the future relationship between theatre and its audiences into view. This is most clearly visible in the independent and artist-led contemporary theatre and performance scene, and is emerging out of the decisions and choices that artists are making about how their work meets an audience, and what that contract should look like, now. It is directly informed by the calls for change in the sector that came through loud and clear during the pandemic. Many of these calls for change were first voiced when the divide between the securely and precariously employed suddenly became acute in the first period of lockdown. These were subsequently worked through (to varying degrees of success) in online networks, such as The Freelance Task Force, an initiative set up by the producers of Fuel to demonstrate solidarity and financial support for the industry's freelance workers (Morris Hargreaves McIntyre 2020). This initiative led to a number of outputs being generated by smaller self-organizing groups of freelancers who came together via the Task Force, and were often directed at venues and those in secure positions of employment, asking them to sit up and listen, and to activate change. Outputs were disseminated across the sector through social media channels, and many of these are listed, and can be accessed via the *Freelance Task Force 2020 Evaluation Report* including 'A Manifesto for (Better) Representation in UK Performing Arts' and 'Reject Better (a collective of art makers who believe that the best way to support unsuccessful applicants is to offer constructive feedback)' (Morris Hargreaves McIntyre 2020). Such documents exist now as a reminder and legacy of the conversations and call for change across the sector that were strongly voiced throughout 2020 – but they continue to remain relevant.

The calls for change that echoed across the sector in online networks, panels and conversations in many formats during 2020 and into 2021 can largely be distilled into calls to prioritize care, access and sustainability (both financial and environmental). These priorities are now being put into practice most holistically by independent practitioners who are redefining their relationship with audiences and starting to shape a new set of conventions and expectations as they make overt commitments to care, access and sustainability in all aspects of their approach.

Imagining change

This final chapter includes a series of personal interruptions, as have the preceding chapters. In earlier chapters these interruptions have taken the form of personal memories. Here, they are based in the future, envisioning moments in time we are yet to experience and live through. The versions of the future these depict are by no means utopian. Instead, they take the current status quo as evidence to imagine where we might end up. In writing these interruptions, I have been inspired by Carol Weiss's theory of change (1995), in which the change or end goal is outlined or imagined, and then micro-steps for how to reach that point are explicitly designed. They have also been shaped by visualization exercises and questions that I have been asked (and have asked) in my own coaching practice, to describe what a point, time or goal in the future might look or feel like, so that the steps for how to get there can be understood, broken down and realized. These interruptions are rooted in a version of my own reality, and many of the reference points are familiar to me, while other aspects of them might feel unimaginable, or preposterous even. But in order to make any change, we have to imagine the seemingly impossible. They are also inspired by the multiple creative conversations I had about what the future might look like across 2020, 2021 and 2022. Each interruption included here does however contain at least one small suggestion about where we might want to get to, so that we can understand and work out how to get there.

This final chapter also reflects upon some of the key changes for theatre and its audiences that came into being during the pandemic. It highlights those that have remained in place or evolved, and are impacting on the way that this relationship is now unfolding. With reference to several recent contemporary performance works, I identify where shifts towards a more equitable future relationship are already in evidence, and paving the way for a new set of norms and conventions. Each work referenced offers insights into how this process of renegotiation is already underway and points to distinct ways in which the relationship is developing. Each has in some way provided a new shape, or set of priorities or an innovation in this relationship, and represents changes that have come about due to the inadequacies highlighted by the pandemic. Alongside these observations of performance works that I have encountered as an audience member, the ideas and thoughts presented in this chapter are in many ways responsive to those hours (and days) of extended Zoom conversations with artists and other colleagues across the independent and subsidized theatre sector who are, in their own way, boldly reshaping a new future for theatre and its audiences.

Critical conversations

During 2021, I participated in a virtual residency called *Imagining Futures*, initiated by Eunic (EU National Institutes for Culture) in partnership with the Goethe Institute and Transform Festival. This brought together festival directors from across Europe, facilitated and documented by the writer Maddy Costa. Many of the ideas we discussed in this forum were indicative of the changes we wanted to make as a result of the pandemic's interruption to the established flow and form of our festivals. Some of those changes and the imagined futures that we discussed were put into immediate action – shifting from an imagined future into an activated present. Amy Letman, Creative Director of Transform Festival in Leeds, developed the idea of an 'extended festival' that would take place between October 2021 and April 2022 as the result of conversations we had in the group about the need for festivals to slow down as they re-emerged; Baltic Circle Festival in Finland made the decision to partner with a rewilding project for their 2022 edition, putting environmental questions at the heart of their activities; Festival Theatreformen in Germany began working with UK-based artist Touretteshero to develop a relaxed festival, offering more accessible options for audiences; and Ruth McCarthy, artistic director of Outburst Queer Arts Festival in Belfast, inspired everyone by sharing how they keep Fridays free of meetings to allow time to nurture their own creativity and focus on self-care. As detailed in the publication that arose from the residency (Costa 2022), and as evidenced by the examples given here, key themes and preoccupations emerged and framed our conversations. These were notions of care, access and sustainability, themes that recur throughout this chapter. The freedom, support and sense of reimagining conjured in these sessions also led to the original participant group, which comprised solely of festival directors, reshaping the design of the online residency while in the midst of it. Collectively, we chose to move away from the original plan of inviting artists to create new artworks in response to the themes that we had been discussing, and instead asked artists to join our conversations, with an invitation to then come together in person in France for a process-led residency with no requirement for any artistic outcomes. This shift in plan acknowledged the problematic hierarchy initially set up for the project, in that artists would be invited to respond creatively to conversation topics initiated by festival directors, rather than being invited to make their own contributions to the dialogue. This was collectively deemed inappropriate by the group, and instead we agreed a need for artists to be invited into the conversations. The change in direction also removed any pressure on artists to create artistic outputs during the residency. The opportunity for deep peer reflection, combined with the possibility of changing the parameters of a project, was highly empowering. It is through participation in processes like these that different futures can be realized, as well as being imagined.

> *4 April 2026. The Metro is unusually busy for an early Saturday morning. Like us, lots of families are taking advantage of the free travel into town provided for the People's Programme – a new city-wide festival curated by members of the public. I scroll through the listings, and I'm enthused by how eclectic and experimental it feels. My eleven-year-old son is jabbering excitedly. There are rumours that Newcastle United footballers are facilitating craft workshops – making new inventions out of recycled household items. His dream comes true. When we arrive, it seems he is right. The queue for the craft tent stretches from Monument, past the Theatre Royal and all the way down to the river. The entire city has turned out. There are street performers and street food stalls as far as we can see. He says he is happy to wait, that it'll be worth it. I am just happy to be here.*

The sudden loss of income for freelancers, the high level of redundancies and huge personnel upheaval across cultural institutions, and ultimately, the closure of long-standing companies (such as Kneehigh in June 2021), became a lasting legacy of the pandemic, demonstrating Covid's ability to expose inequity and vulnerability. Living through the turbulence of these experiences at sectoral level, while simultaneously witnessing (or participating in) movements and protests that unfolded on a global scale, such as Black Lives Matter, gave increased visibility to the multiplicity of inequalities that permeated theatre's status quo pre-pandemic.

Such experiences, combined with the significant rise in theatre and performance made available online, and the need for better access arrangements to be put in place that this exposed, brought about the momentum for change – as discussed in earlier chapters. Disabled practitioners, activists and audiences have been pressing for decades for better access arrangements in theatre. Jo Verrent, Senior Producer at Unlimited, states, 'We have moaned for the last 30 years, things should change', in the aptly titled essay 'It's taken a pandemic to reimagine the arts' (2020). Theatre needed to be taken out of itself in order to see itself, fully. The shift to online/digital raised questions about access and care, and provided an opportunity for awareness and debate around the need for access to be more fully integrated into the audience experience. It also gave practitioners and online event organizers an opportunity to explore what was possible in this context, to respond readily to the calls for change and to model best practice to wide audiences. In many of the online events that became so commonplace across the sector throughout 2020 and 2021 – including performances, panels, workshops and festivals – rapid adaptations demonstrated that change was indeed possible. Online producers and event organizers – including myself – realized the urgency of the need to embed access functions in their formats so that disabled participants could fully engage. Likewise, the need to ensure panels were not solely populated by white arts professionals, but that they should better represent the diversity of the UK's population, was paramount. There was an increasing pressure for online events to be made available for free, and if a freelance worker was contributing as a speaker – or invited to attend an event – then their time should be paid for. Increasingly, those with caring responsibilities were actively accommodated, too, by both careful considerations given to the timings of events and making recordings available online for a set amount of time, providing wider audiences with an opportunity to engage at times that better suited them.

All of these changes meant there were significant shifts in what became expected norms when presenting theatre online, with a strong commitment to ensuring performance works were either captioned or BSL interpreted, or both, that built rapidly in momentum across the sector. Failure to provide access functions was often questioned and readily criticized by audiences and participants, especially across social media platforms. Disabled audiences and artists have described how the experience of increased levels of online access during the pandemic provided visibility in a way that they had been fighting for, often for many decades (Wreford-Sinnott 2022). Other access practices that became more frequent in online panel conversations, post-show discussions and meetings across the sector included the incorporation of visual self-descriptors as speakers introduced themselves. This, alongside speakers offering their preferred pronouns, became standard practice in many public-facing and private online settings. Their incorporation offered a temporary window into a more accessible mode of coexisting, offering clarity around gender identification and providing partially sighted/blind participants and audiences key information about the individual who was speaking at any one time. Such small shifts in behaviour demonstrated that change could be made, and pointed towards a more inclusive future for the industry. Largely, these practices being included as standard have dissipated with the return to in-person events – although arguably there is now an increased level of awareness of how to incorporate these access practices across a broader spectrum of the sector, and there are audiences for whom these remain vital to participation. The hope for the future here is that these practices will continue to permeate and not just be considered exemplary or exceptional, but expected.

Disabled-led production company Little Cog have highlighted how the 'return to normal' has once again denied equal access to disabled artists and audiences. They argue that many of the changes that came about in the pandemic that created a more accessible experience for all have been forgotten in the rush to return to pre-pandemic norms, leaving disabled artists and audiences excluded once again (Wreford-Sinnott 2022). While I believe there is still a vast amount of work to do in this area, and have critiqued the 'return to pre-pandemic business as usual' elsewhere, urging the sector to uphold its commitments to maintaining digital access (Craddock 2022), I also recognize that it is possible to detect some degree of shift in this area. I would argue that awareness of the *need*, and the knowledge of *how* to make theatre and performance more accessible for audiences has moved significantly up the agenda across the sector. Yet, there is still a great deal of work to do in terms of how that awareness translates into action at all levels. One area where a shift in practice can undoubtedly be identified, however, is via the increase in demand for BSL interpreters. This demand is now so great that interpreters in the UK who are experienced in working in theatre and performance have reported that they now require booking up to a year in advance. There are a number of other approaches that became increasingly common practice when theatre was solely online – when increased commitments to care, access and sustainability were being made – that emerged as expected norms as theatre returned to meet audiences in person.

On returning

One of the new norms to emerge as a result of the volume of theatre and performance being made available to audiences online was an increased level of pre-event audience information sent out ahead of the performance via email by theatre makers and venues. Given that most audiences were initially unfamiliar with many aspects of the format, there was a clear need for detailed information prior to audiences accessing an online performance. This information detailed how to access a link or platform, and how to turn on access options (such as captions, audio description), and explained whether the work would be played in real time, or made available beyond the initial stream, alongside details about which browser it would be better experienced in. Regular reminders about the timing of the event and nudges along the lines of 'we look forward to seeing you tonight' became standard for online events. It seems that this experience encouraged more appreciation of the importance of sending out the equivalent pre-information prior to attending an in-person performance. Since reopening, there has been a noticeable increase in the level of detailed communication that venues send out to audiences. Information about event timings, travel options, catering options and so on, often with messages that pre-empt arriving at the venue and 'we look forward to seeing you tonight' reminders, now appear to have become widely adopted as the standard level of communication between theatres and audiences. This level of detailed communication may have emerged in response to shifting trends in patterns of audience behaviour reported by many venues, artists and programmers since the return to in-person events. On reopening, many theatres noted that there was initially a significant increase in 'no-shows' when tickets were booked in advance. Another reported change in behaviour throughout 2022 was for audiences to book tickets much later for events than pre-pandemic, often in the week of, or on the day of a performance. This change may result from the experience of having plans change suddenly during the crisis, with events cancelled or postponed at short notice, as well as having to isolate due to a positive Covid test. Producers also suspect that audiences have fallen out of the habit of leaving the home for cultural experiences – and therefore need more reassurance and encouragement to return. In this context, information and reminders serve to let audiences know that people at the venue are anticipating their attendance.

Efforts by theatres towards increased levels of transparency and openness in terms of communication with audiences have also come about since venues reopened, including venues seemingly being more prepared to cancel or postpone performances due to Covid (or the general ill health of performers). Pre-pandemic, cancellation was an almost unheard-of occurrence in the UK. 'The show must go on' attitude more regularly prevailed. Theatres and venues have reported that audiences have been very understanding about the cancellation or postponement of performances, and that expectations on both sides have indeed changed. It is now an expected norm for any run of a performance to have some degree of interruption. Cancellation – on the part of theatre, or audience member – is no longer taboo. This shift of behaviour patterns, from the perspective of both audiences and theatres, points to the emergence of an increasingly open and understanding relationship between theatre and its audiences.

One of the major issues that dominated discussions around making work available online throughout the pandemic was the monetary aspect of doing so. Debates circled around whether online content should be charged – and if so, at what scale – or made available for free. Many theatres and companies opted for a variation of 'Pay What You Can/Decide/Feel' approach (discussed in Chapter 4), and were still able to raise income via an online box office as a result, while also demonstrably making content affordable to wide ranging audiences. Throughout 2021 and 2022, many more organizations and festivals adopted the Pay What You Can (PWYC) model for their in-person programmes as they reopened and relaunched, including Transform Festival in Leeds, Barbican Theatre in Plymouth and Mayfest in Bristol. In using this approach, organizations across the industry could be seen to be responding directly to the financial hardship experienced by many during the pandemic, in a bid to make theatre and performance more financially viable for audiences who are often priced out and therefore would not normally attend (MAYK 2022). There are distinctions, however, between those organizations who offered PWYC models pre-pandemic and those who have adopted it since. The latter have tended to take a more cautious approach, offering tickets on a PWYC basis, but with a recommended price or a tiered 'suggested donation' system on a sliding scale. While this maintains a commitment to ensuring cheaper tickets are made available for audiences, the inclusion of suggested scaled amounts also raises difficult questions about how individual performance works are valued. Still, it can be seen as initiating a new level of honesty between theatres and audiences. The pricing makes it clear that the model needs to be financially sustainable for the organization, allowing them to highlight their own need for income to audiences. This tiered approach to PWYC, along with 'Pay It Forward' initiatives used by Brighton Festival and Northern Stage amongst many others (in which an audience member at the point of booking is asked to contribute towards, or buy an additional ticket for, someone else who otherwise could not afford to attend), make the interdependency in this relationship increasingly explicit and transparent.

Alongside the increase in PWYC and Pay It Forward models across the sector, other organizations have made cheaper ticket pricing options more directly available for targeted audience groups who otherwise might experience barriers to access. In 2021, Manchester International Festival offered 10 per cent of their tickets for £10 to residents of wider Manchester who were on a low income (defined as earning £18,000 and under a year), while The Royal Shakespeare Company launched TikTok £10 Tickets in 2022 for fourteen- to twenty-five-year-olds, students and state schools, with these tickets being 'targeted particularly at those living in communities facing structural disadvantage' (RSC 2022). Alphabetti Theatre in Newcastle developed initiatives such as a 'no questions will be asked' £3 ticket option, for audiences who 'can't afford any of the other ticket prices but still want to see the show' (Alphabetti Theatre 2022). While the act of singling out certain audience groups or integrating sliding scales into PWYC models and cheaper ticket options increases risk for venues, it is hoped that as initiatives such as these become more commonplace across the sector they will have a cumulative effect, removing financial barriers in order for many more people to have increased levels of access to theatre and performance.

Care in practice

The value and importance of 'care' in practice was already subject to discussion across the theatre industry before the pandemic, and used as a frame for analysis in scholarship (Stuart Fisher and Thompson 2020). The term and concept gained greater currency during the crisis – unsurprisingly, given the intense need for greater care and the pressures on those trying to care for others, and for themselves. There was increased industry interest in the principle of 'care' from 2020 onwards, from organizations describing care as central to their approach to working with artists and audiences (Horizon 2020), to artists articulating care as an urgent strategy for survival for the future (Geraghty 2020). Reflecting on pre-pandemic experiences alongside hopes for the future, many practitioners highlighted their experience of the absence of care in the contexts that they had previously been working, arguing that it should be prioritized and centred in the future for artists, audiences and communities. Practitioners such as Chrissie Tiller proposed that this was the time to consider care as a radical act and embrace notions of collective care (2020), while Maddy Costa argued that although the term is widely used in processes of co-creation and in work with community groups, it operates in complex ways, and should not be thought of as 'fluffy'. Costa reminds us that it is a privilege to be able to give care, and that organizations and artists operating on a precarious hand-to-mouth basis may not always have a place of privilege to consider how best to provide care for others. Likewise, Costa observes that those that often talk about the importance of care in creative processes are not always the best at caring for themselves, reminding us of the need for self-care in order to be better able to support others. Costa also notes that different people within a single group can require differing levels and types of care, and points to this as something that can be negotiated by generating equitable spaces in creative processes, such as that established by theatre company Common Wealth who establish an open dialogue with participants as part of each creative process (Costa 2021).

How can performance practitioners demonstrate care for audiences? In the context of the relationship between audiences and performers, care becomes apparent when consideration has been given to what the overall experience is for the audience, and how cared for they might feel.

It is expressed through the decisions that shape the exchange between theatre and its audiences; through the quality of communication between the two; and in how an audience is 'held' by a venue (or artist) during the time that they spend together. This approach to care starts from an understanding that audiences are not one homogenous grouping, but a disparate and diverse group of individuals who should be invited into an exchange in nuanced ways. In the essay 'Crisis Change Care', artist Toni-Dee Paul encourages readers to make 'care the first thing we bring into rooms that we lead', and to use care 'to transform' (2020). As we have returned to in-person performances, it is possible to identify where artists have adopted this sentiment and this care-centred approach in their relationship with audiences.

Care can be identified as a key component and guiding principle for many contemporary theatre makers creating work today. This manifests in different ways in performance works, and in how those works meet their audience. It is often implicit in the environment or setting that is established for an audience. Works such as the multi-dimensional work *Exposure*, by artist and mental health activist Vacuum Cleaner demonstrate this kind of consideration. When I experienced the work at Lyra Arts Centre in Edinburgh as part of the Horizon Showcase at Edinburgh Festival Fringe in August 2022, audience members were welcomed into a large, airy room that offered different options for how to be in that space. There were options to sit on the floor with cushions, or on benches or on chairs – and blankets for those who wanted to wrap up. The work contained film, storytelling, music and installation, bound together in a highly considered audience experience. There was chai tea freshly brewing by the doorway, with smells of cardamom and cinnamon infusing the space. The invitation to be comfortable and cared for in this environment was deliberate and direct, and can be seen as a response to the challenge of its content. The films contained within the production are built around interviews that the artist carried out with forty-seven health workers in Newham in London about their experiences working during the first wave of the pandemic. The audience are informed of the potentially disturbing and upsetting content, and the performance comes with content warnings, about racism, death from Covid, and mental health (Vacuum Cleaner 2022). The audience are reassured that it is an option to leave the space. They are informed there is a calm, safe space outside of the main room to retreat to, and told there is a trained mental health support worker/facilitator on hand to talk to, or just to be with, if needed. Audience members are invited to pick coriander leaves from plants with fellow audience members, establishing a sense of copresence and community. The distressing content of the work is held in balance with the way in which the needs of the audience are considered throughout their encounter with it.

This Endless Sea, an installation work by artist and choreographer Chloe Smith, also demonstrates how artists have been working to ensure that audiences feel cared for while encountering potentially distressing content through consideration of the experiential environment in which the event takes place. I experienced this work in September 2022. Created for a rugged coastal location on the edge of Chloe's hometown of Berwick, the work took place inside a small wooden hut that was purpose-built to house the experience. The hut was sited in an open grassy expanse that merged into sand dunes, then into the beach and finally into the North Sea. Inside, a film unfolded across several screens. This explored and linked grief and the sea, with Chloe's personal experience of grief being the original catalyst and inspiration that led to the development of the artwork. Consideration of how the audience would be supported in their experience of the work was made apparent in several different ways. People were invited to experience it alone or with one other person – or as part of a small family group. Chloe and the team were available for conversations with audience members before and after their experience – holding a space for conversations, for reflection, for silence and for tears. The proximity of the sea and the elements also provided an immediate environment for escape and solace for audiences following the experiencing of the work. Both *This Endless Sea* and *Exposure* share and demonstrate their consideration of audience needs in the level of detail paid to the environments they set up, and the steps taken to establish a strong connection between artist and audience. The care in evidence across these works can be regarded as a response to calls being made to adopt and approach 'care as a radical act' (Tiller 2020).

Offering online versions of work in tandem with in-person delivery can also be a product of care, and informed by principles of care. One of the key discoveries that practitioners made as a result of the shift to working online induced by the pandemic was the increased level of self-care and attention to well-being that could be built into audience experiences in an online context. This approach has been visible, palpable even, in a number of works created across the sector throughout 2022 when the risks of exposure to Covid remained a source of deep concern for the clinically vulnerable. The durational, hybrid performance *What If?*, created by Two Destination Language for April's GIFT 2022, included a number of artists who participated in the performance via a Zoom call, alongside in-person performers at BALTIC Centre for Contemporary Art in Gateshead. The in-person audience were encouraged to make themselves comfortable on a mixture of bean bags, cushions, seats and benches – while an online audience joining via a livestream watched from the comfort of their own homes, and reported dancing along from their kitchens. The combination of committing to a mode of online participation for both audiences and performers in this work demonstrated a level of considered care across the full experience – allowing for both performers and audiences to make choices about which mode was right for them. *This Endless Sea*, discussed earlier, also offered an online version of the experience. Alongside the in-person installation that took place in Berwick, there was an online, captioned iteration of the work available for audiences to engage with from anywhere in the world without the need to travel. The commitment to running an online experience in tandem signalled a care-led approach by the artist, allowing for wider access to the work and increased levels of choice for audience members about how they might want to engage with material that dealt with sensitive and potentially distressing subject matter. The decisions taken by the company Yewande 103 around how audiences experienced their dance film *The Fountain* (2022) were also visibly care-led. Their Creative Director, Alexandrina Hemsley, wants the company to uphold values of care and connection (2020), qualities that were demonstrated in the multiple presentation choices they made for *The Fountain*. Originally releasing the dance film as a screening to select cinemas across the UK, *The Fountain* was then also presented in an online screening, which allowed it to reach those who might not otherwise be able to attend. I viewed this online iteration in November 2022. It included an introduction by the company in which the work was introduced and the range of access options were shared. Audiences were then invited to select a version of the work that most suited their access requirements. The screening was followed by a conversation in Zoom Webinar between Alexandrina and therapist Foluke Taylor, complete with integrated BSL and captioning. The conversation included reflection on the process of making the artwork itself, and touched on grief, mental health, Black identity, disability, intersectionality, interdisciplinarity, collaboration and the potential of the digital sphere. The effort to consider audience access needs and the preparation which had clearly gone into the wide-ranging and frank conversation were indicative of investment in care for the audience. Audience members responded to the conversation enthusiastically by contributing comments and posting questions via the chat function. Many, including myself, took advantage of the heart emoji to demonstrate connection and solidarity – returning the care and respect that was in evidence on screen.

These works were made by artists who predominantly work in live performance, defining themselves as theatre makers or choreographers. Their confident and deliberate use of video and digital media can be seen, in some cases, as a result of their exploration of the potentials of online and digital formats brought about by the conditions of the pandemic. These works demonstrate a strong commitment to not simply returning to 'normal' but continuing on the creative journey that the pandemic brought about, seeing through commitments made to ensuring performance work remained accessible to wide audiences

– as the pandemic had shown was possible. Their work highlights the flexibility and control that can be cultivated by adopting a digital approach, as these artists show that care and copresence can shape the experience both online and offline.

14 August 2031. It's an unusually hot afternoon for Edinburgh, but as I walk into the Traverse Theatre, I feel the immediate benefit of their newly installed eco air con. I am not the only one who has sought this out. My phone buzzes in my hand, confirming my whereabouts, and the 'Trav Venue' app pings open on my phone. There are several staff members standing where the box office used to be, on hand to support anyone struggling with the app. It seems some phones need an update for the app to work effectively. The staff are enthused and being great with those who haven't used it before. Two of them are kneeling down, chatting warmly to a small group of pre-school-aged children who are gathering for the theatre creche. The app contains all the information I need about the venue for my visit – including a venue map, the names of staff working today, a list of access options both for the venue and for the show, programme notes, the QR code ticket, the vegan bar menu and more. I'm here for a new play written by a friend I went to university with thirty years ago – I'm bursting with pride that (finally) they have a play on in the main house. I've chosen to come today so I can join the post-show conversation, and hopefully have a catch-up after. As I take my seat, I open the access options on the app, and select the ones that apply to me, opting for my electronic seat to widen and to pivot by 90 degrees – accommodating my bad back, and so I can outstretch my arthritic knee. I note the location of the safe space and the name of the in-house support worker – just in case – as my friend, the writer, had a tendency to dwell on harrowing topics when we were young. The house lights fade gradually, giving us time to adjust our eyes. The show opens with a voice-over. As I read along with the projected captions, I find myself thinking I can't quite believe how much progress has been made. Despite this, my pal is still opening their play in the same way as they did all their student productions at university – with a voice-over. Chuckling inside, I sink into my seat, and listen.

Access first

Commitment to care and access as core principles when designing audience experience often go hand in hand. One necessitates the other, though they can manifest in different ways. Concern for care and access can be detected in the increased levels of commitment from venues to offer clearer access information on their websites, from detailing the width of their seats, to offering 360-degree video tours so that orientation can happen prior to arrival, to providing Alt Text and image descriptions positioned alongside photographs and detailed outlines of what to expect in a relaxed performance. If these practices become standardized across the sector in the future – as I believe they should be – they will empower audiences to make more informed decisions about whether – and how – they want to participate or attend.

As discussed in previous chapters, access considerations and access technologies for audiences have undergone significant growth in recent years. Yet, these are most often add-ons to the creative process, serving an additional or functional role rather than a creative one. There are, however, a small but growing number of performance works developed over recent years where access considerations have been incorporated into the creative process from the very start and developed throughout rehearsals. This approach prevents access from being an afterthought or an addition in response to a venue request, but instead positions it as an intrinsic part of the artwork itself. Examples include *joey* by sean burn/gobscure (2019) directed by Selma Dimitrijevic, in which two performers, Scott Turnbull and Faye Alvi, play the same character, with Scott speaking sean's scripted text, while Faye performs simultaneously in British Sign Language (BSL). No one language is prioritized or presented as interpreting the other, rather the actors work collectively and physically, side by side, to tell the same story. Similarly, Sophie Woolley's solo autobiographical performance *Augmented* (2020), in which Sophie shares her personal experience of being 'activated/switched on' and becoming a self-defined 'real life cyborg' (having gone deaf in her twenties), integrates access tools into the art of the performance itself. Throughout the production, creative captions are projected across the set alongside Sophie's spoken text, existing as a creative stage partner to Sophie rather than an access tool. Practice is developing fast in this area. *The Dan Daw Show* by choreographer Dan Daw demonstrates a new level of concern for audience care and access, for example. This work began its creative journey prior to the pandemic, yet was only fully realized in front of audiences as a finished work in 2021, premiering at Newcastle's Dance City, before going on to widespread national and international tours. Care and access as combined commitments are palpable – even visceral – in Dan's work. The complexity of how care operates as a concept is played out in all its messiness onstage, between Dan, a queer, crip (disabled) artist and fellow performer, non-disabled Christopher Owen. Access and care are paramount at every stage of the work, both thematically and in its form. Dan spends considerable time at the start of the performance explaining how the audience and the performers will be in the space together – outlining the relaxed rules of engagement and how access and content descriptions will work throughout the performance. The audience are given a demonstration of the brightest lighting state and the loudest sounds that will feature in the show as part of this integrated introduction, with each having a distinctive visual marker attached – such as a small warning light that will come on prior to these states taking place so that audience members are alerted and can prepare accordingly. Though audiences may have encountered notes outside auditoria which highlight the use of strobe lighting in the past, the detail provided by Dan and its presentation in this way is both novel and potentially empowering for audiences, as it enables them to make informed choices about how they wish to engage with the work.

Integrated access as an approach has become more widespread since the return to in-person performances, and is increasingly being used by artists who do not define themselves as d/Deaf or disabled. In *Gamble* by Hannah Walker, performed in May 2022 at Newcastle's Northern Stage, Hannah was joined on stage throughout the performance by BSL interpreter and performer Faye Alvi. Faye's presence alongside Hannah was integrated as part of the rehearsal process, and there are many sections of the show where they perform as though they are a comedic double act. The strong rapport established between Hannah and Faye and their overall approach to integrated BSL allows for a strong sense of interdependence to be established between the two performers. The integrated BSL in *Gamble* is far from an 'add-on' or an afterthought, but an essential element of the work. The incorporation of BSL from the beginning of the work's creative development ensured that the work could be targeted to d/Deaf audiences, whom the artists particularly want to reach. Hannah's research for this production revealed that d/Deaf communities face a number of barriers to accessing support with gambling addictions, hence the decision to integrate BSL to reach audiences, with the aim of connecting d/Deaf audience members for whom the subject matter resonated to a wider community of support. This approach to integrated BSL is not just for this work, however. In post-show discussion, Hannah reveals a commitment to integrated performances for all of their future productions.

> *14 February 2056. My son has come to visit me in Newcastle. It has been several months since we had the opportunity to touch, hug or hold hands. We make the most of the temporary lift in restrictions and squeeze each other so tightly that I worry he might break my ribs. He has brought me a new house plant, one that he has grown from a clipping of a plant I gave him almost a decade ago when he eventually moved out. He gives me very clear instructions about how much light and water it needs. Together we choose a suitable spot for it in my studio – his old bedroom. We sit facing one another as we did when he was young, making up stories together – taking it in turns, a line at a time. He tells me enthusiastically about the new nationalized inter-city train he travelled on to get here – a high-speed non-stop connection from Bristol. We laugh about the time we flew that route when he was seven, when the flight attendant gave him an adult-sized mask to wear which covered his entire face. We shake our heads in disbelief that we were ever able to take domestic flights. Holding hands, we take it in turns to update each other, listening attentively and with love as new stories and old memories merge.*

Sustainable futures

Restrictions on travel brought about by the pandemic created a heightened awareness across the industry of the need to respond more urgently to the climate crisis. This encouraged reconsideration of how artistic practice developed in the UK might find international audiences in the future, and the possible formats international touring might take. Beyond transitioning existing creative work designed for in-person delivery to the digital sphere, a considered movement towards developing ways of working that were more environmentally sustainable gathered pace. Initiatives such as *Concept Touring*, a commissioning programme led by LIFT (London International Festival of Theatre), saw artists develop and test out models for touring concepts, ideas, processes and live performance as opposed to touring individuals in 2020 and 2021 (Peterson 2022). This represented a development of ideas that emerged and increased in popularity prior to the pandemic, in which a performance would tour, but be recast with local performers, or participants, in different locations. Examples include *Any Table Any Room* by Jonathan Burrows and Matteo Fargion (2017), a performance that is re-rehearsed over a few days, and performed by four professional dancers/artists who are local to each community where the work is presented; *Ah kissing* by Glasgow-based choreographer Rosanna Irvine (2017), a work which is realized by a large group of participants in pairs who are tasked with the act of kissing – as a choreography – in a public space; as well as works that can be performed entirely by participating audience members rather than a professional cast, such as *work.txt (a play without actors)* by Nathan Ellis (2019). The shared experience of strict constraints on international and national travel during the crisis gave this type of work a new urgency and relevance, however. Appetite to explore and expand on its potential developed as people began to see that it would become a necessity in the future.

One of the outcomes of artists creating online iterations of existing performance works during the pandemic is that many artists are now able to tour online versions of their works, instead of the in-person show, giving both artists and curators the opportunity to make more considered choices around environmental responsibility and international touring. Some examples of performances that were reimagined as digital works include *As Far As Isolation Goes* by Basel Zara and Tania El Khoury (2020), *A Crash Course in Cloud Spotting* by Raquel Meseguer Zafe (2021) and *Rich Kids: A History of Shopping Malls in Tehran* by The Javaad Alipoor Company (2020). These were all in-person works created by UK-based artists in the immediate years preceding the pandemic (2018–19), which then had online, digital iterations subsequently created in conjunction with support from UK programmers, before being picked up and presented in international venues and festival contexts (in Germany, Australia and the United States). While the development of these online iterations came about as a creative response to the constraints of the pandemic, they can also be seen to be generating increased levels of flexibility and opportunity for UK artists to reach wider audiences. Equally, they allow artists the opportunity to truly centre sustainability as well as care and access in their practice – as their presentation does not require any artist travel.

Through my work as a festival director operating across different international contexts, I have become acutely aware of the urgency of the conversation around the need for artists, programmers and audiences to continue to develop international networks and opportunities for engagement, while maintaining a commitment to environmental sustainability. The brief examples offered here such as Concept Touring models, and digital versions of existing stage works (as opposed to streamed versions of in-person shows), provide glimpses into the way these relationships will develop in the future. Only time will tell how rapid and how sustained the evolution of such practices might be.

23 December 2037. I arrive home from the Christmas market, laden with paper bags stuffed with locally crafted items: a lino print, some Northumberland honey, a scented candle, two necklaces, a pair of gloves and a collage. I thaw out my fingers on a hot cup of tea, and switch on Radio 4. The newly appointed Country Manager for Amazon UK is being interviewed. I don't quite catch her name. She is being quizzed for her views on #osb, the online shopping boycott that has gathered pace, and being asked why she hasn't published her own personal carbon footprint this year – despite the new legislation. The questioning gets increasingly heated, as they ask for her views on why Amazon UK workers resorted to hunger strikes last Christmas. The interviewee goes silent. She has no more answers. No more counter arguments. Then, live on air, she resigns. I have an overwhelming feeling of familiarity, like déjà vu. This is it. This is the beginning of the end.

The works discussed in this chapter have been created by artists who believe that the future relationship between performance and audience needs to be one in which care is centred and understood as an essential ingredient for an equitable and accessible industry. It is worth noting that they were developed outside of major large-scale UK venues, and created by independent artists and companies. This is no coincidence. Independent artists do not enjoy the security and shelter of association with large cultural organizations – a position which made them uniquely vulnerable in March 2020. This also means, however, that they can be flexible and responsive in ways that building-based institutions cannot. They do not have to accommodate the constraining structures of centuries of inherited tradition but can jettison outmoded approaches and adopt new ones as they see fit. They can select the time, space, technology and forms of communication that will best serve the aims of the experience they are attempting to create – if they can find the resources to do so. The ability to think about future needs rather than attempting to cling to the past was perhaps most apparent in the differing approaches to digital programming adopted by independent artists and larger venues and organizations. The latter rapidly dropped their commitments to digital programming or to livestreaming performances once in-person events returned to their venues. In contrast, the artist-led sector held on to this commitment where they could, understanding its worth and its potential.

Other experiences which many independent artists working in the UK share may also encourage greater sensitivity to the needs of audiences and consideration of the sustainability of their practice.

Many of these artists fund their practice by making applications to Arts Council England's highly competitive Project Grants scheme. As part of the application process to this funding stream, applicants must successfully address a series of questions about their audience. They need to be able to identify who their target audience is and articulate how they will reach them. They have to explain how they will engage with that audience beyond being just observers, and describe how that audience will benefit from engagement with their project. Similarly, there are questions that invite applicants to consider diversity, environmental responsibility, to outline a value for money budget and to describe how they will make their work accessible. It is important to acknowledge that questions such as these receive ongoing critique. Commentators note that arts funding is becoming increasingly instrumental, as artists are compelled to adopt an approach that does not prioritize the art itself but that generates activity that addresses social problems. It could also be argued, however, that artistic innovation and experimentation which has enabled deeply thoughtful and meaningful relationships between theatre and its audiences has come about as a result of engagement with this application process.

Each of the performances discussed throughout this chapter, and the insights into movements and conversations across the sector that I have drawn attention to, offer a vision for the future relationship between theatre and audiences with a set of priorities and values that are optimistic, but not unrealistic. They show how care can become the frame through which all decisions are made about how theatre meets audiences, and that access can and should be integrated into creative practice from the outset. They point to a developing relationship between performance and its audiences that is defined by openness, inclusivity, transparency, understanding, conversation and honesty. I believe that the principles of care, access and sustainability that are currently guiding the contemporary, independent, artist-led theatre and performance sector will soon be absorbed and appropriated by the mainstream. As with all avant-garde movements, practice that appears unconventional or even shocking today eventually becomes standard.

I believe that the relationship between theatre and its audiences will be more responsive and equitable, and that, just as audiences are asked to listen in the theatre, theatre will listen and respond to the needs of its audiences in the future.

> *27 July 2078. Nobody thought I would get here. Everyone said it would be too far for me to travel. But here I am. Three trains later, in Avignon. One last chance to immerse myself and fully soak up the festival. I arrive for the first of several shows that I have booked to see – a hit show from Romania. I don't recognize the names in the programme, but I don't care. A young woman greets me and shows me directly to my isolation pod. I can't risk catching anything. She warns me there are scenes in the production I might find 'offensantes'/offensive. I reassure her I will be fine. From my pod, my view of the audience is as good as my view of the stage. Everyone is here, I think. All of life. But nobody I know. Not anymore. It's thrilling. The bright light warns us the show will start soon and the audience chatter gradually fades. The action begins, but I turn my attention instead to the audience. Gathered, held, accommodated, together.*

References

Aebischer, P. (2020), *Shakespeare, Spectatorship and the Technologies of Performance*, Cambridge: Cambridge University Press.

Aebischer, P. (2022), *Viral Shakespeare: Performance in the Time of Pandemic*, Cambridge: Cambridge University Press.

Aebischer, P., Greenhalgh, S. and Osborne, L. (2018), *Shakespeare and the 'Live' Theatre Broadcast Experience*, London: Bloomsbury.

Alberti, F. B. (2019), *A Biography of Loneliness: The History of an Emotion*, Oxford: Oxford University Press.

Alexander, N. (2017a), 'Speed Watching, Efficiency, and the New Temporalities of Digital Spectatorship', in P. Hesselberth and M. Poulaki (eds), *Compact Cinematics: The Moving Image in the Age of Bit-Sized Media*, 103–12, London: Bloomsbury.

Alexander, N. (2017b), 'Rage Against the Machine: Buffering, Noise, and Perpetual Anxiety in the Age of Connected Viewing', *Cinema Journal*, 56 (2): 1–24.

Alexander, N. (2021), 'The Waiting Room: Rethinking Latency After Covid-19', in P. D. Keidl, V. Hediger and L. Melamed (eds), *Pandemic Media*, 25–32, Lüneberg: Meson Press.

Alland, S. (2018), 'The Development of Captioning in the Performing Arts', *Disability Arts International*, 3 December. Available online: https://www.disabilityartsinternational.org/resources/the-development-of-captioning-in-the-performing-arts/ (accessed 4 December 2022).

Allred, G. K. and Broadribb, B. (2022), 'Introduction: Cultural Cartography of the Digital Lockdown Landscape', in K. Allred, B. Broadribb and E. Sullivan (eds), *Lockdown Shakespeare: New Evolutions in Performance and Adaptation*, 1–22, London: Bloomsbury.

Alphabetti (2022), 'Support Us', *Alphabetti*. Available online: https://www.alphabettitheatre.co.uk/support-us (accessed 16 January 2023).

Alston, A. and Welton, M., eds (2017), *Theatre in the Dark: Blackout, Gloom, and Shadow in Contemporary Theatre*, London: Bloomsbury.

Anderson, L. (2019), 'Debunking Audience Loyalty: What Does Your Data Tell You?', *Uktheatre.org*, 10 June. Available online: https://uktheatre.org/who-we-are-what-we-do/uk-theatre-blog/debunking-audience-loyalty-what-does-your-data-tell-you/ (accessed 1 December 2021).

Angelaki, V. (2017), *Social and Political Theatre in 21st-Century Britain: Staging Crisis*, London: Bloomsbury.

Ansell, S. and Bonczek, R. B., eds (2017), *One Minute Plays: A Practical Guide to Tiny Theatre*, London: Routledge.

ARC Stockton (2021), 'Taking the Time Interview', *Vimeo*, 24 May. Available online: https://vimeo.com/553652831 (accessed 6 January 2023).

Armstrong, S. (2017), 'Theatre tickets: where does the money go?', *The Sunday Times*, 25 June. Available online: https://www.thetimes.co.uk/article/theatre-tickets-price-expensive-book-of-mormon-6rv9pvvh9 (accessed 10 August 2023).

Armstrong, W. (1958), 'The Nineteenth Century Matinee', *Theatre Notebook*, 14 (2): 56–9.

Arts Council England (2016), 'From Live-to-Digital: Understanding the Impact of Digital Developments in Theatre on Audiences, Production and Distribution', *Arts Council England*, 11 October. Available online: https://www.artscouncil.org.uk/sites/default/files/downloadfile/From_Live_to_Digital_OCT2016.pdf (accessed 22 November 2022).

Asquith, R. (1980), 'Subversion at Lunchtime: Or Business as Usual?', in S. Craig (ed.), *Dreams and Deconstructions: Alternative Theatre in Britain*, 145–52, Ambergate: Amber Lane.

Aston, E. (2022), '"Something's Missing": Feeling the Structures of Project Neoliberal Dystopia', in M. Tönnies and E. Voigts (eds), *Twenty-First Century Anxieties: Dys/Utopian Spaces and Contexts in Contemporary British Theatre*, 11–26, Berlin: de Gruyter.

Auerbach, N. (1987), *Ellen Terry: Player in Her Time*, New York: W. W. Norton.

Bakhshi, H., Mateos-Garcia, J. and Throsby, D. (2010), 'Beyond Live: Digital Innovation in the Performing Arts', *Nesta*, 1 February. Available online: https://media.nesta.org.uk/documents/beyond_live.pdf (accessed 22 November 2022).

Balme, C. (2008), 'Surrogate Stages: Theatre, Performance and the Challenge of New Media', *Performance Research*, 13 (2): 80–91.

Balme, C. (2014), *The Theatrical Public Sphere*, Cambridge: Cambridge University Press.

Balme, C. (2020), 'Theatre-historiographical Patterns in the Global South 1950–1990: Transnational and Institutional Perspectives' in T. C. Davis and P. Marx (eds), *The Routledge Companion to Theatre and Performance Historiography*, 269–89, London: Routledge.

Balme, C. and Davis, T. C. (2015), 'A Cultural History of Theatre: A Prospectus', *Theatre Survey*, 56 (3): 402–21.

Bancroft, S. and Bancroft, M. (1969 [1909]), *The Bancrofts: Recollections of Sixty Years*, New York: Benjamin Blom.

Banks, M. and O'Connor, J. (2021), '"A Plague Upon Your Howling": Art and Culture in the Viral Emergency', *Cultural Trends*, 30 (1): 3–18.

Barber, S., Brown, J. and Ferguson, D. (2021), 'Coronavirus: Lockdown Laws', *House of Commons Library*, 22 December. Available online: https://researchbriefings.files.parliament.uk/documents/CBP-8875/CBP-8875.pdf (accessed 23 February 2022).

Barker, M. (2013), *'Live to Your Local Cinema': The Remarkable Rise of Livecasting*, Basingstoke: Palgrave McMillan.

Barstow, S. T. (2001), '"Hedda Is All of Us": Late-Victorian Women at the Matinee', *Victorian Studies*, 43 (3): 387–411.

Batsleer, J. and Duggan, J. (2020), *Young and Lonely: The Social Conditions of Loneliness*, Bristol: Policy Press.

Battersea Arts Centre. (2015), 'Scratch 15', *Google Arts and Culture*. Available online: https://artsandculture.google.com/story/pAVRQ-DJIxwA8A (accessed 25 January 2023).

Bauer, M., ed. (1995), *Resistance to New Technology: Nuclear Power, Information Technology and Biotechnology*, Cambridge: Cambridge University Press.

Bay-Cheng, S. and Holzapfel, A. S. (2010), 'The Living Theatre: A Brief History of a Bodily Metaphor', *Journal of Dramatic Theory and Criticism*, 25 (1): 9–27.

Bennett, S. (1997), *Theatre Audiences: A Theory of Production and Reception*, 2nd edn, London and New York: Routledge.

Bennett, S. and Polito, M. (2014), 'Thinking Site: An Introduction', in S. Bennett and M. Polito (eds), *Performing Environments: Site-Specificity in Medieval and Early Modern English Drama*, 1–16, Basingstoke: Palgrave Macmillan.

Berlant, L. (2011), *Cruel Optimism*, Durham: Duke University Press.

Berry, L. L. (1983), 'Relationship Marketing', in L. L. Berry, G. L. Shostack and G. D. Upah (eds), *Emerging Perspectives in Services Marketing*, 25–38, Chicago: AMA.

Biggs, K. M. (2021), 'COVID-19 Pandemic Increases Accessibility to Theatre Performances', *Ideas* 3 (1). Available online: https://docs.lib.purdue.edu/ideas/three/issue3/1/ (accessed 4 December 2022).

Billington, M. (2019), 'Pinter Five and Six Review – Starry Cast Bring Shorter Works into the Spotlight', *The Guardian*, 6 January. Available online: https://www.theguardian.com/stage/2019/jan/06/pinter-five-and-six-review-starry-cast-bring-shorter-works-into-the-spotlight (accessed 29 December 2022).

Bilodeau, C., ed. (2022), *The Future Is Not Fixed: Short Plays Envisioning a Global Green New Deal*, Lanham: Rowman & Littlefield.

Blume, C., Schmidt, M. H. and Cajochen, C. (2020), 'Effects of the COVID-19 Lockdown on Human Sleep and Rest-activity Rhythms', *Current Biology*, 30 (14): R795–R797.

Bogart, A. (2019), 'Foreword: Embodied Time', in M. Evans, K. Thomaidis and L. Worth (eds), *Time and Performer Training*, 3–6, London: Routledge.

Booth, M. V. (2022), 'The Theatre Scheme Seeking to Tackle Loneliness', *B24/7*, 22 June. Available online: https://www.bristol247.com/culture/theatre/theatre-scheme-tackles-loneliness/ (accessed 10 January 2023).

Botsman, R. (2017), *Who Can You Trust?: How Technology Brought us Together – and Why It Could Drive us Apart*, London: Penguin.

Bowler, L. M. (2016), 'Theatre Architecture as Embodied Space: A Phenomenology of Theatre Buildings in Performance', PhD thesis, Ludwig-Maximilians-Universität.

Bradley, H. J. (2012), '"Speaking to the Eye Rather Than the Ear": The Triumvirate's Autumn Dramas at the Theatre Royal, Drury Lane', *Nineteenth Century Theatre and Film*, 39 (1): 26–46.

Brandreth, G. (2021), 'No More Intervals at the Theatre? But They're the Best Bit!', *The Daily Telegraph*, 26 March. Available online: https://www.telegraph.co.uk/theatre/what-to-see/no-intervals-theatre-best-bit/ (accessed 31 December 2022).

Bratton, J. (2004), 'The Music Hall', in K. Powell (ed.), *The Cambridge Companion to Victorian and Edwardian Theatre*, 164–82, Cambridge: Cambridge University Press.

Briscoe, R. (2022), 'Hello, You've Reached Tech Support – Or 10 Things We Learnt About Digital Theatre and Access Online', *Fast Familiar*, 7 January. Available online: https://workroom.fastfamiliar.com/digital-theatre-access-online/ (accessed 4 December 2022).

Brook, P. (1968), *The Empty Space*, London: Penguin.

Brooks, L. (2019), 'A Play, a Pie and a Pint: How Glasgow Pulls in the Theatregoers', *The Guardian*, 4 May. Available online: https://www.theguardian.com/uk-news/2019/may/04/a-play-a-pie-and-a-pint-how-glasgow-pulls-in-theatregoers (accessed 4 January 2023).

Brosnan, M. J. (2002), *Technophobia: The Psychological Impact of Information Technology*, London and New York: Routledge.

Brown, I. (1929), 'The Sunday Night Plays', *Fortnightly Review*, 126: 794–801.

Brown, M. (2019), *Modernism and Scottish Theatre Since 1969: A Revolution on Stage*, London: Palgrave Macmillan.

Bullock, P. R. (2017), 'Ibsen on the London Stage: Independent Theatre as Transnational Space', *Forum for Modern Language Studies*, 53 (3): 360–70.

Burkeman, O. (2021). *Four Thousand Weeks: Time Management for Mortals*, London: Penguin.

Butterworth, P. (2017), 'The Mechanycalle "Ymage off Seynt Iorge" at St Botolph's, Billingsgate, 1474', in P. Butterworth and K. Normington (eds), *Medieval Theatre Performance: Actors, Dancers, Automata and Their Audiences*, 215–38, Cambridge: Boydell & Brewer.

Butterworth, P. and Harrop, P. (2022), *Staging, Playing, Pyrotechnics and Magic: Conventions of Performance in Early English Theatre: Shifting Paradigms in Early English Drama Studies*, London and New York: Routledge.

Carlson, M. (1989), *Places of Performance: The Semiotics of Theatre Architecture*, Ithaca and London: Cornell University Press.

Carlson, M. (2022), 'Reflections on Theater in the Age of Covid', Lecture hosted by Cyprus House and the Open University of Cyprus, 31 October.

Chakrabarty, D. (2021), *The Climate of History in a Planetary Age*, Chicago: University of Chicago Press.

Chambers, J. and Gearhart, S. S., eds (2018), *Reversing the Cult of Speed in Higher Education: The Slow Movement in the Arts and Humanities*, London and New York: Routledge.

Chatzichristodoulou, M., Brown, K., Hunt, N., Kuling, P. and Sant, T. (2022), 'Covid-19: Theatre Goes Digital – Provocations', *International Journal of Performance Arts and Digital Media*, 18 (1): 1–6.

Churchill, C. (2012), *Love and Information*, London: Nick Hern Books.

Claessens, B. J., Van Eerde, W., Rutte, C. G. and Roe, R. A. (2007), 'A Review of the Time Management Literature', *Personnel Review*, 36 (2): 255–76.

Clark, C. D. (2005), 'Tricks of Festival: Children, Enculturation, and American Halloween', *Ethos*, 33 (2): 180–205.
Clark, D. (1998), 'Bawdy Panto Raises Cash', *Evening Chronicle*, 9 January.
Clarke, N. and Smurthwaite, N. (2020), 'From Pandemics to Puritans', *Opera Holland Park*, 22 April. Available online: https://operahollandpark.com/news/chorus-magazine-from-pandemics-to-puritans-when-theatre-shut-down-through-history-and-how-it-recovered/#:~:text=In%201642%2C%20the%20Puritan%2Dled,of%20lascivious%20mirth%20and%20levity%E2%80%9D.(accessed 1 November 2022).
Clarke, R. (2021), *Breathtaking: Inside the NHS in a Time of Pandemic*, London: Little, Brown.
Clarke, V. (2022), 'Child Speech Delays Increase Following Lockdowns', *BBC*, 7 November. Available online: https://www.bbc.co.uk/news/education-63373804 (accessed 9 January 2023).
Cochrane, C. (2011), *Twentieth-century British Theatre: Industry, Art and Empire*, Cambridge: Cambridge University Press.
Cochrane, C. and Robinson, J., eds (2019), *The Methuen Drama Handbook of Theatre History and Historiography*, London: Bloomsbury.
Collins-Hughes, L. (2020), 'Digital Theater Isn't Theater: It's a Way to Mourn Its Absence', *The New York Times*, 8 July. Available online: https://www.nytimes.com/2020/07/08/theater/live-theater-absence.html (accessed 20 November 2022).
Collins, J. (2018), 'Playing With Materials: Performing Effect on the Indoor Jacobean Stage', in A. Aronson (ed.), *The Routledge Companion to Scenography*, 215–23, London: Routledge.
Colvile, R. (2017), *The Great Acceleration: How the World is Getting Faster, Faster*, London: Bloomsbury.
Connor, S. (1999), 'The Impossibility of the Present: Or, From the Contemporary to the Contemporal', in R. Luckhurst and P. Marks (eds), *Literature and the Contemporary: Fictions and Theories of the Present*, 15–35, Harlow: Pearson/Longham.
Conroy, C. (2019), 'How Can the Theatre Be Fully Accessible?', in M. Bleeker, A. Kear, J. Kelleher and H. Roms (eds), *Thinking Through Theatre and Performance*, 47–57, London: Bloomsbury.
Cornford, T. (2017), 'Backpages: The Editing of Emma Rice', *Contemporary Theatre Review*, 27 (1): 134–7.
Corry, J. (1980), 'News of the Theater Ionesco Play Coming', *The New York Times*, 25 June: 23.

Costa, M. (2021), 'Circles of Care', *Battersea Arts Centre*. Available online: https://bac.org.uk/moving-roots/circles-of-care/ (accessed 20 January 2023).

Costa, M. (2022), 'What If?', *Imagining Futures*, May. Available online: https://www.goethe.de/resources/files/pdf264/imagining-futures-publication-may-20222022.pdf (accessed 20 January 2023).

Craddock, K. (2019), 'Festival Time', in M. Evans, K. Thomaidis and L. Worth (eds), *Time and Performer Training*, 194–203, London: Routledge.

Craddock, K. (2021), 'Curating Community and Connection in a Crisis: GIFT 2020', in L. Bissell and L. Weir (eds), *Performance in a Pandemic*, 135–44, London: Routledge.

Craddock, K. (2022), 'An (In)visible Field', in A. Lownie (ed.), *Field Notes Two*, 32–7, Stockton-on-Tees: Two Destination Language.

Crompton, S. (2017), 'Theatre Needs Intervals and Not Just for Toilet Breaks', *WhatsOnStage*, 11 September. Available online: https://www.whatsonstage.com/london-theatre/news/interval-works-follies-sarah-crompton-blog_44587.html (accessed 31 December 2022).

Crouch, T. (2023), 'Regional Theatres Are on Their Knees – Support Your Local One', *The Guardian*, 10 February. Available online: https://www.theguardian.com/stage/2023/feb/10/covid-live-performance-regional-theatres (accessed 14 April 2023).

Dalrymple, R. (2019), '"The Thrill When It Suddenly Went Pitch Black!": Blackout Cultures in *A Murder Is Announced* and *The Mousetrap*', in R. Mills and J. Bernthal-Hooker (eds), *Agatha Christie Goes to War*, 155–66, London and New York: Routledge.

Daly, N. (1999), 'Blood on the Tracks: Sensation Drama, the Railway, and the Dark Face of Modernity', *Victorian Studies*, 42 (1): 47–76.

Davis R. B. (1993), 'The Scheduling of the Chester Cycle Plays', in K. J. Harty (ed.), *The Chester Mystery Cycle*, 231–57, London: Routledge.

Davis, J. (2007), 'Boxing Day', in T. C. Davis and P. Holland (eds), *The Performing Century: Redefining British Theatre History*, 13–31, Basingstoke: Palgrave Macmillan.

Davis, J. (2017), 'Looking and Being Looked At: Visualising the Nineteenth-Century Spectator', *Theatre Journal*, 69 (4): 515–34.

Davis, T. C. and Marx, P. W., eds (2020), *The Routledge Companion to Theatre and Performance Historiography*, London and New York: Routledge.

Delfont Mackintosh Theatres (2023), 'Accessibility at Delfont Mackintosh Theatres', *Delfont Mackintosh Theatres*. Available online: https://www.delfontmackintosh.co.uk/accessibility (accessed 23 January 2023).

Delgado, M. and Svich, C., eds (2002), *Theatre in Crisis? Performance Manifestos for a New Century*, Manchester: Manchester University Press.

Dessen, A. (2002), *Rescripting Shakespeare: The Text, the Director, and Modern Productions*, Cambridge: Cambridge University Press.

de Waal, A. (2017), 'Expel, Exploit, Exfoliate: Taking on Terror in Mark Ravenhill's *Shoot/Get Treasure/Repeat* (2007)', in K. Frank and C. Lusin (eds), *Finance, Terror, and Science on Stage: Current Public Concerns in 21st-Century British Drama*, 59–82, Tübingen, Narr Francke Attempto Verlag.

Dillon, J. (2006), *The Cambridge Introduction to Early English Theatre*, Cambridge: Cambridge University Press.

Dixon, S. (1999a), 'Digits, Discourse, and Documentation: Performance Research and Hypermedia', *TDR/The Drama Review*, 43 (1): 152–75.

Dixon, S. (1999b). 'Remediating Theatre in a Digital Proscenium', *Digital Creativity*, 10 (3): 135–42.

Dixon, S. (2007), *Digital Performance: A History of New Media in Theater, Dance, Performance Art, and Installation*, Cambridge, MA: MIT Press.

Double, O. (2012), *Britain Had Talent: A History of Variety Theatre*, London: Bloomsbury.

Draaisma, D. (2004), *Why Life Speeds up as You Get Older: How Memory Shapes Our Past*, Cambridge: Cambridge University Press.

Duffin, C. (2020), 'Free Tickets for Walliams Shows to Fill Empty Seats', *Scottish Daily Mail*, 6 January.

Dundee Rep (2023), 'Access', *Dundee Rep*. Available online: https://dundeerep.co.uk/access (accessed 23 January 2023).

Dunnett, H. (2017), 'The Importance of Having a CRM Strategy', *Uktheatre.org*, 30 October. Available online: https://uktheatre.org/who-we-are-what-we-do/uk-theatre-blog/importance-of-crm-strategy/ (accessed 1 December 2021).

Easterling, H. C. (2022), '"Surging Like the Sea": Re-Thinking the Spectacle of the Crowd in Early Modern London', *The London Journal*, 47 (1): 36–48.

Edelman, L. (2004), *No Future: Queer Theory and the Death Drive*, New York: Duke University Press.

Ekirch, R. (2006), *At Day's Close: A History of Nighttime*, London: Phoenix.

Elliott, M. ([1973] 1995), 'On Not Building for Posterity', in R. Mulryne and M. Shewring (eds), *Making Space for Theatre: British Architecture and Theatre Since 1958*, 16–20, Stratford-upon-Avon: Mulryne and Shewring Ltd.

Emeljanow, V. (2014), 'Challenging Space and Time: Popular Theatregoing and the Anxieties of Modernity', *Nineteenth Century Theatre and Film*, 41 (1): 54–67.

Fabian, J. (1983), *Time and the Other: How Anthropology Makes Its Object*, New York: Columbia University Press.

Fair, A. (2018), *Modern Playhouses: An Architectural History of Britain's New Theatres, 1945–1985*, Oxford: Oxford University Press.

Fair, A. (2019), *Play on: Contemporary Theatre Architecture in Britain*, London: Lund Humphries.

Falassi, A. ed (1987), *Time Out of Time: Essays on the Festival*, Albuquerque, NM: University of New Mexico Press.

Farman, J. (2018), *Delayed Response: The Art of Waiting from the Ancient to the Instant World*, New Haven and London: Yale University Press.

Faull, E. (2022), 'Memory. "False," "faulty" or "creative": The After-life of Theatre Performance in Children's Memory', in M. Reason, L. Conner, K. Johanson and B. Walmsley (eds), *Routledge Companion to Audiences and the Performing Arts*, 465–71, London and New York: Routledge.

Fayolle, S., Gil, S. and Droit-Volet, S. (2015), 'Fear and Time: Fear Speeds up the Internal Clock', *Behavioural Processes*, 120: 135–40.

Featherstone, V., Payne-Frank, N., Sprenger, R. and Wiegand, C. (2014), 'The Royal Court Meets the Guardian in Microplays Series – Video', *The Guardian*, 17 November. Available online: https://www.theguardian.com/stage/video/2014/nov/17/royal-court-guardian-microplays-video-off-the-page (accessed 30 December 2022).

Fenton, M. and Williams, R. (2017), 'Board Diversity: Young People at the Heart of Decision Making', *Culturehive*. Available online: http://www.culturehive.co.uk/resources/board-diversity-young-people-at-the-heart-of-decision-making/ (accessed 15 January 2023).

Fischer-Lichte, E., Sugiera, M., Jost, T., Hartung, H. and Soltani, O., eds (2022), *Entangled Performance Histories: New Approaches to Theater Historiography*, London: Routledge.

Fisher, P. (2012), 'Ding Dong the Wicked', *British Theatre Guide*, 1 October. Available online: https://www.britishtheatreguide.info/reviews/ding-dong-the-w-royal-court-the-8108 (accessed 31 December 2022).

Fitzgerald, C. M. and Sebastian, J. T., eds (2018), *The York Corpus Christi Play: Selected Pageants: A Broadview Anthology*, London: Broadview Press.

Fitz-Gerald, S. J. A. (1890), 'Play-Bills – Old and New', *Theatre*, 15: 304–9.

Frayn, M. (1970), *The Two of Us*, London: Samuel French.

Frayn, M. (2014), *Matchbox Theatre: Thirty Short Entertainments*, London: Faber & Faber.

Freeman, D., Waite, F., Rosebrock, L., Petit, A., Causier, C., East, A. and Lambe, S. (2022), 'Coronavirus Conspiracy Beliefs, Mistrust, and Compliance With Government Guidelines in England', *Psychological Medicine*, 52 (2): 251–63.

Freestone, E. (2014), 'What Live Theatre Screenings Mean for Small Companies', *The Guardian*, 20 January. Available online: https://www.theguardian.com/stage/theatreblog/2014/jan/20/live-theatrescreenings-elizabeth-freeman (accessed 22 November 2022).

Freshwater, H. (2009a), *Theatre & Audience*, Basingstoke: Palgrave Macmillan.

Freshwater, H. (2009b), *Theatre Censorship in Britain: Silencing, Censure and Suppression*, Basingstoke: Palgrave Macmillan.

Freshwater, H. (2022), 'Histories of Audiencing: On Evidence, Mythology and Nostalgia', in M. Reason, L. Conner, K. Johanson and B. Walmsley (eds), *Routledge Companion to Audiences and the Performing Arts*, 37–52, London and New York: Routledge.

Fryer, L. and Cavallo, A. (2022), *Integrated Access in Live Performance*, London: Routledge.

Fuchs, B. (2022), *Theater of Lockdown: Digital and Distanced Performance in a Time of Pandemic*, London: Bloomsbury.

Gallagher-Ross, A. and Makonnen, B. (2018), 'Reshuffling the Deck: Selina Thompson Asks 1,000 Questions in "Race Cards"', *Sightlines*, 12 April. Available online: https://sightlinesmag.org/selina-thompson-race-cards (accessed 31 December 2022).

Gardner, L. (2013), 'The Late Show: Should Theatres Change Their Start Times?', *The Guardian*, 11 January. Available online: https://www.theguardian.com/stage/theatreblog/2013/jan/11/late-show-theatre-start-times (accessed 1 January 2023).

Gardner, L. (2015), 'The Cost of Staging an Edinburgh Fringe Show: Artists Open Their Account Books', *The Guardian*, 4 August. Available online: https://www.theguardian.com/stage/2015/aug/04/the-cost-of-staging-an-edinburgh-fringe-show-artists-open-their-account-books (accessed 2 January 2023).

Gardner, L. (2021), 'Don't Give Us a Break – Intervals Are an Outmoded, Unnecessary Theatre Convention', *The Stage*, 29 March. Available online: https://www.thestage.co.uk/opinion/lyn-gardner-dont-give-us-a-break-intervals-are-an-outmoded-unnecessary-theatre-convention (accessed 31 December 2022).

Geraghty, E. (2020), 'We Will Care Deeply: A Manifesto', in Lownie, A. (ed.), *Field Notes*, 37–42, Stockton-on-Tees: Two Destination Language.

GETINTHEBACKOFTHEVAN (2013), 'Making Progress: Questioning the Culture of "scratch"', 3 May. Available online: http://www.getinthebac kofthevan.com/files/transcript-making-progress.pdf (accessed 25 January 2023).

Giesekam, G. (2007), *Staging the Screen: The Use of Film and Video in Theatre*, Basingstoke: Palgrave Macmillan.

Gillespie, B. (2021), 'Pre-Pandemic Memories: Performance in the Before Times', *PAJ: A Journal of Performance and Art*, 43 (3): 31–2.

Giraud, C. and Miles-Wildin, N. (2018), 'Demystifying Access: A Guide for Producers and Performance Makers: How to Create Better Access for Audiences to the Performing Arts', *Unlimited*. Available online: https://weareunlimited.org.uk/wp-content/uploads/2018/08/Unlimited -Demystifying-Access.pdf (accessed 4 January 2023).

Gleick, J. (1999), *Faster: The Acceleration of Just About Everything*, New York: Pantheon.

Glow, H. (2012), 'Cultural Leadership and Audience Engagement: A Case Study of the Theatre Royal Stratford East', in J. Caust (ed.), *Arts Leadership: International Case Studies*, 131–43, Melbourne: Tilde University Press.

Goldhill, S. (1997), 'The Audience of Athenian Tragedy', in P. E. Easterling (ed.), *The Cambridge Companion to Greek Tragedy*, 54–68, Cambridge: Cambridge University Press.

Gomme, R. (2015), 'Not-so-close Encounters: Searching for Intimacy in One-to-One Performance', *Participations: Journal of Audience & Reception Studies*, 12 (1): 281–300.

Goodhart, C. (2020), 'Television Through the Ages', *Museum of the Home*, 12 November. Available online: https://www.museumofthehome.org .uk/explore/stories-of-home/television-through-the-ages (accessed 22 November 2022).

Gowen, D. (1998), 'Studies in the History and Function of the British Theatre Playbill and Programme 1564–1914', PhD thesis, University of Oxford.

Griffiths, P. (2008), *Lost Londons: Change, Crime and Control in the Capital City, 1550–1660*, Cambridge: Cambridge University Press.

Groarke, J. M., Berry, E., Graham-Wisener, L., McKenna-Plumley, P. E., McGlinchey, E. and Armour, C. (2020), 'Loneliness in the UK During the COVID-19 Pandemic: Cross-Sectional Results from the COVID-19 Psychological Wellbeing Study', *PloS one*, 15 (9), 1–18. e0239698.

Grobe, C. (2012), 'Refined Mechanicals; or, How I Learned to Stop Worrying and Share the Stage: New Scholarship on Theater and Media', *Theater*, 42 (2): 139–46.

Grotowski, J., Wiewiorowski, T. K. and Morris, K. (1967), 'Towards the Poor Theatre', *The Tulane Drama Review*, 11 (3): 60–5.

Gummesson, E. (2011), *Total Relationship Marketing*, London: Routledge.

Gurr, A. (2004), *Playgoing in Shakespeare's London*, Cambridge: Cambridge University Press.

Hadley, B. (2014), *Disability, Public Space Performance and Spectatorship: Unconscious Performers*, Basingstoke: Palgrave Macmillan.

Hadley, B. (2022), 'A "Universal Design" for Audiences with Disabilities?', in M. Reason, L. Conner, K. Johanson and B. Walmsley (eds), *Routledge Companion to Audiences and the Performing Arts*, 177–89, London and New York: Routledge.

Hadley, B., Paterson, E. and Little, M. (2022), 'Quick Trust and Slow Time', *The International Journal of Disability and Social Justice*, 2 (1): 74–94.

Hall, C. (2019), 'From the Archive: Britons' Most Loved and Hated Buildings', *The Guardian*, 27 January. Available online: https://www.theguardian.com/theobserver/2019/jan/27/from-the-archive-britons-most-loved-and-hated-buildings (accessed 13 February 2022).

Hall, L. and Wilshaw, P. (2022), 'Relaxed', in M. Reason, L. Conner, K. Johanson and B. Walmsley (eds), *Routledge Companion to Audiences and the Performing Arts*, 503–8, London and New York: Routledge.

Handley, L. (2020), 'UK PM Boris Johnson's 'Stay Alert' Coronavirus Campaign Sparks Countless Memes', *CNBC*, 12 May. Available online: https://www.cnbc.com/2020/05/12/boris-johnsons-stay-alert-coronavirus-campaign-sparks-countless-memes.html (accessed 9 January 2023).

Harker, J. M. and Egan, J. (2006), 'The Past, Present and Future of Relationship Marketing', *Journal of Marketing Management*, 22: 215–42.

Harline, C. (2011), *Sunday: A History of the First Day from Babylonia to the Super Bowl*, New Haven and London: Yale University Press.

Harry Potter and the Cursed Child. (2016), 'Behind the Scenes at the Palace Theatre', *YouTube*. Available online: https://www.youtube.com/watch?v=Fpm_N6PLESY&t=1s (accessed 22 January 2023).

Harvie, J. (2018), 'Review of *Social and Political Theatre in 21st-Century Britain: Staging Crisis* by Vicky Angelaki', *Modern Drama* 61 (4): 585–7.

Harvie, J. (2020), 'International Theatre Festivals in the UK: The Edinburgh Festival Fringe as a Model Neo-liberal Market', in R. Knowles (ed.), *The Cambridge Companion to International Theatre Festivals*, 101–17, Cambridge: Cambridge University Press.

Haslett, R. (2019), A Story With, as Yet, No End', *Live Theatre*, 17 June. Available online: https://www.live.org.uk/blogs-resources/story-yet-no-end (accessed 26 January 2023).

Hatfull, R. (2018), '"The Other RSC": The History and Legacy of the Reduced Shakespeare Company', PhD thesis, University of Warwick.

Hatton, N. (2021), *Performance and Dementia: A Cultural Response to Care*, Basingstoke: Palgrave Macmillan.

Healy, K., McNally, L., Ruxton, G. D., Cooper N. and Jackson A. L. (2013), 'Metabolic Rate and Body Size are Linked with Perception of Temporal Information', *Animal Behaviour*, 86 (4): 685–96. https://Doi.org/10.1016/j.anbehav.2013.06.018 (accessed 12 December 2022).

Healy, R. (2023), '"We've Had to Stop People Fighting and Urinating in Their Seats": The Ugly New Side of Theatre Audiences', *The Guardian*, 10 April. Available online: https://www.theguardian.com/stage/2023/apr/10/bodyguard-police-fighting-urinating-seats-ugly-new-side-of-theatre-audiences (accessed 19 April 2023).

Heddon, D., Iball, H. and Zerihan, R. (2012), 'Come Closer: Confessions of Intimate Spectators in One-to-One Performance', *Contemporary Theatre Review*, 22 (1): 120–33.

Hegarty, S. (2020), 'The Chinese Doctor Who Tried to Warn Others About Coronavirus', *BBC*, 4 February. Available online: https://www.bbc.co.uk/news/world-asia-china-51364382 (accessed 9 January 2023).

Heim, C. (2016), *Audience as Performer: The Changing Role of Theatre Audiences in the Twenty-first Century*, London and New York: Routledge.

Hemsley, A. (2020), 'Compassion I Embodiment I Advocacy I Action'. Available online: http://alexandrinahemsley.com/yewande-103/ (accessed 12 January 2023).

Hemley, M. (2022), 'Planned Cuts at Birkbeck Labelled a "Recipe for Managed Decline"', *The Stage*, 2 November. Available online: https://www.thestage.co.uk/news/planned-cuts-at-birkbeck-labelled-a-recipe-for-managed-decline (accessed 3 November 2022).

Hemming, S. (2018), 'Director James Macdonald on the Rise of "slow Theatre"', *Financial Times*, January 5. Available online: https://www.ft.com/content/000b9402-f084-11e7-bb7d-c3edfe974e9f (accessed 9 December 2022).

Hendlin, Y. H. (2014), 'From Terra Nullius to Terra Communis: Reconsidering Wild Land in an Era of Conservation and Indigenous Rights', *Environmental Philosophy*, 11 (2): 141–74.

Hewison, R. (1995), 'The Empty Space and the Social Space', in R. Mulryne and M. Shewring (eds), *Making Space for Theatre: British Architecture and Theatre Since 1958*, 52–60, Stratford-upon-Avon: Mulryne and Shewring Ltd.

Higgins, A. (1995), 'Work and Plays: Guild Casting in the Corpus Christi Drama', *Medieval and Renaissance Drama in England*, 7: 76–97.

Hill, M. (2022), 'Immensa Lab Errors May Have Led to 23 Covid-19 Deaths', *BBC News*, 1 December. Available online: https://www.bbc.co.uk/news/uk-england-63795285 (accessed 4 December 2022).

Hills, M. (2021), 'The National Theatre, London, as a Theatrical/architectural Object of Fan Imagination', in N. van Es, S. Reijnders, R. Stijn, L. Bolderman and A. Waysdorf (eds), *Locating Imagination in Popular Culture*, 297–311, London: Routledge.

Hindson, C. (2014), 'Heritage, Capital and Culture: The Ghost of "Sarah" at the Bristol Old Vic', in M. Luckhurst and E. Morin (eds), *Theatre and Ghosts*, 82–95, London: Palgrave Macmillan.

Hoggatt, M., Capobianco, J. and Pyzynski, S. (2014), 'So Many Playbills, So Little Time: A Case Study in Fugitive Theatrical Material', *RBM: A Journal of Rare Books, Manuscripts, and Cultural Heritage*, 15 (1): 31–9.

Holland, P. (2007), 'Shakespeare Abbreviated', in R. Shaughnessy (ed.), *The Cambridge Companion to Shakespeare and Popular Culture*, 26–45, Cambridge: Cambridge University Press.

Honigsbaum, M. (2016), *Living with Enza: The Forgotten Story of Britain and the Great Flu Pandemic of 1918*, Basingstoke: Palgrave.

Honoré, C. (2004), *In Praise of Slowness: Challenging the Cult of Speed*, San Francisco: HarperOne.

Horizon. (2020), 'Notes on Our Working Culture', *Horizon*. Available online: https://www.horizonshowcase.uk/wp-content/uploads/2022/07/Noteson OurWorkingCulture_updated.pdf (accessed 27 January 2023).

Horswill, R. (2022), '12 Last Songs – An Interview with Richard Gregory', *The State of the Arts*, 14 September. Available online: https://www.thestateofthearts.co.uk/features/12-last-songs-an-interview-with-richard-gregory/ (accessed 6 January 2023).

Hughes, M. (2021), 'SHOUT Festival Statement on Birmingham Repertory Theatre's Decision to Host a Nightingale Court', *Birmingham LGBT*, 5 January. Available online: https://blgbt.org/shout-festival-nightingale-court/ (accessed 23 February 2021).

Humphrey, C. (2000), 'Bakhtin and the Study of Popular Culture: Re-thinking Carnival as a Historical and Analytical Concept', in C. Brandist and G. Tihanov (eds), *Materializing Bakhtin: The Bakhtin Circle and Social Theory*, 164–72, Basingstoke: Macmillan.

Hutchings, M. (2013), 'The Interval and Indoor Playmaking', *Studies in Theatre and Performance*, 33 (3): 263–79.

Hutton, D. (2021), *Towards a Civic Theatre*, Glasgow: Salamander Street.

Jacobson, K. (2020), 'Theatre Companies Are Pushing Storytelling Boundaries with Online Audiences Amid COVID-19', *The Conversation*, 21 July. Available online: https://theconversation.com/theatre-companies-are-pushing-storytelling-boundaries-with-online-audiences-amid-covid-19-141583 (accessed 22 November 2022).

Jeong, T. H., Volkmer, A., Jiang, J., Brotherhood, E. V., Dobson, L., Harding, E., Suarez-Gonzalez, A., Crutch, S. J., Warren, J. D., Hardy, C. J. D. and Agustus, J. L. (2021), 'Communication During Covid-19: Impacts of Face Coverings on People Living With Dementia', *Alzheimer's & Dementia*, 17 (7): e057733.

Johansson, M. (2020), 'City Festivals and Festival Cities', in R. Knowles (ed.), *The Cambridge Companion to International Theatre Festivals*, 54–69, Cambridge: Cambridge University Press.

Johnson, D. (2015), *The Art of Living: An Oral History of Performance Art*, Basingstoke: Palgrave Macmillan.

Johnson, S. (1763), 'PROLOGUE SPOKEN BY Mr. GARRICK, At the Opening of the Theatre in Drury-lane', in R. Dodsley (ed.), *A Collection of Poems in Six Volumes. By Several Hands*, Vol. I., 200–2, London: J. Hughs.

Jolley, D. and Paterson, J. L. (2020), 'Pylons Ablaze: Examining the Role of 5G COVID-19 Conspiracy Beliefs and Support for Violence', *British Journal of Social Psychology*, 59 (3): 628–40.

Jones, K., Poore, B. and Dean, R. (eds). (2018), *Contemporary Gothic Drama: Attraction, Consummation and Consumption on the Modern British Stage*, London: Palgrave Macmillan.

Jones, R. (2015), 'West End Grrs: Best Seats in the House up 300% for Top Shows', *The Guardian*, 8 June. Available online: https://www.theguardian.com/money/2015/jun/08/west-end-best-seats-top-shows-price-rises-theatres (accessed 16 January 2023).

Jowett, P. (2022a), 'British Council Restructure Threatens Sector, Strikers Say', *ArtsProfessional*, 23 March. Available online: https://www.artsprofessional.co.uk/news/british-council-restructure-threatens-sector-strikers-say (accessed 3 November 2022).

Jowett, P. (2022b), 'NPO Decisions: Changes in Regional Funding Distribution', *ArtsProfessional*, 8 November. Available online: https://www.artsprofessional.co.uk/news/npo-decisions-changes-regional-funding-distribution (accessed 9 November 2022).

Kalb, J. (2011), *Great Lengths: Seven Works of Marathon Theater*, Ann Arbor: University of Michigan Press.

Kanem, N. (2020), 'Protecting Our Elders', 23 October, UNA-UK, SDGs: Building Back Better. Available online: https://www.sustainablegoals.org.uk/protecting-our-elders/ (accessed 16 August 2022).

Katritzky, M. A. and Drábek, P. eds (2019), *Transnational Connections in Early Modern Theatre*, Manchester: Manchester University Press.

Katz, I. (1992), 'Box Office Politics: London's Biggest Shows Always Sell Out. Or do They?', *The Guardian*, 9 April: 26.

Kawalko Roselli, D. (2011), *Theater of the People: Spectators and Society in Ancient Athens*, Austin: University of Texas Press.

Kedward, R. (1931), 'Sunday Performances (Regulation) Bill', *Hansard: House of Commons Debates*, 20 April: 251 cc633–765. Available online: https://api.parliament.uk/historic-hansard/commons/1931/apr/20/sunday-performances-regulation-bill (accessed 2 January 2023).

Kershaw, B. (1999), *The Radical in Performance: From Brecht to Baudrillard*, New York and London: Routledge.

Kirwan, P. (2007), '"Eke Out Our Imperfections with Your Minds": The Festival's Impact on Audience Expectations and Involvement', *Cahiers Élisabéthains*, 71 (1): 99–102.

Kirwan, P. (2020), 'Streaming Shakespeare: The Theatre Industry in Lockdown', *University of Nottingham*, n.d. Available online: https://www.nottingham.ac.uk/vision/vision-streaming-shakespeare (accessed 9 December 2022).

Kitcher, N. (2020), 'Electrophone: The Victorian-era Gadget That Was a Precursor to Live-streaming', *The Conversation*, 12 November. Available online: https://theconversation.com/electrophone-the-victorian-era-gadget-that-was-a-precursor-to-live-streaming-148944 (accessed 22 November 2022).

Lakoff, G. and Johnson, M. (1980), *Metaphors We Live By*, Chicago: University of Chicago Press.

Landes, D. S. (1983), *Revolution in Time: Clocks and the Making of the Modern World*, Cambridge, MA: Harvard University Press.

Latimer, A. (2022), 'Beyond "Geordierama": Theatre and Performance in North East England, 2017–18', PhD thesis, Newcastle University.

Lavender, A. (1989), 'Theatre in Crisis: Conference Report, December 1988', *New Theatre Quarterly*, 5 (19): 210–16.

Lawson, M. (2021), 'What If If Only Review – Short and Sharp, with Shades of Scrooge', *The Guardian*, 1 October. Available online: https://www.theguardian.com/stage/2021/oct/01/what-if-if-only-review-short-and-sharp-with-shades-of-scrooge (accessed 31 December 2022).

Lawson, R. (2017), 'Go See Events', *Culturehive*. Available online: https://www.culturehive.co.uk/wp-content/uploads/2018/01/Cultural-Spring-CultureHive-Case-Study.pdf (accessed 15 January 2023).

Lefebvre, H. (1991 [1974]), *The Production of Space*, translated by D. Nicholson-Smith, Oxford and Cambridge, MA: Blackwell.

Lewis, L. (2018), *Performing Wales: People, Memory and Place*, Cardiff: University of Wales Press.

Liedke, H. L. (2022), 'Transmedial Experience in Nineteenth-Century Live Theater Broadcasting', in Meyer C. and Pietrzak-Franger, M. (eds), *Transmedia Practices in the Long Nineteenth Century*, 62–78, London and New York: Routledge.

Lindley, D. (2004), 'The Stuart Masque and Its Makers', in J. Milling and P. Thomson (eds), *The Cambridge History of British Theatre*, 383–406, Cambridge: Cambridge University Press.

Linford, M. (2018), 'Secrets of the Seat Fillers: London's Labyrinth of Free Theatre Tickets', *The Guardian*, 31 October. Available online: https://www.theguardian.com/stage/2018/oct/31/secrets-of-the-seat-fillers-london-free-theatre-tickets (accessed 17 January 2023).

Lister, D. (1993), 'Theatre Thrives on "Pay What You Can"', *The Independent*, 7 January.

Machon, J. (2013), *Immersive Theatres: Intimacy and Immediacy in Contemporary Performance*, Basingstoke: Palgrave Macmillan.

MacKay, E. (2017),'Knowledge Transmission: Theatre at the Crossroads of Concept, Medium and Practice', in R. Henke (ed.), *A Cultural History of Theatre in the Early Modern Age*, 183–204, London: Bloomsbury.

Mackintosh, I. (1993), *Architecture, Actor and Audience*, New York and London: Routledge.

Maguire, H. (2000), 'The Victorian Theatre as a Home from Home', *Journal of Design History*, 13 (2): 107–21.

Maguire, T. (2020), 'Alternative Worlds: The Emergence of Theatre for Young Audiences from the Conflict in Northern Ireland', *Strenæ*, 16.

Mantell, O. (2022), 'Cultural Participation Monitor: Quarterly Key Findings', *The Audience Agency*, October. Available online: https://www.theaudienceagency.org/evidence/covid-19-cultural-participation-monitor/recent-key-insights (accessed 3 November 2022).

Marshalsay, K. (1993), 'Seaside Entertainers', *The Waggle o' the Kilt: Popular Theatre and Entertainment in Scotland*. Available online: https://www.arts.gla.ac.uk/STELLA/STARN/crit/WAGGLE/seaside.htm (accessed 3 January 2023).

Martin, A. (2017), 'The Sunday Post: What's in a Name?', *BBC*, 2 April. Available online: https://www.bbc.co.uk/blogs/genome/entries/884d3352-36f1-471b-8cb8-6e6ceb38b7e7 (accessed 22 January 2023).

Masura, N. (2020), *Digital Theatre*, Basingstoke: Palgrave Macmillan.

Mathers, M. (2020), 'Coronavirus: UK Government Urged to Include Sign Language Interpreter in Daily Briefings', *The Independent*, 6 April. Available online: https://www.independent.co.uk/life-style/health-and-families/health-news/coronavirus-lockdown-uk-government-sign-language-daily-press-briefing-a9449576.html (accessed 11 January 2023).

Maxmen, A. (2021), 'Why did the World's Pandemic Warning System Fail When COVID Hit?', *Nature*, 23 January. Available online: https://www.nature.com/articles/d41586-021-00162-4 (accessed 9 January 2023).

MAYK. (2022), 'Some Reflections on Pay What You Can Pricing', *MAYK*, 12 September. Available online: https://www.mayk.org.uk/blog/pay-what-you-can-reflections (accessed 20 January 2023).

McAuley, G. (1999), *Space in Performance: Making Meaning in the Theatre*, Ann Arbor: University of Michigan Press.
McDowell, E. (2022), 'Mixing Methods in Audience Research Practice: A Multi-method(ological) Discussion', in M. Reason, L. Conner, K. Johanson and B. Walmsley (eds), *Routledge Companion to Audiences and the Performing Arts*, 264–77, London and New York: Routledge.
McNeill, J. R. and Engelke, P. (2016), *The Great Acceleration: An Environmental History of the Anthropocene Since 1945*, Cambridge, MA: Harvard University Press.
McWilliam, R. (2020), *London's West End: Creating the Pleasure District, 1800–1914*, Oxford: Oxford University Press.
Mecanoo (2022), 'Home Arts Centre', *Mecanoo*, n.d. Available online: https://www.mecanoo.nl/Projects/project/66/HOME-Arts-Centre (accessed 10 March 2022).
Meier, H. (2018), 'Mary Cassatt's Women at the Opera: Representations of Modern Femininity', *Creative Matter*, 21, n.d. Available online: https://creativematter.skidmore.edu/art_history_stu_schol/21 (accessed 2 December 2022).
Merriam-Webster. (2022), 'Words We're Watching: Remembering How It Was in the "Before Times"', *Merriam-Webster*, n.d. Available online: https://www.merriam-webster.com/words-at-play/before-times-covid-history-and-usage (accessed 6 November 2022).
Mével, P., Robinson, J. and Tennent, P. (2022), 'Immersive, Creative, Inclusive: Areas of Cross-fertilization Between Accessible Captions for D/deaf Audiences for the Stage and for the Screen', *Journal of Audiovisual Translation*, 4 (1): 176–93.
Mével, P., Robinson, J. and Tennent, P. (2023), 'Integrated Immersive Inclusiveness: Rethinking Captioning for Creative Accessibility', in L. Kostopoulou and V. Misiou, (eds), *New Paths in Theatre Translation and Surtitling*, 199–220, London: Routledge.
Milling, J. (2004), 'The Development of a Professional Theatre, 1540–1660', in J. Milling and P. Thomson (eds), *The Cambridge History of British Theatre, Origins to 1660*, 139–77, Cambridge: Cambridge University Press.
Moores, Z. (2020), 'Fostering Access for All Through Respeaking at Live Events', *The Journal of Specialised Translation*, 33: 207–26.
Moran, J. (2022), *The Theatre of Fake News*, London: Anthem Press.

Morris Hargreaves McIntyre. (2020), 'Freelance Task Force 2020 Evaluation Final Report', *Fuel*, December. Available online: https://fueltheatre.com/wp-content/uploads/2020/12/Freelance-Task-Force-2020-Evaluation-Final-Report.pdf (accessed 20 January 2023).

Moskowitz, G. B., Olcaysoy Okten, I. and Gooch, C. M. (2015), 'On Race and Time', *Psychological Science*, 26 (11): 1783–94.

Muse, A. (2023), *The Drama and Theatre of Annie Baker*, London: Bloomsbury.

Muse, J. H. (2017), *Microdramas: Crucibles for Theatre and Time*, Ann Arbor: University of Michigan Press.

National Theatre of Scotland. (2022), 'About', https://www.nationaltheatrescotland.com/about (accessed 17 February 2022).

National Theatre Wales. (2022), 'About Us', https://www.nationaltheatrewales.org/about-us/we-are-ntw/ (accessed 17 February 2022).

Neff, E. (2022), 'Plague-Time Aesthetics', *PAJ: A Journal of Performance and Art*, 44 (1): 42–8.

Nesher Shoshan, H. and Wehrt, W. (2022), 'Understanding "Zoom Fatigue": A Mixed-method Approach', *Applied Psychology*, 71 (3): 827–52.

Neves, J. (2018), 'Subtitling for Deaf and Hard of Hearing Audiences: Moving Forward', in L. Pérez-González (ed.), *The Routledge Handbook of Audiovisual Translation*, 82–95, London and New York: Routledge.

NHS (2020), '7 Simple Tips to Tackle Working from Home', *NHS*, n.d. Available online: https://www.nhs.uk/every-mind-matters/coronavirus/simple-tips-to-tackle-working-from-home/ (accessed 5 December 2022).

Nichols, D. (2017), 'New Writing in a Populist Context: A Play, a Pie and a Pint', *Theatre History Studies*, 36 (1): 266–85.

Nicholson, H. (2023), 'Local Theatres: Cultures of Participation', in H. Nicholson, J. Hughes, G. Edwards and C. Gray, *Theatre in Towns*, 12–40, London: Routledge.

Nicoll, A. (1981), *The Garrick Stage: Theatres and Audience in the Eighteenth Century*, Manchester: Manchester University Press.

Nield, S. (2017), 'Technologies of Performance', in P. W. Marx (ed.), *A Cultural History of Theatre in the Age of Empire*, 203–26, London: Bloomsbury.

Niven, A. (2019), *New Model Island: How to Build a Radical Culture Beyond the Idea of England*, London: Repeater Books.

Northern Stage (2023), 'Become a Supporter', *Northern Stage*. Available online: https://northernstage.co.uk/support-us/become-a-supporter-2/ (accessed 16 January 2023).

Novak, D. A. (2016), 'Caught in the Act: Photography on the Victorian Stage', *Victorian Studies*, 59 (1): 35–64.

O'Connor, M. (2002), 'Reconstructive Shakespeare: Reproducing Elizabethan and Jacobean Stages', in S. Wells and S. Stanton (eds), *The Cambridge Companion to Shakespeare on Stage*, 76–97, Cambridge: Cambridge University Press.

Ogden, R. (2020), 'The Passage of Time During the UK Covid-19 Lockdown', *PLOS ONE*, doi:10.1371/journal.pone.0235871.

Ogden, T. (2009), *Haunted Theaters: Playhouse Phantoms, Opera House Horrors, and Backstage Banshees*, London: Rowman & Littlefield.

O'Gorman, R. and Werry, M. (2012), 'On Failure (On Pedagogy): Editorial Introduction', *Performance Research*, 17 (1): 1–8, doi:10.1080/13528165.20 12.651857.

Ouellet, C., Tétreault, É. and Grondin, S. (2023), 'Politically Biased Time Perception and Perspective', *Timing & Time Perception*, 11: 1–17 (published online ahead of print 2022). https://doi.org/10.1163/22134468-bja10046 (accessed 12 December 2022).

Pakula, P. (2011), 'Jerzy Grotowski's Influence on British Theatre, 1966–1980: Histories, Perspectives, Recollections', PhD Thesis, University of Kent.

Palmatier, R. W., Burke Jarvis, C., Bechkoff, J. R. and Kardes F. R. (2009), 'The Role of Customer Gratitude in Relationship Marketing', *Journal of Marketing*, 73 (5): 1–18.

Palmer, S. (2017), 'Harnessing Shadows: A Historical Perspective on the Role of Darkness in the Theatre', in A. Alston and M. Welton (eds), *Theatre in the Dark: Shadow, Gloom and Blackout in Contemporary Theatre*, 37–63, London: Methuen Drama.

Pardes, A. (2020), 'There Are No Hours or Days in Coronatime', *Wired*, 8 May. Available online: https://www.wired.com/story/coronavirus-time-warp -what-day-is-it/ (accessed 5 December 2022).

Paul, T-D. (2020), 'Crisis, Change, Care', in Lownie, A. (ed.), *Field Notes*, 82–8, Stockton-on-Tees: Two Destination Language.

Paxton, C. (2020), 'Birmingham Rep Accused of "Breaking Trust" as It Leases Space for "Nightingale Courts"', *Birmingham Mail*, 15 December. Available online: https://www.birminghammail.co.uk/news/midlands-news/ birmingham-rep-accused-breaking-trust-19462569 (accessed 23 February 2022).

Pearson, M. (1998), 'My Balls/your Chin', *Performance Research*, 3.2 (39): 35–41.

Peterson, M. (2022), 'Concept Touring: Evaluation Report', *LIFT*, January. Available online: https://d8989d5044934ffdd9e3.b-cdn.net/wp-content/uploads/2022/10/Concept-Touring-Report.pdf (accessed 20 January 2023).

Pettman, D. (2016), *Infinite Distraction*, Cambridge: Polity.

Pinter, H. (2018), *The Short Plays of Harold Pinter*, London: Faber & Faber.

Pitts, S. E. and Price, S. M. (2020), *Understanding Audience Engagement in the Contemporary Arts*, London and New York: Routledge.

Postlewait, T. (2009), *The Cambridge Introduction to Theatre Historiography*, Cambridge: Cambridge University Press.

Ptacek, K. (2003), 'Avatar Body Collision: Enactments in Distributed Performance Practices', *Digital Creativity*, 14 (3): 180–92, doi:10.1076/digc.14.3.180.27873.

Putnam, L. (2022), 'Taxis and Toilets and Pools, Oh My!: 13 Unusual Venues at Edinburgh Fringe', *Playbill*, 25 July. Available online: https://playbill.com/article/taxis-and-toilets-and-pools-oh-my-13-unusual-venues-at-edinburgh-fringe (accessed 2 January 2023).

Pye, T. (2017), 'The Language of Space', *Theatre and Performance Design*, 3 (1–2): 99–106.

Ravenhill, M. (2009), 'The Joy of Slow Theatre', *The Guardian*, 20 April. Available online: https://www.theguardian.com/stage/2009/apr/20/mark-ravenhill-slow-theatre (accessed 8 December 2022).

Ravenhill, M. (2013), *Plays: 3*, London: Bloomsbury.

Reason, M., Conner, L., Johanson, K. and Walmsley, B., eds (2022), *Routledge Companion to Audiences and the Performing Arts*, London and New York: Routledge.

Reicher, S. and Drury, J. (2021), 'Pandemic Fatigue? How Adherence to Covid-19 Regulations Has Been Misrepresented and Why It Matters', *BMJ (Clinical Research Ed.)*, 372 (137).

Reinelt, J. (2014), 'What UK Spectators Know: Understanding How We Come to Value Theatre', *Theatre Journal*, 66 (3): 337–61.

Rhine, A. S. and Murnin, P. M. (2018), 'Day, Duration, and Start Time: Are the Arts Providing What Their Audiences Require?', *Arts and the Market* 8 (1): 19–29. https://doi.org/10.1108/AAM-12-2017-0027 (accessed 12 December 2022).

Richards, D. (2019), 'Does "Pay What You Can" Pay Off?', *ArtsProfessional*, 21 November. Available online: https://www.artsprofessional.co.uk/magazine/article/does-pay-what-you-can-pay (accessed 17 January 2023).

Ridout, N. (2006), *Stage Fright, Animals and Other Theatrical Problems*, Cambridge: Cambridge University Press.

Rings, J. (2017), 'Selina Thompson Interview: "As a Queer Black Woman I Am Often Expected to Educate People on Race, Class and Gender. Enough! Time for You to Think for Yourself"', *Brighton Dome*, 14 December. Available online: https://brightondome.org/news_blog/selina_thompson_interview_race_cards/ (accessed 6 January 2023).

Ritter, T. and Geersbro, J. (2010), 'Antecedents of Customer Relationship Termination', Paper presented at ISBM Academic Conference 2010, Boston, MA.

Robinson, J. (2016), *Theatre & the Rural*, Basingstoke: Palgrave Macmillan.

Robson, M. (2019), *Theatre & Death*, London: Red Globe Press.

Rokison, A. (2013), *Shakespeare for Young People: Productions, Versions and Adaptations*, London: Bloomsbury Academic.

Rose, S. (2020), 'Heaven Can Wait: What Will Happen to the Films Delayed by Coronavirus?', *The Guardian*, 23 March. Available online: https://www.theguardian.com/film/2020/mar/23/what-will-happen-to-the-films-delayed-by-coronavirus (accessed 5 January 2023).

Roy, A. (2020), 'The Pandemic Is a Portal', *The Financial Times*, 3 April. Available online: https://www.ft.com/content/10d8f5e8-74eb-11ea-95fe-fcd274e920ca (accessed 6 November 2022).

RSC. (2022), 'Henry VI Part One Open Rehearsal Project Highlights', *YouTube*, 29 April. Available online: https://www.youtube.com/watch?v=b6HRmfaVbhI&t=11s (accessed 22 January 2023).

Ruhl, S. (2015), *100 Essays I Don't Have Time to Write: On Umbrellas and Sword Fights, Parades and Dogs, Fire Alarms, Children, and Theater*, New York: Farrar, Straus & Giroux Inc.

Russell, G. (2020), *The Ephemeral Eighteenth Century: Print, Sociability, and the Cultures of Collecting*, Cambridge: Cambridge University Press.

Rutrecht, H., Wittmann, M., Khoshnoud, S. and Igarzábal, F. A. (2021), 'Time Speeds up During Flow States: A Study in Virtual Reality with the Video Game Thumper', *Timing & Time Perception*, 9 (4): 353–76.

Salman, S. (2016), 'Street Theatre Show Highlights Modern Loneliness Epidemic', *The Guardian*, 4 October. Available online: https://www.theguardian.com/social-care-network/2016/oct/04/street-theatre-show-modern-loneliness-epidemic (accessed 10 January 2023).

Saunders, G. and Bull, B. (2015), 'Series Editors' Preface', in G. Saunders and J. Bull (eds), *British Theatre Companies: 1980–1994*, viii–xi, London: Bloomsbury Publishing.

Saunders, G. H., Jackson, I. R. and Visram, A. S. (2021), 'Impacts of Face Coverings on Communication: An Indirect Impact of COVID-19', *International Journal of Audiology*, 60 (7): 495–506.

Sauter, W. (2010), 'Cyclic Perseverance and the Linear Mobility of Theatrical Events', in C. M. Canning and T. Postlewait (eds), *Representing the Past: Essays in Performance Historiography*, 117–41, Iowa City: University of Iowa Press.

Schneidner, R. (2001), 'Archives: Performance Remains', *Performance Research*, 6 (2): 100–8.

Schechner, R. (2002), *Performance Studies: An Introduction*, London and New York: Routledge.

Scott, C. (1899), *The Drama of Yesterday and Today*, vols I and II, London: Macmillan & Co.

Secară, A. (2018), 'Surtitling and Captioning for Theatre and Opera', in L. Pérez-González (ed.), *The Routledge Handbook of Audiovisual Translation*, 130–44, London: Routledge.

Sedgman, K. (2016), *Locating the Audience: How People Found Value in National Theatre Wales*, Bristol: Intellect Books.

Sedgman, K. (2018), *The Reasonable Audience: Theatre Etiquette, Behaviour Policing, and the Live Performance Experience*, Basingstoke: Palgrave Macmillan.

Sedgman, K. (2022), 'Fans and Fandom in the Performing Arts' in M. Reason, L. Conner, K. Johanson and B. Walmsley (eds), *Routledge Companion to Audiences and the Performing Arts*, 190–202, London: Routledge.

Shaffer, P. (2005 [1973]), *Equus*, New York: Scribners.

Shalson, L. (2013), 'Waiting', *Contemporary Theatre Review*, 23 (1): 79–82.

Shaw, D. (2020), 'Zoom Meetings Targeted by Abuse Footage Sharers', *BBC*, 23 April. Available online: https://www.bbc.co.uk/news/uk-52391531 (accessed 26 January 2023).

Sherman, J. F. (2016), *A Strange Proximity: Stage Presence, Failure and the Ethics of Attention*, New York and London: Routledge.

Sherwood, H. (2022), '"Sums up 2022": Permacrisis Chosen as Collins Word of the Year', *The Guardian*, 1 November, https://www.theguardian.com/

culture/2022/nov/01/sums-up-2022-permacrisis-chosen-as-collins-word-of-the-year (accessed 1 November 2022).
Shillito, I. J. and Walsh, B. (2007), *Haunted West End Theatres*, Stroud: The History Press.
Short, A. (2011), '"Turn the Theatre Inside Out": Curve, Leicester', in C. A. Short, Barrett, P. S. and Fair, A., *Geometry and Atmosphere: Theatre Buildings From Vision to Reality*, 137–66, Farnham: Ashgate Publishing.
Short, C. A., Barrett, P. S. and Fair, A. (2011), *Geometry and Atmosphere: Theatre Buildings from Vision to Reality*, Farnham: Ashgate Publishing.
Siddique, H. and Denis Campbell, D. (2020), 'Chief Nurse Dropped From No. 10 Briefing "For Not Backing Cummings"', *The Guardian*, 12 June. Available online: https://www.theguardian.com/politics/2020/jun/12/chief-nurse-dropped-from-no-10-briefing-for-not-backing-cummings (accessed 9 January 2023).
Simon, F. M. and Camargo, C. Q. (2021), 'Autopsy of a Metaphor: The Origins, Use and Blind Spots of the "Infodemic"', *New Media & Society*, 1: 1–22.
Smyth, P. (2010), 'Beyond the Picture-frame Stage: Late Nineteenth-Century Pictorial Theatre Posters', *Nineteenth Century Theatre and Film*, 37 (2): 4–27.
Snow, G. (2019), 'West End Toilets Survey: Exclusive Research Reveals Theatreland Caught Short by Sub-par Toilet Provision', *The Stage*, 2 January. Available online: https://www.thestage.co.uk/news/west-end-toilets-survey-exclusive-research-reveals-theatreland-caught-short-by-sub-par-toilet-provision (accessed 8 January 2023).
Snow, G. (2021), 'Birmingham Rep to Face Critics Over Decision to Become Temporary Court', *The Stage*, 19 January. Available online: https://www.thestage.co.uk/news/birmingham-rep-to-face-critics-over-decision-to-become-temporary-court (accessed 23 February 2021).
Snyder-Young, D. (2020), *Privileged Spectatorship: Theatrical Interventions in White Supremacy*, Evanston, IL: Northwestern University Press.
Snyder-Young, D. and Omasta, M., eds (2022), *Impacting Theatre Audiences: Methods for Studying Change*, London and New York: Routledge.
Sörgel, S. (2020), *Contemporary African Dance Theatre: Phenomenology, Whiteness, and the Gaze*, Basingstoke: Palgrave Macmillan.
SPI-B: Scientific Pandemic Insights Group on Behaviours Committee (2020), 'Public Health Messaging for Communities from Different Cultural Backgrounds', *Scientific Pandemic Influenza Group on Behaviours*, 22 July.

Available online: https://assets.publishing.service.gov.uk/government/ uploads/system/uploads/attachment_data/file/914924/s0649-public-health -messaging-bame-communities.pdf (accessed 9 January 2023).
Spracklen, K. and Spracklen, B. (2018), *The Evolution of Goth Culture: The Origins and Deeds of the New Goths*, Bingley: Emerald Group Publishing.
Stagetext (2022), 'About Us', *Stagetext*, n.d. Available online: https://www .stagetext.org/about-us/about-stagetext/ (accessed 4 December 2022).
Staples, D. (2021), 'Postscript – "The Ghost Light"', in D. Staples (ed.), *Modern Theatres, 1950–2020*, 550–1, New York and London: Routledge.
Stengers, I. (2018), *Another Science Is Possible: A Manifesto for Slow Science*, translated by S. Muecke, Cambridge: Polity.
Stern, T. (2007), *Rehearsal from Shakespeare to Sheridan*, Oxford: Oxford University Press.
Stern, T. (2006), '"On Each Wall and Corner Poast": Playbills, Title-pages, and Advertising in Early Modern London', *English Literary Renaissance*, 36 (1): 57–89.
Stone, A. R. (1996), *The War of Desire and Technology at the Close of the Mechanical Age*, Cambridge, MA: MIT Press.
Stronks, M. (2022), *Grasping Legal Time*, Cambridge: Cambridge University Press.
Stuart Fisher, A. (2020), *Performing the Testimonial: Rethinking Verbatim Dramaturgies*, Manchester: Manchester University Press.
Stuart Fisher, A. and Thompson, J., eds (2020), *Performing Care: New Perspectives on Socially Engaged Performance*, Manchester: Manchester University Press.
Sullivan, E. (2020), 'Live to Your Living Room: Streamed Theatre, Audience Experience, and the Globe's *A Midsummer Night's Dream*', *Participations: Journal of Audience & Reception Studies*, 17 (1): 92–119.
Sullivan, E. (2022), *Shakespeare and Digital Performance in Practice*, Basingstoke: Palgrave Macmillan.
Sullivan, O. and Gershuny, J. (2018), 'Speed-up Society? Evidence from the UK 2000 and 2015 Time Use Diary Surveys', *Sociology*, 52 (1): 20–38.
Syler, C. (2022), 'Prioritizing Black Experience, or the Inevitability of Educating White Audiences: A Discourse Analysis', in Snyder-Young, D. and Omasta, M. (eds), *Impacting Theatre Audiences*, 39–51, London and New York: Routledge.

Tan, Y. (2022), 'China Signals Ease in Covid Policy After Mass Protests', *BBC News*, 2 December. Available online: https://www.bbc.co.uk/news/world-asia-china-63805188 (accessed 4 December 2022).

Tawil-Souri, H. (2017), 'Checkpoint Time', *Qui Parle*, 26 (2): 383–422.

Thomas, D., Carlton, D. and Etienne, A. (2007), *Theatre Censorship: From Walpole to Wilson*, Oxford: Oxford University Press.

Tiller, C. (2020), 'Care as a Radical Act', *Heart of Glass*, 19 May. Available online: https://www.heartofglass.org.uk/news-and-resources/thoughts/care-as-a-radical-act (accessed 20 January 2023).

Trott, M., Driscoll, R., Irlado, E. and Pardhan, S. (2022), 'Changes and Correlates of Screen Time in Adults and Children During the COVID-19 Pandemic: A Systematic Review and Meta-analysis', *EClinicalMedicine*, 48, 101452.

Turkle, S. (2011), *Alone Together: Why We Expect More from Technology and Less From Each Other*, New York: Basic Books.

Turnbull, O. (2008), *Bringing Down the House: The Crisis in Britain's Regional Theatres*, Bristol: Intellect.

Turpin, A. (2015), 'Here's What Happened When We Asked Audiences to Set Their Own Ticket Prices', *The Guardian*, 8 July. Available online: https://www.theguardian.com/stage/theatreblog/2015/jul/08/audiences-ticket-prices-arc-stockton (accessed 17 January 2023).

Tynan, C. (1997), 'A Review of the Marriage Analogy in Relationship Marketing', *Journal of Marketing Management*, 13: 695–703.

UK Government (2020), 'Prime Minister's Statement on Coronavirus (Covid-19)', 23 March. Available online: https://www.gov.uk/government/speeches/pm-address-to-the-nation-on-coronavirus-23-march-2020 (accessed 23 February 2022).

UK Theatre. (2022), 'UK's Most Welcoming Theatre Award', *UK Theatre*, 23 October. Available online: https://uktheatre.org/training-events/uk-theatre-awards/uks-most-welcoming-theatre/ (accessed 23 January 2023).

Vallee, M. (2021), 'COVID-19 & Touch', *Solidarity and Care During the COVID-19 Pandemic*, 24 February. Available online: https://www.solidarityandcare.org/stories/essays/covid-19-touch (accessed 10 January 2023).

Van Drie, M. (2020), 'Know It Well, Know It Differently: New Sonic Practices in Late Nineteenth-Century Theatre-Going. The Case of the Theatrophone in Paris', in M. Bull, L. Back and D. Howes (eds), *The Auditory Culture Reader*, 205–16, London: Bloomsbury.

Van Lennep, W., Avery, E. F. and Scouten, A. H., eds (1965), *The London Stage, 1660–1800: A Calendar of Plays, Part I: 1660–1700*, Carbondale, IL: Southern Illinois University Press.

Verrent, J. (2020), 'It's Taken a Pandemic to Reimagine the Arts', in Lownie, A. (ed.), *Field Notes*, 99–102, Stockton-on-Tees: Two Destination Language.

Vickers, H. (1993), 'Obituary: Martin Tickner', *The Independent*, 20 February.

Virilio, P. (1986 [1977]), *Speed and Politics: An Essay on Dromology*, translated by M. Pollizotti, New York: Semiotext(e).

Vuga, B. (2021), 'Theatres and Publicness', in D. Staples (ed.), *Modern Theatres, 1950–2020*, 17–26, London and New York: Routledge.

Wajcman, J. (2015), *Pressed for Time: The Acceleration of Life in Digital Capitalism*, Chicago: University of Chicago Press.

Walford, R. and Dolley, C. (2015), *The One-Act Play Companion*, London: A&C Black.

Wallace, C., Escoda, C., Monforte, E. and Prado-Pérez, J. R., eds (2022), *Crisis, Representation and Resilience: Perspectives on Contemporary British Theatre*, London: Bloomsbury.

Walmsley, B. (2019), 'The Death of Arts Marketing: A Paradigm Shift From Consumption to Enrichment', *Arts and the Market*, 9 (1): 32–49.

Walmsley, B. and Franks, A. (2011), 'The Audience Experience: Changing Roles and Relationships', in B. Walmsley (ed.), *Key Issues in the Arts and Entertainment Industry*, 1–16, Oxford: Goodfellow.

Walmsley, B. et al. (2022), 'Culture in Crisis Impacts of Covid-19 on the UK Cultural Sector and Where we go From Here', *Culture Hive*, n.d. Available online: https://www.culturehive.co.uk/CVIresources/culture-in-crisisimpacts-of-covid-19/ (accessed: 4 December 2022).

Walsh, F. (2021), 'Grief Machines: Transhumanist Theatre, Digital Performance, Pandemic Time', *Theatre Journal* 73 (3): 391–407.

Ward, S. (1973), 'The Greatest Play on Words: The Amazing History of Theatre Posters and Playbills', *Art and Antiques*, 9 June: 31–5.

Warstat, M. (2020), 'Theatre History as Contemporary History', in T. C. Davis and P. Marx (eds), *The Routledge Companion to Theatre and Performance Historiography*, 383–96, London and New York: Routledge.

Webster, L. (2021), '"We Know They Can Do It When It Suits Them": Theatre Became More Accessible During Covid. Will it Last?', *The Guardian*, 15 October. Available online: https://www.theguardian.com/stage

/2021/oct/15/we-know-they-can-do-it-when-it-suits-them-theatre-became-more-accessible-during-covid-will-it-last (accessed 4 December 2022).

Wedderburn, A. (2020), 'Pandemic Time', *Soundings: A Journal of Politics and Culture*, 75: 31–5.

Weiss, C. H. (1995), 'Nothing as Practical as Good Theory: Exploring Theory-Based Evaluation for Comprehensive Community Initiatives for Children and Families', in J. Connell, A. Kubisch, L. Schorr and C. Weiss (eds), *New Approaches to Evaluating Comprehensive Community Initiatives*, 65–92, New York: The Aspen Roundtable Institute.

Welton, M. (2020), 'Going Dark: The Theatrical Legacy of Battersea Art Centre's Playing in the Dark Season', in T. Edensor and N. Dunn (eds), *Rethinking Darkness*, 179–91, London and New York: Routledge.

West, R. (2002), 'The Sun King: James I and the Court Masque', in *Spatial Representations and the Jacobean Stage*, 59–81, Basingstoke: Palgrave Macmillan.

White, G. (2012), 'On Immersive Theatre', *Theatre Research International*, 37 (3): 221–35.

White, M. (2014), '"When Torchlight Made an Artificial Noon": Light and Darkness in the Indoor Jacobean Theatre', in A. Gurr and F. Karim-Cooper (eds), *Moving Shakespeare Indoors: Performance and Repertoire in the Jacobean Playhouse*, 115–36, Oxford: Oxford University Press.

Whitrow, G. J. (1988), *Time in History: The Evolution of Our General Awareness of Time and Temporal Perspective*, Oxford: Oxford University Press.

Wiles, D. (2003), *A Short History of Western Performance Space*, Cambridge: Cambridge University Press.

Wiles, D. (2014), *Theatre & Time*. Basingstoke: Palgrave Macmillan.

Wiles, D. (2021), 'Theatre/Performance Historiography for the 2020s: A Review Essay', *Theatre Survey*, 62 (3): 364–74.

Williams, R. (1977), *Marxism and Literature*, Oxford: Oxford University Press.

Wise, L. (2018), 'The Joy of the Theatre Interval', *The Evening Standard*, 6 December. Available online: https://www.standard.co.uk/esmagazine/the-joy-of-the-theatre-interval-a4008641.html (accessed 31 December 2022).

Wittmann, M. and Mella, N. (2021), 'Having Children Speeds up the Subjective Passage of Lifetime in Parents', *Timing & Time Perception*, 9 (3): 275–83.

World Health Organization (2020), 'Mental Health and Psychosocial Considerations During the COVID-19 Outbreak'. Available online:

https://www.who.int/docs/default-source/coronaviruse/mental-health
-considerations.pdf?sfvrsn=6d3578af_2 (accessed 5 December 2022).

Worthen, W. B. (2020), *Shakespeare, Technicity, Theatre*, Cambridge: Cambridge University Press.

Worthen, W. B. (2021), 'Zoom; or, Obsolescence', *TDR*, 65 (3): 181–200.

Wreford-Sinnott, V. (2022), 'Crucial Conversations With Disabled Artists. Just What is the New Normal?', *Little Cog*, 28 March. Available online: http://www.littlecog.co.uk/news/crucial-conversations-with-disabled-artists-just-what-is-the-new-normal (accessed 20 January 2023).

Wyver, J. (2011), 'In the Beginning: *When We Are Married* (BBC, 1938) 1', *Screen Plays: Theatre Plays on British Television*, 22 September. Available online: https://screenplaystv.wordpress.com/2011/09/22/in-the-beginning-when-we-are-married-bbc-1938-1/ (accessed 21 November 2022).

Young Vic. (2023), 'What to Expect', *Young Vic*. Available online: https://www.youngvic.org/visit-us/what-to-expect (accessed 23 January 2023).

Youngs, I. (2014), 'Sir Alan Ayckbourn Voices Fears over Theatre Screenings', *BBC News*, 11 June. Available online: https://www.bbc.co.uk/news/entertainment-arts-27761568 (accessed 22 November 2022).

Zaiontz, K. (2014), 'Narcissistic Spectatorship in Immersive and One-on-One Performance', *Theatre Journal*, 66 (3): 405–25.

Zárate, S. (2021), *Captioning and Subtitling for D/deaf and Hard of Hearing Audiences*, London: UCL Press.

Zerubavel, E. (2021), 'The Sociology of Time', in J. Reinecke, R. Suddaby, H. Tsoukas and A. Langley (eds), *Time, Temporality, and History in Process Organization Studies*, 44–9, Oxford: Oxford University Press.

Index

12 Last Songs, Quarantine 53–4

Abuses Stript and Whipt, George Wither 127–8
access 108–11, 140–1, 154–6, 166–8
Aebischer, Pascale 32, 97
Ah kissing, Rosanna Irvine 169
Alphabetti Theatre, Newcastle 142, 159
amphitheatres 64–6, 77
Angels in America, Tony Kushner 49
anonymity 67, 97, 99–101, 113–16
anti-theatrical prejudice 35, 123, 127
Any Table Any Room, Jonathan Burrows and Matteo Fargion 169
applause 125, 132, 142
architecture, *see* buildings
ARC Stockton 53, 139
Arts Council 68
    Arts Council England (ACE) 9, 139, 172
As Far As Isolation Goes, Basel Zara and Tania El Khoury 170
audio description 108–10
Augmented, Sophie Woolley 166

backstage 73, 115, 124, 131, 134
Baker, Annie
    The Flick 51
    John 51
Ballycarry Amphitheatre, County Antrim, Northern Ireland 65
Balme, Christopher 5, 93, 95, 102, 126–8
Barbican, London 79, 104
Barbican Theatre, Plymouth 158

barriers 66, 82, 95–6
bars 72, 73, 104–5
Battersea Arts Centre, London 112, 137, 140
Before I Sleep, dreamthinkspeak 75
Belgrade Theatre, Coventry 69
Bennett, Susan 11, 65–6, 95–6, 113, 129
Berlant, Lauren 17
binge-watching 32
Birmingham Rep Theatre 85
Black audiences 85, 108, 114
Blackfriars playhouse 78, 112
Black Lives Matter 54, 136, 154
BOAT, The (Brighton Open Air Theatre) 65
bodies 17–18, 22, 33, 114, 121
Bogart, Ann 31
boxes 62–3, 77, 129
brevity 42–9, *see also* speed
Britain isn't Eating, Laura Wade 48
broadcasting theatre 106–7, 131
Brook, Peter 7, 95
buildings 13, 30, 60–85, 123, 128, 134–5, 141

cancellations 149, 157–8
captioning 108–10, 155–6, 163–4, 167
care 154–6, 159–65
CAST, Doncaster 69, 79
cast size 41–2, 46
censorship 79, 122
change 1–6, 20–3, 25–7
    theory of 151
Chichester Festival Theatre 68
children 16, 26, 27, 41, 87, 122, 132, 138
Churchill, Caryl
    Ding Dong the Wicked 44

Here We Go 52
Love and Information 43
What If If Only 44
citizenship 65–6, 68
class 62–4, 76, 81
climate 19–21, 48–9
closures
  of public amenities 58
  of schools 16
  of theatre companies and
    venues 1, 4, 31, 35, 58,
    153–4
Cochrane, Claire 21
comfort 63, 81–2, 140–1, 161–3
commemoration 53
communication 14, 119–28,
    143–4
  failure of 123, 143–4
community 85, 100, 106
  programming 139
Composed, Rosa Postlethwaite 110
compression 40–2
concealment, *see* secrecy
concept touring 169–70
Contact Theatre, Manchester 139–40
convention 3–9, 22–3, 33, 38–9, 45,
    49–50, 55–6, 61, 71, 75, 83,
    130–1, 141, 145
copresence 60, 90–1, 97, 101,
    104–6, 118
Corpus Christi cycles 34, 50, 80, 91
Costa, Maddy 152, 160
Court performances 36, 66, 77–8,
    92, 112, 123
Covid 1–5, 16–17, 25–7, 57–60, 85,
    87–9, 91, 119–22
A Crash Course in Cloud Spotting,
    Raquel Meseguer
    Zafe 170
crisis 1–5, 17–19
Crucible, The, Sheffield 68

Dance City, Newcastle 141, 167
Dan Daw Show, The Dan Daw 167

dark festival 14–16, 25, 30–1, 56,
    76, 101, 121, 143–5
dark play 15
Davis, Tracy C. 5, 21
d/Deaf and hard of hearing
  audiences 109–10, 168
death 15
  of theatre 22, 32, 148
  and theatre 30, 103
Death of England, Roy Williams 48
democracy, *see* citizenship
Devil is an Ass, The Ben Jonson 83
digital performance 10, 23, 59,
    101–6, 108, 114–18, 154–6,
    163–5, 170, 171
direct address 104, 125–6, 142
disabled audiences and artists 56,
    108, 110–11, 114, 141,
    154–6, 167–8
disruptive behaviour 20, 67, 99
distance 71, 82, *see also* proximity
division, *see* hierarchy
domestic abuse 82
doorstep theatre 60
Douglas, John Home 132
duration 40–56

economics, *see* funding
Edinburgh Festival Fringe 37, 41–4,
    161
Edinburgh International
    Festival 68
electrophone, *see* theatrophone
Elision, Gudrun Soley
    Sigurdardottir 116
End, The Bert and Nasi 108
endurance 50–1
entrances 62–3, 69, 123
Evidence Chamber, The Fast
    Familiar 117
exclusion 61–2, 71, 77, 128, 156
exclusivity 63, 73, 77–9, 92, 105,
    134–5
exposure, *see* visibility, of audiences
Exposure, Vacuum Cleaner 161–3

Index

façade 69, 79, 124
Facebook, *see* social media
face coverings, *see* masks
fans 42, 100–1, 134
feedback 137–9, 141–2, 150
festivals 31, 34, 37, 46–7, 50, 75, 145, 152–3, *see also* Edinburgh Festival Fringe; Edinburgh International Festival; Gi60 (Gone in Sixty Seconds) One Minute Theatre Festival; GIFT (Gateshead International Festival of Theatre)
Festival Theatre Edinburgh 69
Finborough Theatre 82
Fountain, The Yewande 163–4
foyers 55, 69, 72–3
freelance artists 1, 60–1, 145, 149–50, 152–4, 171–2
frontage, *see* façade
Fuchs, Barbara 18
funding 9, 36, 42, 45, 60–2, 68, 70, 71, 73, 77, 78, 172
future 1–3, 21–3, 147–52, 171–3

Gamble, Hannah Walker 167–8
Garrick, David 125–6, 130–1
gaze 96–7, 113–14
ghost lights 2, 58, 112
ghosts, *see* haunting
Gi60 (Gone in Sixty Seconds) One Minute Theatre Festival 46–7
GIFT (Gateshead International Festival of Theatre) 8, 12, 104, 116, 138, 147, 163
Gododdin, Brith Gof 75
Grandpa's Great Escape, David Walliams and Kevin Cecil 137
Great Yes, No, Don't Know Five-Minute Theatre Show, The National Theatre of Scotland 47–8

Greek theatre 34, 64–6, 76–7
grief, *see* mourning
Grotowski, Jerzy 94–5

Harry Potter and the Cursed Child, Jack Thorne 134
haunting 30, 84
Heim, Caroline 96, 101, 113–14, 126, 130–1
hierarchy 15, 62–3, 67, 71, 77, 153
historiography 3, 5–7, 9, 20–1
home 57–60, 81–2
HOME, Manchester 81, 108
honesty 141–2, 159
Hotel, Geraldine Pilgrim 75

I, Malvolio, Tim Crouch 80
iMelania, Varjack Lowry 104
immersive theatre 75, 98–100
improvisation 41, 45, 72, 99
inclusion 15, 25, 40, 48, 56, 64–9, 71–5, 108–11, 149, 155
independent artists, *see* freelance artists
inequality 3, 14, 26, 58, 144–5, 148–9
information 141–2, 156–7
In Many Hands, Kate McIntosh 73
interaction 52, 59, 64–7, 82, 96, 99–101, 104–6
interruption 16–18, 39
intervals 17, 38–9, 56
intimacy 59–60, 73, 83, 134
It Don't Worry Me, Atresbandes (in collaboration with Bertrand Lesca and Nasi Voutsas) 104

joey, sean burn/gobscure 166
Jones, Inigo 78, 92, 94
Jonson, Ben 83, 94

Key Theatre, Peterborough 69
Kneehigh Theatre Company

closure 153–4
Nights at the Circus 73

labour 51–4, 97, 100, 117
Leeds Playhouse, *see* West Yorkshire Playhouse/ Leeds Playhouse
Leicester Haymarket 65
Life and Adventures of Nicholas Nickleby, The David Edgar 49, 50
lighting 13, 36, 71, 95–8, 111–14
 candlelight 36, 39, 78
Little Cog 155–6
Live Action Relay, Sue Healey 57
liveness 33, 90, 102, 103, 106
Live Theatre, Newcastle 46, 74
lockdown 13, 23, 26–7, 57–9, 120–2
long-form performance 49–50
loss 1–2, 16, 103–4, 118, 154
Lowry, The, Salford 139
lunchtime theatre 38, 45

marketing 14, 50, 126–9
 reciprocal marketing 135–6
 relationship marketing 133–4, 142–3
Marx, Peter 21
masks 88, 89, 99, 101, 113, 121–2
matinees 38
memory 17, 30, 55, 85
Mermaid, The, London 65
microdramas 43–4
midnight matinees 37
Minack Theatre, Cornwall 65
Miniaturists, The 44
mortality 15, 27, 28, 30, 112
mourning 102–4, 106, 118, 162, 164
music hall 37, 44, 129
myth 3, 20, 76–7, 84

National Theatre of Scotland 47–8, 74
 Home 74
National Theatre of Wales 74–5

A Good Night Out in the Valleys 74
For Mountain, Sand & Sea 75
Shelf Life 75
The Weather Factory 74–5
New Theatre Royal, Glasgow 128
New World Order, The Harold Pinter 43
Nield, Sophie 96–7, 101
Northern Stage 159, 167
nostalgia 3, 20, 32, 98

An Ode to Drury Lane, Samuel Johnson 126–7, 130
Old Red Lion Theatre, London 82
Old Vic Theatre, London 72
one-to-one performance 83
online performance, *see* digital performance
open-air venues and performances 36, 39, 60, 64–7, 74–5, 80–1
Òran Mór, Glasgow 46

Palace Theatre, London 134
Palmer, Scott 111–13, 116
pandemic, *see under* Covid
pantomime 36, 42
papering 137
participation 13, 53, 59, 64–7, 72–4, 76, 84, 96–7, 99–100, 137–40, 155, 163–4
passivity 3, 65, 70–4, 95, 113
peripatetic theatre companies 74–5
playbills 127–9, 131
precarity 19, 61, 64, 150, 160
Prince of Wales Theatre, London 38, 81
private
 lives 13, 57–9, 82
 property 81
 space 63, 77, 79–81, 124, 144
 theatres and theatre clubs 5, 35, 66, 78–9, 106, 112

programmes   129–31
promenade   72, 74
proximity   32, 59, 60, 65–6, 82–3
public space   58–9, 80–1, 114, 127, 169
Punchdrunk   75, 98–100
    Faust   75
    Sleep No More   98

Quizoola! Forced Entertainment   49

Race Cards, Selina Thompson   54
racism   48, 54, 85, 162
Reduced Shakespeare
    Company   41–2
rehearsals   134–5, 139, 166, 168
religion   34, 36, 66
repetition   30, 51–2, 55
rhythm   36, 46, 58
*Rich Kids: A History of Shopping
    Malls in Tehran*, The Javaad
    Alipoor Company   170
Ridout, Nicholas   96, 101
risk   15, 30, 60, 83, 163
Robinson, Jo   21, 110
Roy, Arundhati   2, 22, 145
Royal Court   44, 48, 72
Royal Exchange Theatre,
    Manchester   68
Royal National Theatre, London   49,
    51, 59, 65, 70, 72, 106, 109
Royal Scots Club   37
Royal Shakespeare Company   49,
    135, 159

scenography   78, 94, 113
    and machines   91, 93
    and scene changes   39, 92
School Gate, Rachel De-lahay   48
Scratch performances, *see* feedback
Search for Power, The Tania El
    Khoury   73
seasons   36
seating   63–5, 67–8, 71, 79, 92, 99

and social segregation   77, 92
on stage   39, 72, 83
secrecy   61–2, 123–4, 137
    and casting   124
Sedgman, Kirsty   101, 114
Shakespeare, William   30, 40–1,
    67, 97
    *Complete Works of William
        Shakespeare (Abridged)*   41
    Hamlet   41
    Henry IV Part 1   41
    Henry IV Part 2   41
    Henry VI Part 1   135
    A Midsummer Night's Dream   125
    Shakespeare for Breakfast   37
Shakespeare's Globe   37, 39–41, 67,
    84, 97
Sheffield Amphitheatre   65
Shoot Get Treasure Repeat, Mark
    Ravenhill   44
silence   51, 58, 113, 131
site-specific performance   74–5, 85
slow theatre   51–2
small theatres   82–3
social distancing   60, 119
social media   20, 47, 73, 85, 89, 100,
    105, 135–6
Soho Theatre   45
Some Enchanted Evening, C. P.
    Taylor   74
space   42, 57–85, 99, 104–5, 124,
    134–5, 141–2, 161–2
Speak Bitterness, Forced
    Entertainment   49
spectacle   75, 78, 91–2, 94–4, 97,
    113, 123
speed   29, 40–3, 48, 49, 51–2, 56, 88,
    89, 93
'stay at home' orders, *see* lockdown
Stephen Joseph Theatre,
    Scarborough   68
A Streetcar Named Desire, Tennessee
    Williams   131
street theatre   34, 60, 80

Sullivan, Erin   17, 106–7
Summit Conference, R. D.
    MacDonald   133
Sunday   34–5
sustainability   16, 65, 169–70

Taking the Time, Gillian Jane
    Lees and Adam York
    Gregory   53
technology   13
    definitions of   90
    distrust of   89–90
    limitations and failures of   88–9,
        116–17
Telephone, Coney   105
theatre
    and death   30, 103
    definition of   10, 102
Theatre Royal, Drury Lane,
    London   63, 93, 125, 130
Theatre Royal, Haymarket,
    London   62
Theatre Royal, Stratford East   139
Theatre Royal, York   69, 139
theatrophone   107–8
This Endless Sea, Chloe Smith   162–3
Thoringham Theatre, Suffolk   65
Three Estates, The Tyrone
    Guthrie   67–8
thrust stage   67–8
ticket pricing   37, 128, 136–7,
    140–1, 158–9
time   25–9, 33
    Coronatime   25–7
    management of   28
    poverty   29
    slow   56
toilets   18, 63, 69, 131
touring   36, 41, 54, 73–4, 77, 107,
    169, *see also* concept
    touring
tradition, *see* convention
transience   30, 55, 56
transparency   69, 79, 136, 141–2,
    157–9

travel   5, 9, 36, 58, 74, 108, 169
Traverse Theatre, Edinburgh   37, 46
Twitter, *see* social media

unification   3, 64, 66, 76
Uninvited Guests
    *It Is Like It Ought To Be: A
        Pastoral*   72
    *Love Letters Straight From Your
        Heart*   72
Unlimited   111, 154

variety theatre   37, 44, 48, 74
Victoria Theatre, Stoke-on-Trent   68
visibility, of audiences   13, 114–16,
    see also exposure
voyeurism   13, 99, 115

waiting   27, 29, 51–2
Waiting for Godot, Samuel
    Beckett   51
Walsh, Fintan   103–4, 118
welcome   81, 105, 134, 140, 142, 161
West Yorkshire Playhouse/Leeds
    Playhouse   46, 53, 65, 138
What If?, Two Destination
    Language   163
When We Are Married, J. B.
    Priestley   107, 131
Wiles, David   35–6, 61, 65
work.txt (*a play without actors*),
    Nathan Ellis   169
Worthen, W. B.   90, 98–101, 113
Wyndham's Theatre, London   140–1

You Me Bum Bum Train, Katie Bond
    and Morgan Lloyd   98
Young Vic, The, London   141–2

Zeldin, Alexander
    Beyond Caring   52
    Love   52
Zoom   82, 88, 104–6, 114–15, 121,
    163–4

www.ingramcontent.com/pod-product-compliance
Lightning Source LLC
Chambersburg PA
CBHW071841230426
43671CB00012B/2034